MANULIFE

MANULIFE

How Dominic D'Alessandro
Built a Global Giant and Fought to Save It

ROD McQUEEN

VIKING
CANADA

VIKING CANADA

Published by the Penguin Group

Penguin Group (Canada), 90 Eglinton Avenue East, Suite 700, Toronto, Ontario, Canada M4P 2Y3
(a division of Pearson Canada Inc.)

Penguin Group (USA) Inc., 375 Hudson Street, New York, New York 10014, U.S.A.
Penguin Books Ltd, 80 Strand, London WC2R 0RL, England
Penguin Ireland, 25 St Stephen's Green, Dublin 2, Ireland (a division of Penguin Books Ltd)
Penguin Group (Australia), 250 Camberwell Road, Camberwell, Victoria 3124, Australia
(a division of Pearson Australia Group Pty Ltd)
Penguin Books India Pvt Ltd, 11 Community Centre, Panchsheel Park, New Delhi – 110 017, India
Penguin Group (NZ), 67 Apollo Drive, Rosedale, North Shore 0745, Auckland, New Zealand
(a division of Pearson New Zealand Ltd)
Penguin Books (South Africa) (Pty) Ltd, 24 Sturdee Avenue, Rosebank, Johannesburg 2196, South Africa

Penguin Books Ltd, Registered Offices: 80 Strand, London WC2R 0RL, England

First published 2009

1 2 3 4 5 6 7 8 9 10 (RRD)

Manufactured in the U.S.A.

McQueen, Rod, 1944–
Manulife : how Dominic D'Alessandro built a global giant and fought to save it / Rod
McQueen.

Includes bibliographical references and index.
ISBN 978-0-670-06920-0

1. D'Alessandro, Dominic. 2. Manulife Financial—History. 3. Chief
executive officers—Canada—Biography. 4. Businessmen—Canada—Biography.
I. Title.

HG8764.D35 M38 2009   368.32'0092   C2009-900325-2

Visit the Penguin Group (Canada) website at **www.penguin.ca**

Special and corporate bulk purchase rates available; please see
www.penguin.ca/corporatesales or call 1-800-810-3104, ext. 477 or 474

To Sandy

who makes everything possible

CONTENTS

INTRODUCTION

DOMINIC D'ALESSANDRO MOVED to the microphone and peered out at the black-tie crowd as if assessing their mood or how much wine they had consumed. Would his opening joke still work? Why not? This event on October 29, 2008, at the Four Seasons Hotel in Toronto was, after all, a dinner in his honour. He had been chosen months earlier to receive the Ivey Business Leader Award given by the Richard Ivey School of Business at the University of Western Ontario. The five hundred alumni were in a convivial mood after enjoying beef tenderloin and Mission Hill Estate wines from the Okanagan Valley at the event that raised $317,000 for student scholarships. In return, the attendees were looking to learn leadership secrets from the pugnacious D'Alessandro who, since his 1994 appointment as chief executive officer of Manulife Financial, had taken a sleepy company and created the largest life insurance company in North America and the third largest in the world after AXA of France and Assic Generali of Italy.

Until the very month of the Ivey event, Manulife had avoided the global chaos of collapsing markets that caused once-proud companies to go bankrupt or need government backstopping. That's because

D'Alessandro had wisely kept Manulife away from subprime mortgages, as well as all those synthetic derivatives that wreaked havoc on so many other firms. Prudence, however, could only protect a corporation for so long. In October the financial version of the bubonic plague infected even the healthiest corporate citizens. Manulife share price fell 46 percent in that one month.

As a result, D'Alessandro's personal fortune suffered an unholy hit. At the beginning of October, D'Alessandro held shares and options in Manulife worth $188 million. As he stood before the Ivey crowd, most of the options, which four weeks earlier had accounted for half of that substantial sum, were worth absolutely nothing. The rest of the holdings had also shrivelled; the $188 million had become $50 million. All those bonuses deferred, all those years of taking salary in shares because he believed in what he was doing, all that Herculean effort—and for what?

Little wonder D'Alessandro began his remarks on the anniversary of Black Tuesday, October 29, 1929, somewhat defensively. "I will confess to being very apprehensive about having to speak to you tonight about the important subject of leadership. It's a subject that has been covered so many times by so many other, far more capable, speakers," he said. "In fact, I feel a little like Elizabeth Taylor's seventh husband must have felt on their wedding night. I know what to do, but how do I make it interesting?"

D'Alessandro went on to say that leadership was all about bold vision, self-confidence, the ability to persuade others to pursue an objective, and most of all, integrity. But the lesions of the present tempered the lessons of the past. "The irony of speaking to you tonight about leadership and integrity, given the tumultuous developments in global financial markets, is not lost on me. Every day brings new revelations that these qualities, sadly for everyone, were too often absent in many parts of the financial services industry," he said. "It is simply unbelievable what has happened. Who would have thought a few months ago that we would witness the nationalization or forced sale of major portions of the banking industry in Europe, the United

States, and elsewhere? That investment banking, as we know it, would virtually disappear? That AIG, once the world's largest financial institution, would be on life support almost certainly never to regain anything remotely like its former stature?" Who indeed? Not Dominic D'Alessandro. Not anyone.

———•———

THE STORM THAT sank AIG, American International Group, and was battering Manulife, began gaining force five months earlier in May 2008. Manulife announced that profits in the previous quarter were down 12 percent, hurt by a regulatory change called fair value accounting. In the past, price changes in shares of other companies in which Manulife had invested would have mattered only if Manulife had sold those shares and had to declare a capital gain or loss. Under the new rules, a drop in the share value of a holding in the company's investment portfolio had to be recorded just as if the loss were permanent, as if the shares had been sold at those reduced prices, when in fact they hadn't been.

The stock market decline reduced quarterly profits by $265 million, the first such drop in almost seven years of rising results. (Manulife reports in Canadian dollars, so figures in this book, except where noted, are in C$.) The company was forced to take into account that market tumble despite the fact that year-over-year insurance sales rose 30 percent in Canada, 42 percent in the United States, and 46 percent in Asia.

For the next few months, Manulife shares had held their value—until Black October. That's because D'Alessandro had built one of Canada's most profitable companies. Only the Royal Bank made more money, $5.5 billion versus $4.2 billion for Manulife, but Royal had 65,000 employees to Manulife's 22,000. As a result, annual profit per Manulife employee was $192,000 compared with $85,000 for each Royal banker. Manulife made so much money that the combined profit of the next-two-largest life insurance companies in Canada, Great-West Life and Sun Life, was about the same as Manulife's. On a revenue per employee basis, giant General Motors of Canada topped Manulife, but only by a hair's breadth: $1,667,105 per GM employee to $1,615,136 per Manulife employee.*

GIVEN THAT KIND of relentless strength, the gyrations that Manulife suffered in 2008 were but a blip on the radar screen for a firm founded in 1887, when the president was none other than the prime minister of Canada, Sir John A. Macdonald. While the company grew to become one of Canada's leading insurers, it wasn't until D'Alessandro arrived that the place came alive. One hundred dollars invested in 1999, when Manulife demutualized and became a public company, was worth $267 on December 31, 2008; $100 invested in the S&P/TSX Composite Index during the same period rose to $128. Former policyholders who stayed the course were better off backing D'Alessandro than trusting the broader index even after the market collapse.

D'Alessandro was handsomely rewarded for making other people rich. During the three years from 2005 to 2007 his compensation averaged $15 million a year. "He's done a remarkable job. He has given a new face to the life insurance leader group by showing that, while in the past they might have been collectively very conservative, staid, and quiet, he's out front. He's more typical of American CEOs," said Jim Rogers, who heads Rogers Group Financial of Vancouver and in 2008 was president of the Million Dollar Round Table, an elite group of the top 1 percent of life insurance agents in the world. "He's done wonders for the industry in terms of pushing the regulators and legislators. In terms of speaking out about public policy around financial institutions, he has not been shy or reticent."

In his speech to the 2008 annual meeting, for example, D'Alessandro railed at greedy business leaders who'd caused the financial pox that was slowly spreading around the world. "I am stunned at

---

*Financial Post 500, June 2008; figures are for 2007.

the extent of the problems and at the damage that has been done not just to many of the largest and most sophisticated financial institutions in the world but also to millions of investors and homeowners." D'Alessandro called for vigorous intervention. "Policymakers ought to rid themselves once and for all of the attitude that the 'market is always right.' It is this attitude—which events have shown to be naïve and dangerous—which more than anything else is at the heart of the current crisis." Such activist statements put him in a tiny minority of CEOs, most of whom want to be left alone by governments to do whatever they desire—with little thought for the consequences.

D'Alessandro's candid views expressed that day in May 2008 came with a surprise postscript. He had decided to call it quits. The annual meeting in May 2009 would be his last after fifteen eventful years as chief executive officer. The impact of lower earnings, coupled with D'Alessandro's tidings, sent Manulife shares down 5 percent in less than thirty manic minutes, thereby wiping $3 billion off the value of the company. Other members of the insurance sector were in far worse shape because of poor management and bad investments, not because of anyone's leave-taking. That same day AIG announced a loss of $7.8 billion; CEO Martin Sullivan was fired.

AFTER THE MEETING, D'Alessandro headed for a nearby conference room where a dozen journalists awaited. Watching a business leader enter a room is always an instructive exercise. Some chief executive officers try to dominate through their physical presence, others simply assume proper attention will be paid once the world realizes who is in their midst. Power, they believe, flows from their personality and position. At five feet seven inches, in his trademark blue or grey two-piece suits and matching ties, Dominic D'Alessandro is too short to use his height to control his surroundings. Unlike many men of his height, however, D'Alessandro doesn't suffer from "short-man syndrome." He isn't one of those banty roosters who create a commotion as a way of claiming that there's substance behind all the clamour.

But what D'Alessandro may lack in stature, he makes up in intensity. There's an arresting aspect to the beetling black eyebrows, the distinguished greying hair, and the spring-loaded step that radiates self-confidence. He seems to emit electricity from some secret internal source. His best weapon is his smile, which looks like the familiar happy face with a crescent mouth upturned at the corners.

At first, the media seemed intimidated and sat silently like pigeons in the park waiting for crumbs. To fill the awkward stillness, D'Alessandro launched into a description of the surroundings, pointing out the oil portraits of former leaders of North American Life, one of Manulife's many acquisitions during his time at the top.

Finally, one of the reporters mustered enough moxie to ask D'Alessandro how old he was. Don't they have his bio? "I'm sixty-one," he replied. "When I retire a year from now, I'll be sixty-two and a half." With the logjam broken by that toughie, other queries began to flow. Will there be one more acquisition before he calls it a day? "We're not obsessed with being a mega-organization, but if an opportunity came our way, I'd be derelict in my duties if I didn't pursue it. I don't think my announcement precludes anything."

Why was he leaving? "I've given this job fifteen years. I want some time to decompress and some time with my family. I'll see how satisfying that is. If I should get terribly desperate to want to come and meet with analysts every quarter and have shareholder meetings, I might have to go back to work. But I doubt that will happen."

He will join some boards and he might teach, a vocation he enjoyed thirty-five years ago. As a young chartered accountant with Coopers & Lybrand in Montreal, by day he conducted audits for clients and at night taught those who were studying for their CA designation. His course was one of the more difficult, Financial Accounting Theory, the final session before students wrote their qualifying exams. "Intellectually, he's very bright. He's in the upper category. On the other hand, he's not an intellectual. He's a practical thinker and he's got very strong people skills," said Warren Chippindale, former chairman of Coopers & Lybrand, who hired

D'Alessandro in 1968. "Everywhere he's gone, he's gone straight up. I think it's partly because everybody likes him so much. His integrity is unmistakable. He has the ability to deal with the Queen on the one hand, the homeless guy on the other hand, and everybody in between. He can go up or down the scale and be perfectly at ease. Not everybody can do that."

As the media questioning turned to the topic of succession at Manulife, D'Alessandro refused to be drawn into specific choices, saying only that the board of directors would handle the task. "I'm a colourful person and therefore I attract a lot of attention, but there are a lot of excellent people in this company. I'm not sure we need a clone. I have no doubt that Manulife will go from success to success. They replace even the Pope and life goes on."

When asked to describe his legacy, D'Alessandro gave a quick summation of what he saw as his successes since his arrival in 1994. In his first year at Manulife he bought the group life and health insurance business of the defunct Confederation Life and in 1995 took over North American Life. In 1996 Manulife was the second foreign insurance company to gain access to China and in 1999 the first into Vietnam. In 2005, when a hedge fund called Portus Alternative Asset Management collapsed, he ordered a full refund of the $260 million invested by Manulife clients, a generosity matched by no other financial firm.

But the capstone of his career was Manulife's $15 billion takeover of Boston-based John Hancock Financial Services in 2004, at the time the largest cross-border transaction by any Canadian company. That record stood until 2007, when Thomson Corp. bought Reuters Group for US$17 billion. The Hancock acquisition doubled Manulife's size and elevated D'Alessandro's leadership to legendary status.

In 2002, he even took a run at Canadian Imperial Bank of Commerce. Although he did not pull off the deal, at least he tried, which is better than most CEOs who keep their boards of directors mollified by meeting more modest goals. "I consider him one of our most outstanding alumni. Having had seven years with Royal Bank, he moved on to Laurentian and on to Manulife, and has just done an outstanding job. I've been an admirer all through those years," said Allan Taylor, chairman and CEO of Royal Bank when D'Alessandro worked there from 1981 to 1988. "The takeover of Hancock really put Manulife on the map. It was no surprise to me that he was chief executive of the year a couple of years ago."

As the news conference wound down, D'Alessandro tried to give the members of the media some institutional context by which to measure his career. To do so, he reached far back into business history for a fitting comparison. "The original J.P. Morgan said he wanted to run a first-class company in a first-class way. We've done that at Manulife." The questions dwindled away like the last flickers of an evening campfire. "Are we done?" asked D'Alessandro, then responded to his own query by abruptly taking his leave. For the next year at least, he had a company to run.

ONE

Coming to Canada

IF ADVERSITY DURING CHILDHOOD can create a driven leader, Dominic D'Alessandro endured more than enough to succeed. Born January 18, 1947, in Frosolone, a village in central Italy, he was one of four children of Anthony and Angelina D'Alessandro. As was the case with many of his fellow countrymen following the Second World War, Anthony immigrated to Canada in 1949. He found work in Montreal as a labourer, saved his money, and the following year sent for his family to join him.

D'Alessandro was three years old during that Atlantic crossing on the S.S. *Canberra*. He vividly recalls his fascination with the band on board and how he would edge closer and closer to the musicians, only to be gently shooed away by the clarinet player. At one point, a passenger picked up the little boy and carried him to the rail of the ship, saying, "I'm going to throw you overboard." The purser took the threat seriously and warned the passenger not to pull that stunt again.

D'Alessandro arrived in Halifax at Pier 21, where 1.5 million immigrants, war brides, evacuee children, and Canadian military service personnel were processed during the years 1928 to 1971. The immigration shed was part of a series of buildings connecting the dock to the railway station for trains west. As the family sat huddled together, their belongings gathered around them, D'Alessandro watched wide-eyed as a woman nearby ate slices of fresh bread. Finally, she took pity on the boy and gave him some. This was not the bread he was used to, dipped in olive oil. This came smothered in butter, a first-time taste sensation. Dominic D'Alessandro had arrived in The Promised Land where there were many new flavours to discover and a future that could be whatever he wanted.

—•—

THE FAMILY LIVED in Little Burgundy, a working-class Montreal neighbourhood across a series of railway tracks southwest of the city's downtown core. The cold-water brick walkups stood shoulder-to-shoulder, hard against the sidewalk. It was years before D'Alessandro saw a house on a lot with a lawn. While French-Canadian families dominated, there were pockets of Anglos, Italians, Native Canadians, and blacks from the Caribbean. He spoke Italian at home and learned English at school and French in the streets.

His street, Rue des Seigneurs, ran south from St-Antoine to the Lachine Canal, where the neighbourhood children fished and swam. Each summer some lad would drown and everyone would be warned away for a while. There was a Bank of Montreal at the corner, a grocery, and a Salvation Army thrift shop. The neighbourhood also boasted a club. "We knew all the dancers. They'd come by and give us a soft drink, a chocolate bar, or a little kiss, depending on how cute you were," said D'Alessandro.

D'Alessandro was six in 1953 when he and his brother, eight-year-old Felix, were walking home from Belmont Public School. A friend hollered, "Hey, you guys better get home, your father is dead." When they entered the house, everything seemed normal. Their mother was in the hall teaching their ten-month-old sister, Elvira, how to walk.

"Mom, Mom, did you hear Dad's dead?"

"What are you saying?" she replied in disbelief.

A few minutes later, friends and relatives arrived with the news that Anthony was indeed dead. He'd been laying pipe in a deep trench of soft, wet earth that was not properly supported by timbered sides. Without warning, the soil collapsed and he was buried alive. So disfigured was he that the family was not even allowed to view the remains.

THE HOUSE, which had always been filled with fun, friends, and neighbours, became a sad and solemn place as Angelina, widowed at thirty-six, struggled to make ends meet. She spoke neither French nor English but was determined to carry on and raise her children without help. "She was a fiercely proud woman. She never collected a nickel of welfare—that would have been unheard of. She never put a hand out to anyone, not her relatives, nobody," said D'Alessandro. At first, Angelina did piecework at home, sewing gloves. Then she rented the house next door and filled it with boarders, as many as ten at a time, mostly Italian men coming ahead on their own to Canada as had her Anthony. She not only housed them, she also did their laundry and made their meals.

Out of those tragic circumstances, none of D'Alessandro's siblings fared as well as he did. His oldest brother, Nicholas, left school and went to work at fifteen to help support the family. At first he delivered bread and then spent forty years as a taxi driver. He is now retired. Felix was a gambler who drifted in and out of relationships. At one point, he made $6 million by selling a business he'd built, but he frittered away every dollar. He is now dead. Elvira married and had a son. "We are different, very different. I think I had a mind; that was my big gift. None of my siblings are stupid, they're just average people. They weren't as clever or as curious. I've always had a facility, I loved ideas and started to read at an early age. While others were doing other things, I would go someplace and read a good book. I got encouraged by my teachers," said D'Alessandro. "It's the luck of the draw."

He also spent more time with his mother than the others did. "I was more reliable than my brother Felix. If my mother asked me to do something, it would get done. If she asked Felix, it might or might not get done. I'd accompany her to different things and we'd talk. It gave me motivation to see just how hard a life she had."

Every Saturday morning Angelina would take Dominic to the Salvation Army shop to buy second-hand clothing. The only new outfits Dominic wore while growing up were purchased once a year when Nick took him shopping. The family was so poor that his first Christmas gift came from the Santa at a community centre after D'Alessandro watched a seasonal variety program. Still, he was better off than most in the neighbourhood. "I had friends that we used to play with and they became murderers. I can remember going to their homes, there was nobody in the house and the place was stark, cold, and full of garbage. I remember one kid, a nice boy, he couldn't have been more than nine, going into his house. His sister was all made up, she was twelve or thirteen and he asked, 'Where did you get the makeup?' She told him she'd stolen it at the five-and-dime. He said, 'Where's Mom?' She said, 'She's out with her boyfriend.' Contrast that to my house where my mother always had a meal for us. These were very poor people who only ate well when they got their welfare cheque or the baby bonus. They used to wait for the postman."

D'Alessandro riles easily when he thinks about those lucky stiffs who were born with a silver spoon in their mouth or got ahead by lolling along at half-speed. "There are a lot of comfortable middle-class people who don't have any appreciation for poor people. They say, 'Why don't you just get a job?' Well, if you don't have the exposure and it's not part of your environment and everybody around you is behaving badly, it's difficult to break that cycle."

Having fought his way out of such a background, he has not forgotten the experience. "I've always been sympathetic to the underdog. If I categorize myself, I'd certainly be left of centre. I find it very facile for people to prescribe for others. A lot of very success-ful people, because the system has worked well for them, are remarkably unsympathetic. They don't make allowances that maybe they were successful because they had some gifts, they had drive or IQ points or some skill. If they'd just been average, they'd still be there, shining hubcaps. Poverty is not a good thing." He worked every summer, starting at age twelve, doing delivery or factory jobs.

Religion was not part of his upbringing. Sundays were chaotic as Angelina tried to get herself ready for church and organize all four children. She would take Elvira to mass and tell Dominic and Felix to attend an earlier service. The boys usually went elsewhere. "I'm not religious. It never made sense to me even as a child; it sounded improbable. I didn't like the incense; I didn't like the smell." A life-size statue of Christ on the Cross frightened him as a six year old. "I remember looking up at it and seeing the blood. It scared me half to death."

Saturdays, however, were different. While his mother sought bargains among the clothing bins at the Salvation Army, D'Alessandro scoured the used book tables. The clerks soon got to know him and charged him twenty-five cents for as many volumes as he could carry. At home, he'd spread out his treasures on the kitchen floor, up to twenty books per trip, while his mother made hot chocolate as a treat.

Those books became a haven from his surroundings. "I was drawn to stories about heroic types who had strength of character. I think it was a form of escape." He read all the G.A. Henty novels of derring-do, as well as other classics, such as Mark Twain's *Tom Sawyer* and *Huckleberry Finn*. At twelve he was devouring Dickens and Dostoyevsky. D'Alessandro skipped grades four and six and finished high school at fourteen. On graduation day, he won most of the academic awards.

———◆———

D'ALESSANDRO ENROLLED at Loyola, a Jesuit college in Montreal that has since merged with Sir George Williams University to become Concordia. After his mother remarried when he was sixteen, he left home to live with his brother Nick. It wasn't that he disliked his new stepfather, David Benyani, he just wasn't happy to have a man around the house, even though his mother's lot had improved. "She was more comfortable. He wasn't a wealthy man but she didn't need to struggle quite as hard." (Angelina died in 2004 at eighty-seven with a photo of the S.S. *Canberra*, the boat that brought her to Canada, on her night table. Benyani, who is in his nineties, is still alive.)

In those days, Loyola was small and had recently become co-ed. The five hundred students included about fifty women. He did well during his first two years, but as he began third year, the seventeen-year-old D'Alessandro attended the first football game of the season. After, he went with friends to a bar and met a divorced mother of two children who was six years older than he was. He moved in with her and enjoyed his first real sexual relationship so much that he lost all interest in his studies, dropped out of school, and smoked pot. "Everybody did it. Now I drink a little bit of Scotch, but back then I didn't like alcohol so you'd have a joint and you'd feel like everybody else did who drank twenty beers."

Looking back, D'Alessandro blames his actions on his immaturity. Because he advanced through public and high school so quickly, his classmates and friends were always older, so he wasn't as emotionally developed. By Christmas the relationship was over, but by then he'd missed so much of his maths and physics program with its thirty hours of labs and classes every week that he did not write the exams.

Loyola was small enough that faculty members knew all the students. In the new year, one of D'Alessandro's professors, Father Aloysius McPhee, sent a message that he wanted to see D'Alessandro. During their subsequent meeting, the priest said, "You should finish what you start. You won't have much of a future if you don't get a degree." D'Alessandro complained that he didn't like science. "Just because you're studying science now doesn't mean you have to do it for the rest of your life. It'll stand you in good stead," said the priest.

D'Alessandro took his advice, went back to Loyola, and excelled. During fourth year he also taught physics part-time at Lower Canada College to grade twelve students who were the same age as he was. He earned $2500, half the pay of a full-time teacher, for covering such topics as mechanics, specific gravity, and magnetism. That experience brought him into contact for the first time with old Montreal money. The students, including members of the Molson brewing family, lived in baronial homes and represented a world that seemed forever beyond his reach.

That same year he met his future wife, Pearl Fiore, through mutual friends. Pearl, who was born in Canada, was seventeen and a student at Marianopolis College, an all-girls school. Her father was of Italian origin, and her mother was French-Canadian and German, thus her blonde hair. The two were in love, but D'Alessandro was not ready for marriage.

After graduation from Loyola in 1967 with his Bachelor of Science, he worked briefly at Northern Electric as an inventory control management trainee, a job he quickly grew to detest. He rode a bus back and forth to work. One day it poured rain; he got drenched and asked himself "What am I doing here?" Said Paul Nantel, a friend, "Why don't we go to Europe?" D'Alessandro had saved some money from his teaching job, so the two took off for London and then Paris. They paid $180 for a plumber's used yellow truck, tossed a mattress in the back, and spent a year touring France, Spain, Portugal, Italy, Greece, and Turkey.

Word eventually reached D'Alessandro that Pearl was upset. Was he serious about her or not? If he didn't come home soon, she would start dating others. Realizing he didn't want to lose her, D'Alessandro headed for Montreal, ready to get on with his personal and professional life. They were wed in 1968. Said D'Alessandro, "It took only twenty years or so for me to convince my mother-in-law that her daughter had not married beneath herself."

—◦—

IN ORDER to decide what he would do professionally, D'Alessandro underwent career counselling at the Loyola placement office. Included in the process was a test that found him suited to law, writing, and accounting, in that order. "I came up through a classical education system. People who studied accounting were dummies. If you were smart you went into the sciences or the arts. If you weren't, you went into commerce. I didn't have any idea whatsoever what accounting was. All I knew was that it had a stigma about it," he said. "I'd never thought of a career in business. I thought I'd do something entrepreneurial. The aspirations weren't very high. The hero in our neighbourhood was the guy who had a steady job as an electrician."

The top two options, law or writing, offered him no chance to earn immediate money. As a prospective accountant, he could work full-time during the day while studying at night for his CA designation. His interest piqued, D'Alessandro asked for the names of accounting firms and was told Clarkson, Gordon and McDonald, Currie. He applied to both, and both offered him a job. "What their recruiting people saw in me I'll never know. I had never held a job before, my hair was down to my shoulders, my attitudes were decidedly anti-business, and I had none of the requisite background education," he said. "I think he's exaggerating," said Warren Chippindale, personnel partner at McDonald, Currie, who offered him $525 a month, $25 more than Clarkson, Gordon. "He looked like a typical young Italian boy. We'd gotten away from the WASP syndrome sometime before that. We were hiring the people we thought were best."

In 1968 D'Alessandro joined McDonald, Currie. (Founded in Montreal in 1910, the firm became part of Coopers & Lybrand in 1973 and merged with Price Waterhouse in 1998 to become PricewaterhouseCoopers.) "We liked to hire people who were not necessarily accounting graduates because we found, particularly the arts students, they'd learned how to think a little bit. One could tell right away that he had a good head on his shoulders," said Chippindale. "He was a star from day one. He became an audit manager quicker than almost anybody."

D'Alessandro had found his métier. The workplace was intense, collegial, and professional. "I worked with people my own age and they had a whole vocabulary that I'd never heard. These people talked about the stock market, shares, and bonds, language I wasn't familiar with, but I learned fast," he said. "I never felt inferior to anybody, anybody, even though I should have because I didn't dress as well, I wasn't polished. I felt the opposite. I felt, I can *think* better than these people, despite their privileges."

D'Alessandro started working with smaller clients, then moved up to larger firms, such as Quebec Hydro, Sorel Steel, and Genstar. As an outsider working with clients, he was able to see clearly a firm's strengths and weaknesses while learning analytical skills that would be useful later in life. At the same time, he attended night classes in accounting. "I was never really what you'd call a terribly diligent student. I was best known for being an eager card player and passing exams in courses for which I hadn't attended a single lecture." Spurred on by Pearl, he changed his ways and attended all his classes in the CA program. After taking twenty credits in three years at McGill University, he wrote the Uniform Final Exam for his Chartered Accountant designation in 1971. He won the bronze medal for Quebec and finished in the top twenty among the several thousand across Canada who wrote the exam.

——•——

FOR D'ALESSANDRO, his time at Coopers included a year in the firm's Paris office, from 1970 to 1971. This time, there was no plumber's truck. The couple and their first-born son, Anthony, lived in a small apartment in the sixteenth arrondissement, a residential and commercial area near the Bois de Boulogne, a fashionable park that attracts walkers, cyclists, and horseback riders.

At the time, the more aggressive French companies were beginning to look beyond the nation's borders. They were eager to be listed on the London Stock Exchange in order to gain the kind of exposure that would give them access to more sources for capital. Because the Paris office was the accounting firm's only location in France, D'Alessandro travelled the country conducting audits and offering financial advice to a wide range of firms.

Clients included individuals who have since become world-renowned. D'Alessandro worked with a wood and lumber company in Brittany run by François Pinault, now the billionaire head of Artemis (Converse sneakers, Samsonite luggage, and Christie's auction house) who recently restored the Palazzo Grassi in Venice for his collection of contemporary art.

D'Alessandro was hired to check the books prior to Pinault's selling the firm and didn't like what he saw. "His margins had leapt up at the end of the accounting period. We were convinced he had miscounted his inventory, but we couldn't prove it." An angry Pinault summoned D'Alessandro, demanding to know what he thought he was doing. Pinault listened to D'Alessandro's allegation and then told him that the numbers had indeed changed during the year. "The previous numbers are wrong. The right ones are the ones at the end of the year when everything is actually physically counted," said Pinault. D'Alessandro had no choice but to go along. The buyer on that occasion was none other than Tiny Rowland, chairman of Lonrho, a British conglomerate with interests in mining, newspapers, and hotels.

Then twenty-four, D'Alessandro was still learning social skills as well as business savvy. While working with another client, Rhône-Poulenc, the French pharmaceutical firm, he stayed at the corporate guesthouse and dined with senior executives. One particular evening started badly when he decided that the foie gras on the filet mignon looked too rich for his taste. Using his knife, he scraped the offending delicacy to the side of his plate. Everyone was aghast.

His uncouth behaviour continued. "I had just read that California wines on a blind taste were found to be just as good as French wines, so I brought up that subject. This scandalized them. On another occasion, someone in the group was going on about X [pronounced 'eeks']. I said, *'Excusez-moi, qu'est-ce que X?'* It was like the air went out of a balloon. He explained to me X was Polytechnique, the top engineering school in France. Everybody who went there was proud of it and he was laying it on for our benefit. I was just such a goddamn boor."

D'Alessandro later learned that he'd won admiration from others at the dinner who'd studied at Hautes Études Commerciales, another of the "four aces" where the French elite are trained. (The other two are L'École Nationale d'Administration and l'École Normale Supérieure.) "There was enormous rivalry. They all thought I had done it on purpose, saying, 'You put him in his place.' I told them I had no idea, but I have used that technique since. If I sense people are boasting, I'll say, 'What is that, exactly?'"

Before taking on the Paris assignment, he'd agreed to remain with the accounting firm for a year after his posting. He returned to Montreal as planned and then as soon as the promised year was up, he left the firm and the profession. That decision was precipitated by a conversation he had with a senior partner while the two men worked together at a client's office. Herb Spindler was a dapper man, the dean of the tax practice, but on that particular day he was a nervous wreck. When D'Alessandro asked why, Spindler explained he was screwing up his courage to inform the chairman of the client firm about a problem with his personal tax return. "A light bulb went off in my head. I said if I stay at this firm and I'm really successful, one day I could be worrying about somebody's else's tax return. Wouldn't I rather be the guy whose tax return they worry about? I liked the relationships. I liked the intellectual challenge, but I thought that I would enjoy more being the fellow who makes the decisions as opposed to the one who reviews them and the rewards that flow with it."

In 1975 he was offered a job by one of his clients, Genstar, a real estate and construction conglomerate. Warren Chippindale, who'd hired D'Alessandro and was by then chairman of Coopers & Lybrand, tried to talk him out of leaving. "I said, 'Look, Dominic, you're sure-fire partner potential, and you've got a few more years to go, but that's in the future for you.' But he left. He decided he didn't want to spend his life as a public accountant. Luckily for him, he didn't take my advice."

TWO

Learning the Ropes

THE SURROUNDINGS at D'Alessandro's former client, Genstar, were both different from and the same as they had been at Coopers & Lybrand. Different because he was no longer forced to follow a rigorous route to the top; the same because powerful people admired and mentored him. As assistant controller, D'Alessandro was assigned to work with Nick Libertore, a New Yorker hired by Genstar to expand its international interests. D'Alessandro soaked up everything he could from finance to fashion: "He was tall and elegant. His name was Italian and he could cite every Italian opera, but he couldn't speak the language. He took it upon himself to make sure that I understood the finer things in life. We'd be in New York, he'd take me around and explain in great detail how every man lived here and why it was important."

D'Alessandro was soon given his first major assignment—a posting with a Genstar transportation joint venture in Dhahran, Saudi Arabia. At thirty, as general manager of a company that provided port management and freight handling services throughout the Kingdom and the surrounding Gulf States, D'Alessandro oversaw several thousand employees and dealt with clients in the United States, Europe, and Asia.

Because Genstar's West Coast head office was twelve hours behind Saudi time, D'Alessandro might as well have been flying solo. For three years he learned management skills by making his own decisions and his own mistakes. "There were very few telephones back then in the Kingdom, the principal means of communications were those old telex machines. We quickly learned that the best way to deal with 'directives' from home office was to simply unplug the machine and tell everyone later there had been a power outage," said D'Alessandro. "It was a harsh posting—there were no movie theatres, few hotels, and even fewer restaurants. But we did have two company airplanes, a helicopter, and a palace that we rented from a prince to use as a guesthouse. So there were some comforts and it was possible to get away often. What an unbelievable learning experience it all was. You had to be resourceful to survive, you had to make decisions quickly, and you had to accept responsibility for your actions."

In 1979 Genstar sent him to San Francisco, where he served as vice president, material and construction group, and as a deputy to Libertore. Typical of the projects he worked on was a housing development to be financed by Ramon Pimentel-Harding, the scion of a wealthy Venezuelan family that owned vast tracts of land around Caracas. Pimentel-Harding was interested in replicating Genstar's Lake Bonaventure and Lake Bonavista communities in Calgary, with their artificial lakes surrounded by houses and recreational facilities. "We got a team together. I was the guy who made all the numbers work. We'd go to Ramon's house, this vast thing perched on top of a mountain. There were guards all around the place, gates would open and there'd be gardens and groves. How do these people live? Just next door there's unbelievable poverty and there inside is this opulence." Exciting though that world was, many of the projects did not proceed. D'Alessandro itched to see results for his efforts.

———◆———

IN 1981, after six years at Genstar, D'Alessandro received a telephone call from Robert Swidler, who ran his own executive search firm in Montreal. Swidler had been retained by the Royal Bank to find a deputy controller in the finance and investments division in the Montreal head office, a job that paid $60,000 a year. In order to create a list of possible candidates, Swidler had phoned every CA he knew. "They all kept telling me about this Dominic D'Alessandro who I didn't know from a hole in the wall. He was the smartest guy in their classes and a nice guy to boot. He was one of the boys, good people skills, a lot of fun to be with."

D'Alessandro's initial reaction to Swidler's probe was negative. "Are you crazy? Work for a bank? They're so bureaucratic!" But when he got home that night and talked with Pearl, the idea didn't seem so far-fetched. The couple by then had two sons—Anthony, named after Dominic's father, and Michael, named after Pearl's father, in the tradi-tional Italian way. (A daughter, Katherine, was born later.) "I was really homesick. I wanted my boys to grow up near their family. This was a way of coming back to Canada and having someone else pay the freight," said D'Alessandro. Moreover, the job was with one of the country's most prestigious corporations. "It was the Royal Bank of Canada, which for an immigrant Italian family like Dominic's was the most blue blood of blue blood firms. He believed enough in himself that he could rise up through the ranks," said Swidler.

But D'Alessandro was also careful to protect himself against the possibility that the role wouldn't work out. "I went through the interview process and made it clear to everybody that I'm committed to at least one year, but if I didn't like it, I could leave," said D'Alessandro. His fears were unfounded. "I fell in love with the business. It was a business that lent itself to being analyzed and understood. It was a business that provides value and is essential to life. It is a respected profession. There was nothing I didn't like."

Shortly after arriving at the bank, he prepared a report on a possible acquisition. Chief general manager Bob Utting summoned

D'Alessandro to discuss his findings. As the meeting concluded, Utting said, "D'Alessandro, that's Italian, isn't it?" D'Alessandro replied that it was.

"Well, I was raised in Niagara Falls, and there were lots of Italians there," said Utting. "They were hard-working people. They were all gardeners, as I recall."

D'Alessandro paused for a moment and then said, "Well, Mr. Utting, I live in Beaconsfield [a suburb of Montreal]. My gardener's name is Chuck, but I don't know if he's from Niagara Falls. I'll have to ask him."

Utting looked D'Alessandro straight in the eye. D'Alessandro thought his career in banking was over. Then Utting let loose a laugh and became one of D'Alessandro's biggest boosters in the bank.

D'ALESSANDRO WAS QUICKLY PROMOTED to vice president and controller; the man who'd hired D'Alessandro ended up reporting to him. In 1983 D'Alessandro was made a senior vice president, then in 1987 executive vice president with responsibility for the bank's financial planning, financial analysis, taxation, accounting, and investor relations functions. "He learned banking quickly. He's very capable," said Peter Rubenovitch, at the time the youngest vice president ever named at the Royal. They were both frustrated by the tedious pace of decisions. "Large corporations have a certain inertia. We're workaholics both of us. There were times at the Royal where we'd be working on something and then sit around waiting until there was a discussion about it," said Rubenovitch.

D'Alessandro's talents brought him more exposure to the higher-ups than was the case for most of his colleagues. "They identified his intelligence and his strengths. There were a number of people who took Dominic for what he was—an intelligent, driven individual—and supported him as he grew into larger and larger roles," said Roy Firth, who headed investor relations at the bank. "He was refreshing.

He would tell things like they were. A lot of people took him under their wing along the way."

D'Alessandro worked closely with Royal CEO Rowland Frazee and the head of the international division, Allan Taylor, who in 1983 was named president and Frazee's designated successor. "He certainly had things to add to us because of his non-banking experience. We saw some real advantage in that," said Taylor. "He moved quickly. I was always impressed with him. He was very entrepreneurial. In banking, that's a real plus; it's not always there."

D'Alessandro learned which leadership qualities worked and which didn't. "Rowlie [Frazee] took a shine to me. I travelled with him. You felt you automatically wanted to do your best for Rowlie. He never had to ask; you just didn't want to let him down. He liked me. He liked everybody; he was just a very decent person. He was a gentleman." But that leadership style also had a flaw. "Because he was so considerate with everybody, he would procrastinate. He'd insist on getting his whole team together and getting them to agree. The reality is that you can't get strong-willed people to agree all the time and, once in a while, you have to make a call and say, 'This is the way it's going to be.'"

D'Alessandro concluded he'd be better off as a manager by being tough. "I saw things that I should avoid. You can be too nice. You can be too accommodating. You can be too information gathering. You can be too consensual. It is possible to be too collegial. People do have their own agendas and they don't overtly say 'I've got an agenda that is different than yours,' but they're pursuing their own interests and your job as leader is to make sure that things move and they follow." He also learned to loathe high-paid consultants who delayed already laggardly decision-making with their endless studies. "My abhorrence of consultants comes from the Royal Bank because they were besotted with them. One year, McKinsey held sway. The next year it was [Peter] Drucker's group."

As his power grew, D'Alessandro never forgot his modest roots. Among the perks was access to the executive dining rooms at the top of Place Ville Marie, the skyscraper that housed Royal Bank's head office. As a boy, D'Alessandro, along with his brother Felix, would play hooky from school and head across the tracks to watch that very building under construction. Twenty-five years later, D'Alessandro could stand at the upper windows, look southwest to Little Burgundy, and consider just how far he had come. "It was such a kick being in the dining room up there. I'd be able to look down on the very street where I grew up. What a change of circumstance!"

<hr />

IN 1986, when Allan Taylor was named CEO of the Royal Bank and John Cleghorn was appointed president, it was obvious that Cleghorn would get the top job when Taylor retired. Cleghorn, an accountant like D'Alessandro, had obtained his CA at Clarkson, Gordon and joined the Royal Bank in 1974, so he'd been at the bank seven years longer than D'Alessandro. Moreover, he had worked in a number of different business units, whereas D'Alessandro's experience was limited to finance. Cleghorn was also older. In 1986, that year of change, President Cleghorn was forty-five and D'Alessandro was thirty-nine.

Succession at the Royal, Canada's largest bank, was tightly scripted like at no other institution in Canada. Taylor was set to head the bank for six to eight years; Cleghorn would take over in the mid-1990s and would serve as CEO into the twenty-first century. By then, if he stayed around, D'Alessandro would be in his mid-fifties. Maybe he'd be a candidate for the top job, but more likely not; the bank might choose someone younger.

Until then, the gods had smiled on D'Alessandro. "I've had an almost magical career. I've been helped along. I've worked with great people who've given me great opportunity. I believe that you make your own breaks, but on the other hand, other people work hard and never get a chance. I'm mindful that I've earned everything I have, but I'm also mindful that a few things had to go right. I think fondly of everybody I've worked with. There are very few people, there's a few, but I would say I could count them on the fingers of one hand, that I'd care not to see."

Among those very few people was John Cleghorn. "I didn't respect him very much and I don't think he particularly liked me, either. I didn't want to be part of his team. I didn't like his style," said D'Alessandro. "I didn't want to work for somebody that I didn't respect. I had no aspirations to be the CEO of anything at that stage—I just wanted to have progressively increasing responsibility. I certainly didn't have an aspiration of being CEO of the Royal Bank. I left because I had never compromised myself to work with somebody I didn't respect or like, why should I do it now?"

Many bank executives in D'Alessandro's position would have swallowed the defeat and stayed. There's even a phrase at the banks, "the golden handcuffs," referring to the high pay and pleasant perks that keep unhappy officers chained to their executive chairs long after their best-before dates. Not D'Alessandro. At this defining moment in his life, he wanted to get out, so he turned to the same man who put him into the bank in the first place, Robert Swidler. "Dominic thought he would be made president. He thought his experience was more valuable. Maybe he should have been made president, but that's not what the bank decided to do. It was in the cards for Cleghorn. When they named him, Dominic was in effect gone. It was just a matter of when and with whom. He wasn't used to having that type of reversal and he felt they'd made a mistake," said Swidler.

As it happened, Swidler was looking for a chief financial officer at Laurentian Group, a Montreal conglomerate busily acquiring a wide variety of firms in order to create one-stop shopping for financial services. "It was a company that was a pale shadow of the Royal Bank. It wouldn't be fair to mention the two of them in the same breath. I apologized to Dominic for even offering it to him," said Swidler. D'Alessandro wanted to leave the Royal so badly he was willing to take any available role. "He held his nose and agreed to take the job. He was resentful of the Royal Bank for the way in which they failed to recognize his accomplishments and failed to bring him forward as quickly as he would have liked. He always had a desire to get back at them, to thumb his nose at them, and show them what he could do," said Swidler.

As if all that weren't motivation enough, Laurentian offered a potentially lucrative reward that the Royal did not: stock options. D'Alessandro had recently worked on the Royal Bank acquisition of Dominion Securities. The Big Five banks were expanding into wealth management by buying investment dealers with their millionaire partners who did corporate mergers and acquisitions: Scotiabank acquired McLeod, Young, Weir; Bank of Montreal nabbed Nesbitt Thomson; CIBC bought Wood Gundy.

During the Dominion Securities deal, D'Alessandro saw the kind of money investment bankers earned. "It was fabulous. Hell, I worked on Rowlie's retirement package. His basic income was his pension and it wasn't very big by today's standards. Back then, you couldn't get options. Banks weren't allowed to pay their people in that way. It was almost like a priesthood. They lived very, very well and had big homes, drivers, and shoeshine boys, but they didn't accumulate a lot of capital. Here was a chance to get away from the fate that I wasn't sure was going to be what I really liked, to get some equity. So I took it. I had some money but I didn't have what we used to call in the vernacular, f-you money."

———◆———

IN THE 1980S Laurentian Group was one of the fastest-growing financial services conglomerates in Canada. Laurentian's vaulting ambition was fuelled by an unlikely alliance between former Quebec health minister Claude Castonguay, a lifelong federalist Liberal who became CEO of Laurentian Group, and the ground-breaking work of Jacques Parizeau, finance minister in the separatist Parti Québécois government of René Lévesque from 1976 to 1984. Parizeau led the rest of the provinces in knocking down the four pillars of financial services: banking, insurance, investment banking, and trust services. Castonguay seized the opportunity and took Laurentian Group from $80 million in assets in 1976 to a $3.4 billion banking and insurance empire a decade later.

For all Laurentian Group's success, however, D'Alessandro realized that he'd made a mistake as soon as he arrived in July 1988. "He was extremely unhappy. He was in my office almost every week crying to me to get him out of there," said Swidler. Fortunately, in November, an internal opening came available for CEO of the Laurentian Bank of Canada. Not only did the lateral arabesque solve his personal dilemma, but it also offered him professional scope and stock options. "I was attracted to the opportunity. I wasn't guaranteed anything. It was an opportunity to make money but the motivation wasn't—if I do well, I'll get this big a pie. The motivation was my name was on the door. People knew that Dominic D'Alessandro was doing this, so I'll do my damnedest not to screw up. Your pride and self-esteem is very important."

Senior management at Laurentian Bank were well educated and politically aware. General counsel was Louis Bernard, who had been chief of staff to Lévesque and later ran for leader of the Parti Québécois. A major and immediate adjustment for D'Alessandro was working almost totally in French. Laurentian also provided a test kitchen for D'Alessandro to create his own inimitable management style. "I got an opportunity to put some of my own ideas into practice. That was satisfaction in its own right, the notion that you could be excellent and that you could grow, that you could control your own destiny, you could hold your own, it didn't matter that you were small. You could make it more profitable, service clients better, introduce products, just regular bread-and-butter stuff," said D'Alessandro.

Among those ideas, D'Alessandro instituted weekly meetings with the eight most senior executives and once a month expanded the group to include the top twenty-five officers. At those gatherings, he would ream out anyone he felt was ineffective. Within two years of becoming CEO, he'd replaced half of the top eight executives. "He's demanding, he's hard driving, and he expects a lot out of his people. He expects the right answers and for them to know the business in great detail. He gets frustrated and anger comes up. It's not everybody's personality that can work well with Dominic. Some people thrive under that type of leadership and other people don't," said Roy Firth, whom D'Alessandro recruited from the Royal Bank to be chief financial officer of Laurentian. "The organization became much more professional in its financial rigour, administrative policies, and operations, and profitability improved substantially."

D'Alessandro cut costs by getting rid of chauffeurs, including his own. He reduced bureaucracy by removing an entire layer of management so that vice presidents reported directly to him. "He really modernized Laurentian. He brought elements of bigger-bank type approaches of doing things that he had seen from his days at Royal," said Michael Goldberg, who was then an analyst with Dominion Securities.

D'Alessandro expanded Laurentian Bank through seven acquisitions that included Standard Trust, General Trust, Financière Coopérants Prêts-Épargne, and Guardian Trust. "We reached the point where the assets and the income of the bank coming from outside Quebec were as important as those based in Quebec," said Castonguay, who headed the bank's parent company and was also D'Alessandro's chairman at the bank. "All the people who worked for Dominic were very committed to the pursuit of the strategy and the objectives identified by Dominic. The team spirit was very strong. Not only is he a good leader, he can motivate his people. He has a good strategic mind and he doesn't set himself too many objectives, but then he is very determined in their pursuit. He expects people to perform as he does. He works hard and expects other people to do so. If they do, he treats them very well, but if they don't, he won't tolerate that."

The real estate recession of the early 1990s hurt many institutions. "It was a very difficult time to be a small financial institution in Canada in the late eighties, early nineties. They all went out of business, every single one of them. We managed to double the size of Laurentian during that period. I had fun. I loved the people I worked with. I loved my little bank," said D'Alessandro. "People feel energized by the experience of doing something unusual. People want to be active and be challenged and do something notable. They like to read about themselves. They like to be talked about as successful." Under D'Alessandro, Laurentian's share price outperformed the Toronto Stock Exchange bank index by 10 percent.

———————

IN 1993, the ground shifted under D'Alessandro once again. Mouvement Desjardins, a co-operative financial group with a network of *caisses populaires* in Quebec and credit unions in Ontario, bought Laurentian Bank. D'Alessandro's job was secure, but the share-and-share-alike community mentality of Desjardins ran counter to his gung-ho public-company style. Moreover, Desjardins was run by Quebec nationalists. As a staunch federalist, D'Alessandro feared he wouldn't be able to hold his tongue if he heard too much pro-Quebec talk from the new owners. "They were rabid nationalists. There was no way I could work with that group. I can't hide my views on most things and not something like that."

The seven-year itch had come early. D'Alessandro had spent approximately seven years at each of Coopers, Genstar, and Royal. Laurentian held his interest for only five years. He again called on Robert Swidler for help in finding his next role. That step ensured the third fee for Swidler flowing from the career of a repeat candidate in what must be a record in the recruitment field. When D'Alessandro told me about his ongoing relationship with Swidler, he quipped, "He must have a boat someplace named after me." When I repeated the comment to Swidler, he said, "If I have a boat named after Dominic, he has a Caribbean island named after me!"

Swidler, who was by then managing partner for Canada at Egon Zehnder International, did indeed have a role for D'Alessandro—CEO of Manulife Financial—but D'Alessandro would need to leave his beloved Montreal, move to Toronto, and work in life insurance, a sector in which he had no experience. Initially, D'Alessandro was not interested. Work at a life insurance company, he asked himself, particularly a sleepy *mutual* company, a sector known to be full of underachievers?

Even if he consented to let his name stand, D'Alessandro didn't think he stood a chance. The CEO role was vacant because the Manulife board of directors had just fired the incumbent, Tom Di Giacomo. "They'd just had an experience with Di Giacomo," he said to himself. "What are the prospects to give the job to a D'Alessandro?" The question played into a complaint D'Alessandro had about how Canadians in general view Italians in their midst. "He was very conscious of the culture and heritage of Italians, their past and the way the economy of northern Italy was functioning, and that Canadians regarded Italians in a condescending way," said Castonguay. "He came back to this a few times, comparing the culture in Italy to what he considered a not very profound culture in Canada." Before even agreeing to be interviewed, D'Alessandro would think carefully about any possible hindrance caused by his Italian heritage, as well as the personal angst of leaving friends and family for a new life in Toronto. He would measure those negatives against the opportunity to grab hold of this company called Manulife and make it his own.

THREE

In the Beginning

CANADA WAS JUST barely aborning on June 23, 1887, when The Manufacturers' Life Insurance Co was brought into being by an Act of Parliament. The aim was to have $250,000 in paid-up capital, but enthusiasm was so great that investors committed $621,000, of which $126,820 was in hand by January 1888. The president of Manufacturers' was Sir John A. Macdonald, first prime minister of Canada. Macdonald was voted out of office in 1873, then re-elected. It was during his second term, from 1878 to 1891, that Manufacturers' was created. The possibility of a conflict of interest was apparently of no concern in those days.

Such prime ministerial appointments were not uncommon in an era when life insurance was still gaining the trust of citizens. Alexander Mackenzie was president of North American Life from 1881 to 1892; Sir Mackenzie Bowell was at Imperial Life from 1903 to 1912. At Crown Life there were two: Sir Charles Tupper from 1901 to 1904 and Robert Borden from 1928 to 1937. Those four prime ministers, however, became insurance company presidents *after* they were no longer prime ministers. Sir John was the only sitting PM who did double duty.

Moreover, Manufacturers' was the only firm synonymous with a politician's vision, taking its name from the core belief of Sir John's National Policy, a program of high tariffs to protect Canadian manufacturers. Many of the directors of Manufacturers' owned firms that produced goods, such as carriages, hats, gloves, paper, and billiard tables. The company symbol was a working man's powerful arm, wielding a hammer, much like the logo used by Arm & Hammer Baking Soda.

Other than a few newspaper clippings in the corporate archives, little is known about Sir John's business relationship with the firm. Among Sir John's papers in the online National Archives, the only documents that relate to Manufacturers' are a few congratulatory telegrams from directors on the 1891 election, plus some pleas about specific government appointments. While there is no proof one way or the other, it's unlikely that Sir John assumed the presidency without payment. As Richard Gwyn writes in his lively biography *John A.: The Man Who Made Us*, Sir John cared deeply about making money. He had to. At various times in his career he supported an ailing wife, a son, his two sisters, and his mother. His daughter was an invalid; her lifelong care was expensive. "Say nothing on business without receiving a fee in advance," a fellow lawyer advised Sir John.

Directors on the first Manufacturers' board were paid $5 per meeting, but Sir John would surely have received some sort of stipend on top of that. After all, his name gave Manufacturers' an instant and illustrious reputation. In addition to running the country, Sir John chaired meetings of the Manufacturers' board of directors and carried out such honorific duties as signing in his flowing hand all share certificates, as well as letters to employees and agents inviting them to the annual meetings. "I am certain this company is going to be a successful enterprise. If I did not think that I certainly would not be here today, and would not have allowed myself to be placed on the board of directors. The list of directors—with the exception of myself perhaps—shows that you start with a strong impetus, which must soon lead to success," Macdonald told a standing-room-only crowd at the inaugural meeting.

On that occasion Macdonald wore a long steel-grey frock coat and a stylish English scarf around his neck. A newspaper account described him as "unusually buoyant and elastic in carriage, and his eye full of life and vigor. He looked well, decidedly so." After the meeting, Macdonald attended a banquet at the Board of Trade during which policyholders presented him with a portrait done in oils. Said *The Empire*, "He acquitted himself in his usual happy manner and kept the audience in a hilarious mood from first to last."

In failing health Sir John won his last majority in the March 1891 election. The issues were familiar: fights with the provincial premiers, annexation by the United States, foreigners fishing in Canadian waters, and French–English relations. Sir John died at his home in Ottawa on June 6, 1891. He was seventy-four. Since Sir John was a man who liked a drink, it was appropriate that he should be replaced as president of Manufacturers' by George Gooderham, a Toronto businessman who ran Gooderham and Worts, a distillery he inherited from his father, William, which dominated Toronto's east end.

———◆———

INSURANCE HAD ITS BEGINNINGS in seventeenth-century England as protection against marine disasters. Life insurance followed early in the eighteenth century, offered by companies that collected premiums, earned interest on the money invested, and paid beneficiaries at the time of the insured's death. The earliest U.S. life insurance company, Mutual Life of New York, was founded in 1843. The first Canadian company was Canada Life, begun in 1847, followed by Ontario Mutual (later called Mutual Life, then Clarica) in 1868, Sun Life and Confederation Life in 1871, London Life in 1874, North American Life in 1881, Temperance and General in 1884, and Manufacturers' in 1887.

In 1893 Manufacturers' sold its first policy outside of Canada, in Bermuda; Grenada, Jamaica, and Barbados followed in 1894;

Trinidad and Tobago, and Haiti in 1895; then British Honduras, British Guiana, China, and Hong Kong in 1897. "As was often remarked in those heady days, the sun did not set on either the British Empire or Canadian life insurance salesmen," wrote historian Michael Bliss in *Northern Enterprise: Five Centuries of Canadian Business*, a book underwritten by the company on the occasion of its centenary in 1987.

Foreign markets were essential. Canada had too small a population to support so many domestic companies. Sun Life was in Trinidad in 1879 and by the 1890s was operating in Asia, as well as in Central and South America. By 1932 Manufacturers' was active in thirty-five countries, from Burma to the Virgin Islands. Half of the company's business in force, $542,500,000, was outside Canada in what the company lyrically called "Fields Abroad."

———•———

ON MARCH 23, 1901, Manufacturers', run by Gooderham the distiller, announced a most unlikely merger with the Temperance and General Life Assurance Co. of Toronto. Temperance and General had been slow to grow. Even in 1890, six years after the company had been founded, there was no stenographer in head office. "If there was, she could not have been very good looking or I would have remembered her," agent E.R. Machum, of Saint John, later recalled.

Policies were sold to drinkers and abstainers alike, but non-drinkers paid lower rates. Agents were expected to meet equally stringent standards. "As an officer of the Company we expect you to guard its interests with jealous care," said the Temperance and General agents' manual. "We expect you neither to use liquor yourself nor to frequent places where it is sold. By doing either you are brought into contact with men who are very undesirable risks while you lose the confidence and goodwill you should most desire to secure."

The combined company—which dropped the apostrophe and became known as The Manufacturers Life Insurance Co.—was the third-largest life insurance company in Canada, with more than

$25 million worth of insurance in force, $3 million in assets, an annual income of more than $1 million, and a head office staff of twenty-seven. To help seal the deal, George Gooderham stepped aside as president in favour of George Ross, the head of Temperance and General.

When Gooderham died in 1905, he left Toronto some architectural gems. The York Club bought Gooderham's Romanesque mansion, built in 1892, at the corner of St. George and Bloor streets. Gooderham had also commissioned the Flatiron Building at Front and Wellington streets but died before he could move into his new office, which was to have been on the fifth floor, right under the cupola.

Despite giving up the presidency for a time, the Gooderhams, who held a controlling interest in Manufacturers, dominated the company for decades. Two of George Gooderham's sons also served as presidents: William from 1914 to 1935 and his brother Ross from 1935 to 1951. William kept a low profile. "He is a quiet retiring man about whom the newspapers have had little to say," declared the company *News Letter* in May 1914. "His aversion to being photographed or interviewed has been rarely equaled. By the force of his ability and personality he has retained the leadership of the Gooderham 'clan' and his leadership is frankly acknowledged." (Family control of Manufacturers by the Gooderhams was not unusual in the life insurance sector. Confederation Life, for example, was founded in 1871 by John Kay Macdonald, a Scottish immigrant. There were several presidents over the years, but three generations of the Macdonald family ruled for most of the period from 1930 to 1969.)

No sooner had William Gooderham been named president than there was a proposal in 1915 to merge Manufacturers, which had 6 percent of the market share in Canada, with Sun Life, holders of 20 percent of the market. Governments and regulators were no more amenable to the union of giants than they are today. Ottawa investigated for a year and then refused to allow the deal.

At the beginning of the First World War, staff included thirty-nine women and fifty-nine men. Battles abroad did not curtail growth. By the end of the war, the number of women had nearly doubled to seventy-two, with sufficient new men added to keep the number almost constant at fifty-seven. Forty-three men enlisted, of whom six were killed and ten injured. After the war, the already fast pace of growth quickened. It took the first thirty-one years of the company's existence to reach $100 million of business in force in 1918. The second $100 million was in place by 1921. By 1924, Manufacturers was selling more new insurance weekly than the company had sold annually at the beginning of its history.

Any success by an individual agent was usually the result of that person's own efforts, not any grand corporate plan. "I was literally handed a rate book and a pack of applications and told to go to work," said Frank Nicholson, who joined Manufacturers in 1927 and later became agency supervisor of the Canadian division. At one point, he travelled by train with Alf Kinch, inspector of agencies, and George Holmes, who rose to become president but was then with the actuarial department. "I quizzed them both about the difference between various policy contracts. Although they were technically informed in the business, they did not have the knack of imparting knowledge to me in a way that I could absorb during that early stage of my career. I was seriously handicapped by the company's lack of training for both managers and agents."

Still, agents somehow managed to sell the product. The number of employees required to handle applications grew to the point where head office became crowded despite having three full floors in the Dominion Bank building at the southwest corner of Yonge and King streets. The board of directors, realizing that most of the contact between head office and policyholders was by mail, telegraph, and telephone, decided there was no reason to remain in Toronto's financial district. They selected a site two miles north on Bloor Street. The 4.5-acre lot three blocks east of Yonge had a frontage of 300 feet and a depth of more than 700 feet sloping into the Rosedale ravine.

Manufacturers hired Sproatt & Rolph, a local architectural firm, which had designed Hart House and Soldier's Tower on the campus of the University of Toronto. Construction began in 1924 and the building was completed in March 1925 at a cost of $1 million. Four of the six floors were open work areas with no private offices. The fifth floor held the boardroom and offices for executives. On the sixth floor was the dining room and kitchen where the 260 employees daily ate a free lunch.

On the morning of August 26, 1925, Peter C. Larkin, Canadian High Commissioner in London, ceremoniously unlocked the front doors. Gooderham took it upon himself to give the gathering a far too detailed description of the Georgian Renaissance building made of Indiana limestone on a pink Milford granite base. The edifice was 196 feet long and 45 feet deep, and featured a row of six columns at the main entrance. Two 18-foot wings, on both the east and west ends, formed an elongated U. Gooderham went into even greater detail about the construction techniques of the fireproof building.

It was left to general manager J.B. McKechnie to explain the reasons for moving. "Our staff are nearer to their homes; they have more air and better light and finer working conditions, and they have quiet. We have room for expansion here to look after our needs for many years to come." The London *Advertiser* waxed more poetic. "The massiveness of the building suggests a stability which a skyscraper fails to convey, and aroused admiring comments from all who saw it for the first time," enthused the newspaper. "No unsightly outside fire escapes mar its appearance. There is a classic beauty in its straight lines."

———

WHEN PRESIDENT WILLIAM GOODERHAM died in 1935, he was replaced by his younger brother, Ross Gooderham. At fifty-eight, Ross was a dour, pipe-smoking man with hooded eyes, a high forehead, large ears, a strong chin, and a mouth like a letter slot. "He likes to sleep, play golf or billiards, and read detective stories," wrote Kenneth R.

Wilson in the *Financial Post* on December 14, 1935, in what must have been one of the earliest personal profiles of a business leader in Canada. "On Sunday, for example, he sleeps late in the morning and lies down again in the afternoon (except during the golf season)." A member of the Toronto Golf Club, he shot in the low 80s, and he took billiard lessons from a former champion.

Gooderham's education was spotty. He started at the Toronto Model School, attended Eastbourne Preparatory School in England, then returned to Canada at fourteen to attend Jarvis Collegiate, followed by Ridley College, and finally graduated from high school with the help of a private tutor. He did not go to university.

For Ross Gooderham, who served as a member of the Canadian War Loan Committee, the Second World War was a means of showing national mettle. "Never was there a time in the history of nations when the financial resources of their citizens assumed a more important place than is the case at the present day with the peoples engaged in a war costing prodigious sums daily," he told the annual meeting in January 1940. "The war must be prosecuted until victory for the allied, freedom-loving nations is assured. No material cost is too great. The liberty we strive for is as precious as life itself."

By the end of the war, 370 employees out of a total complement of 1624 head office staff and field agents had served in the armed forces. Among those who died were resident secretary E.H. Crumley and assistant secretary A.H. Murray, who were captured when Singapore fell. They perished in 1943 during a 175-mile "Death March" to the Burma border, where they were sent to work on the railway, a project that killed many POWs and forced labourers. In all, twenty-two employees of Manufacturers died in the Middle East, in Hong Kong, on the beaches at Dieppe, over Germany, at Arnheim, and in Holland.

While Paquita Gonzalez did not make the supreme sacrifice, few other employees made a greater wartime contribution. In 1942, when the Japanese invaded the Philippines, where Manufacturers had been in business since 1907, they confiscated corporate assets and records.

Gonzalez, manager Edward Hall, and two other agents hurriedly packed up the contents of the office of the Manila branch before they could be seized. Cashier Ernesto Perlas took 67,000 pesos (US$33,500) in cash and negotiable securities from the safe and hid everything at home, stuffing bills into used clothing, his piano, the ceilings and walls.

The job of safekeeping the records fell to Gonzalez, a slim and dark-eyed woman who had been among the first wave of Filipinas to enter the workforce. She joined Manufacturers in 1935 after women had won the right to vote two years earlier. Because she was a Filipina, the Japanese allowed her to remain free. All the Americans at the branch were sent to internment camps.

Perlas soon decided that it was too dangerous to hide the money and securities, so he turned everything over to Gonzalez. She regularly visited manager Hall in the internment camp and used office funds, always preparing appropriate vouchers, to buy food that supplemented his rations. Even so, he weighed a skeletal 115 pounds when he was finally released.

In October 1944, the Japanese commandeered Gonzalez's home. She demanded that they relocate her belongings. Among the personal and household effects they agreed to move were several boxes of the company's records hidden in a clothes hamper. "It would be thanks to her grit and extraordinary bravery that the Manila Agency would be the first life insurance company to open for business after the war," said the one hundredth anniversary book about Manulife in the Philippines, *From Sea to Sea.* "She could have just as easily been shot, or beheaded, as over a hundred thousand Manileños were in the battle for the city. But Paquita Gonzalez stood her ground." To this day Gonzalez is celebrated at Manulife as an example of how one individual's courage and conviction can make a difference to the success and continuity of the company.

FOUR

Action Jackson

THE SIX-STOREY HEAD OFFICE, opened in 1925 with its fifty thousand square foot of space, had been more than sufficient for twenty years. But as the post-war economy boomed, the staff of seven hundred worked in cramped quarters. Early in 1947, the year of the company's sixtieth anniversary, business in force passed the $1 billion mark and, that May, policy number one million was issued. Manufacturers began construction of a $6 million eleven-storey addition, designed by Toronto architect Marani and Morris, using the same Indiana limestone and welded steel as before.

A major feature of the new premises, completed in 1953, was draft-free indoor climate control. "In effect, the ceiling of each floor acts as a 'sky,' combining air conditioning, radiant heating and cooling, fluorescent lighting, acoustic control and public address system," said *The Telegram*. The only other similar installation was in the Time-Life-Fortune building in New York.

The open floor concept of the original building continued into the new tower. Available office space increased by 145,000 square feet—enough to double the number of employees. Facilities included a main-floor lounge, a library, a health centre, and a 750-seat cafeteria. A Westminster clock chimed the hours and quarter hours; electric amplifiers carried the notes over a wide area. Employees could walk out onto a terrace on the eleventh floor and gaze downtown.

By then, James Hector Lithgow had become president, replacing Ross Gooderham, who died in 1951. Lithgow, who joined the company in 1908 and had been a vice president since 1944, did not last long. He stepped down in 1956, served as the firm's first chairman of the board, and then resigned in 1959 because of poor health. Next in line was George Holmes, a quiet and down-to-earth man who joined the actuarial department in 1919 and worked his way up, becoming vice president and actuary in 1951.

It was during Holmes's time that Manufacturers ordered a new IBM 650 Drum Calculator, the first IBM mainframe computer used in Canada by an insurance company. The circumstances around approval of the 650, which weighed 5300 pounds, were unusual to say the least. Hudson Stowe, comptroller and head of the company's statistical department, had been involved in mechanization since the 1920s, when Manufacturers installed the electronically operated super adding and sorting machines that revolutionized bookkeeping.

Stowe was dispatched to obtain Holmes's approval. Associate actuary Jack Bell knew Stowe was going to point out, as part of his presentation, some of the negative aspects of the 650 so he later asked Stowe if Holmes had any concerns. "Oh, he didn't have much chance to comment on them," said Stowe. "He was sitting in the next cubicle in the washroom to me when I described the 650 to him."

George Holmes, president since 1956, stepped down in 1964 after forty-five years with the firm, remained on the board until 1975, and lived until he was one hundred. After a series of leaders with actuarial backgrounds, the next president, Alf Seedhouse, was of a different stripe. He'd joined Manufacturers in 1925, had been assistant treasurer, and knew investments.

The company Seedhouse headed had 3400 employees and 1150 agents. It took Manufacturers seventy-four years to reach $1 billion in assets in 1961 and only four and a half years to add another $500 million. Some of those assets included a new fourteen-storey office building in Calgary, a one thousand–unit apartment building in Montreal, and a sixteen-storey twin tower office building immediately east of head office to hold the additional staff required by the rapid growth. Seedhouse also led the company into new businesses, such as mutual funds. "Tradition should be a guide, not a gaoler," he said in 1970. "I believe that once a man has fully satisfied his needs for lifelong financial protection through insurance, some money in the stock market, soundly managed by professional investors is, over a reasonable time span, a thoroughly worthwhile aim for any family or for any business man or woman."

But of all the steps Seedhouse took, the most revolutionary occurred in 1968 when he created a twelve-member task force to study management structure. Syd Jackson, a man of the next generation, was appointed to head the group. The future was about to arrive.

WHEN DOMINIC D'ALESSANDRO took over in 1994, Syd Jackson was still on the board of directors. In 1968, Jackson was the man who had taken a strong but directionless firm and begun building a pontoon bridge that would reach all the way to today. Born in Regina in 1922, Jackson served as a lieutenant in the army from 1943 to 1945 and then obtained his Bachelor of Commerce from the University of Manitoba. Named chief actuary in 1956 and senior vice president in 1969, Jackson was among the first modern leaders in a stodgy business. At six feet three inches, he towered over most of his colleagues and kept fit by swimming and skiing.

Unlike most actuaries, who are shy and retiring, Jackson has a ready smile and an animated manner. When I first interviewed him in the 1980s, he acted out some of his wartime training at Fort Benning, Georgia, bouncing around his office to show me how his squad used a landscape model to create a mock artillery battle.

Two issues necessitated the task force launched by Seedhouse. First, Seedhouse and more than half the vice presidents were scheduled to retire within three years. Second, Manufacturers was operating in fourteen different countries, each with its own tax and regulatory regime. The task force recommended dividing the company into separate and autonomous geographic divisions. Although many functions—such as administration, actuarial, and investment—were retained at head office, sales and marketing were moved closer to the clients around the world. The task force also recommended fewer bureaucratic layers and urged a new system of job evaluation, job posting, and performance appraisal.

Women received particular attention. The task force recommended equal opportunity for women, including recruitment, job evaluation, performance appraisal, compensation, access to training, and counselling. Women, who made up three-quarters of staff, had long been second-class citizens. Prior to 1941, when the war caused labour shortages, no married woman had been hired. If a single woman on staff got married, she had to resign. The rules, relaxed in 1941 because of the war, were never again enforced. By 1957, the number of married women on staff outnumbered single women.

To symbolize all the changes, the company adopted a new name in 1971: ManuLife, the version of Manufacturers Life that had been used internally for some time. In the stylized representation, between Manu and Life was positioned a stick man with two legs but only one arm who soon became known as ManuMax, the one-armed bandit. Assets hit $2 billion. "I know that size does not necessarily make us a good company but I confess that this growth makes me feel good," said Seedhouse at the annual meeting in January 1971, his last as president.

———◆———

WHEN SYD JACKSON became president in January 1972, he was forty-nine, the youngest ever to hold that office in a firm that retained Dickensian surroundings. "There were a large number of clerical people in the company, much more than there are now and their jobs in comparison to today's were quite small," said vice president Joe Davin, a member of the task force. "I remember aisles of people who just sat there posting cards. Employees were considered to be almost child-like by management. The company was not a great respecter of its employees. There was no clear expectation of staff by senior management and certainly not much communication between them."

Jackson ordered the walls around private offices torn down and replaced by "office landscaping." Plants and six-foot-high curving acoustic screens were placed among the desks; new carpeting hid the bilious green and black tiles. Even Jackson worked in an open area, albeit with better furniture and more space. "Landscaping got the managers closer. They couldn't sit in their offices. They were right there with their people. This meant a new style of management where a manager had to manage his people—he wasn't just there to solve problems," said Jackson. A new program called OPTime allowed head office staff to work flexible hours. They could work longer hours each day and take a day off every two weeks or a half day every week. Or they could work regular eight-hour days starting any time between 7 A.M. and 10 A.M.

The new decor and organizational changes took two years and cost $1 million. "Life firms have been traditionally as changeless as the basic ingredients of their business, which are life and death. In addition, they have been among the most paternalistic and moralistic of employers. The company knew best, hard work was its own reward, and all that. It's not that many years ago that some employees had to ask their supervisors for permission to go to the bathroom," wrote Robert Catherwood in the *Financial Post* in 1972. "It is unlikely, however, that any Canadian insurer has undergone such a penetrating examination as the 85-year-old Manufacturers is now experiencing. Blowing away the corporate cobwebs has exposed inefficiencies and resulted in some painful changes."

Previous presidents kept out of sight. Jackson often ate lunch in the company cafeteria and once a month invited a dozen employees to the executive dining room so he could hear first-hand their complaints and ideas. At one annual meeting, he donned a T-shirt bearing a likeness of Sir John. In 1975 he attended a meeting of the British division in Switzerland. The three-day affair ended with a black-tie dinner to which Jackson wore a pair of Swiss lederhosen, size extra large. After the meal, when the band played, Jackson took to the dance floor in the local costume. "It must have been 90 degrees," said John Clark, a senior vice president, "but Syd danced all night."

Jackson gave particular prominence to women. Among senior executives reporting to him were three women, a far higher proportion than at other companies. "ManuLife was ahead of its time. I was the first general manager in the insurance industry in North America," said Diane Schwartz, who along with Jalynn Bennett, also an executive, had been a member of the task force. In 1978 Jackson appointed economist Gail Cook-Bennett to the ManuLife board of directors, two years after Royal Bank CEO Earle McLaughlin had outraged the country when he claimed he could not find a competent female director.

The systems department, which in the 1970s grew to four hundred people, led a revolution in office styles as blue jeans replaced grey flannel. "There was a percolating of ideas that enriched the place. We invited guest speakers at lunch, outspoken people like feminist Laura Sabia," said Sy Landau, administrative vice president. "Sometimes we would eat our lunch on the lawn and listen to recitals with string quartets. It was a stimulating place to be."

All the changes brought progress. In 1972, the rate of growth in new business was higher than at any time in the previous twenty-five years. In 1978, Jackson established a corporate affairs department to build a national profile through public relations, advertising, donations, and better liaison with government. In 1982 he launched group life and health insurance in Canada and oversaw the opening of a $50-million twenty-storey office tower called ManuLife Plaza in downtown Los Angeles, followed in 1983 by ManuLife Place, a $100-million thirty-six storey office tower in Edmonton for total real estate holdings of $1 billion.

In 1984 ManuLife opened the North Tower, the second expansion of the original 1925 head office, a $40-million twelve-storey addition of four hundred thousand square feet, clad with reflective gold glass. The executive floor boasted desks of burled Carpathian elm, walls sheathed in Jack Lenor Larsen silk, and ivory wool broadloom bordered and sculpted by women working on their hands and knees with tiny scissors. Joining the North Tower to the rest of the head office complex was a copper-roofed rotunda topped by a cupola with stained glass by Canadian artist David Morgan. This round structure contained the main entrance, the security desk, and a nineteenth-century painting by Cornelius Krieghoff of a First Nations family camped at a portage. The work, done on a cast-iron tabletop that weighed six hundred pounds, was fixed to a wall and could only be moved by forklift truck.

The oval boardroom was a sight to behold, measuring forty by twenty-five feet and containing a custom-designed table that had to be built on site. The cherry wood used was chosen from veneer flitches one-sixteenth of an inch thick, two feet wide and eight to ten feet long. Wood from one hundred trees was examined to find the one tree that supplied all the veneer for the boardroom. Construction of the room and the table took three months. The two-dozen chairs were covered in grey suede; each place had a leather Nienkämper desk pad.

In the rest of the building, the open concept was abandoned for private offices to hold the 1750 head office employees, a relief from the office landscaping that had been a novel experiment but became a noisy barracks that offered no privacy. In the new digs, employees enjoyed a corporate fitness centre with a banked running track, a fully equipped exercise room, a sauna, and showers. The company-subsidized cafeteria served a full-course meal with entrees, such as roast beef, for the bargain price of $1.50, including dessert. The same year the new North Tower was completed, the company changed its logo again, opting for a small green square with Manufacturers and a stylized M, thus bringing to an end the orange logo with the man who had two legs but only one arm.

CREATING BIGGER BUILDINGS was easy. What Jackson wanted was for ManuLife to be Canada's biggest life insurance company. In 1978 he wrote letters to the presidents of eight foreign companies asking if they were interested in being acquired. "To our surprise, Standard Life wrote back and said they were interested," he said. Standard Life Assurance of Edinburgh began in Quebec City in 1833, the first life insurance company to operate in Canada. After the victory of the separatist Parti Québécois in 1976, Standard grew increasingly uncomfortable under the tough new language laws. The 1978 departure of Sun Life from Montreal to Toronto only heightened their anxiety. Selling to ManuLife provided the perfect exit.

Jackson concluded a $1.7 billion takeover that would have made ManuLife Canada's biggest life insurance company. The next step was approval by Ottawa. Previous hopefuls had visited the superintendent of insurance, Richard Humphrys, or his predecessor, Ken MacGregor, both of whom always rejected mergers. Rather than call on Humphrys and hear the wrong answer, Jackson and ManuLife director Yves Fortier, a Montreal lawyer with excellent political connections, went to see Minister of Finance Jean Chrétien. "We're bringing back to Canada ownership of a foreign company," said Jackson. Without hesitation, Chrétien responded, "You've got my approval."

But as the actuaries scrutinized the details, an argument arose. One of the strengths of a mutual company is the ability to move a portion of its surplus around the world. But host countries, including Canada, were beginning to insist that surpluses made in those countries stay in those countries. Would Standard leave behind its $200-million surplus invested in Canada or would Edinburgh repatriate the cash back home as dividends to shareholders? Standard claimed the company was owed that money because of pension loans made after the Second World War, but no record of such a debt could be found.

In addition to such weighty actuarial issues, the members of Standard's Canadian board of directors were miffed that management did not consult them about the deal until the last minute. Life insurance companies come under federal laws for solvency, but the provinces have jurisdiction over property rights. There was a view that merger legislation might be required in every province. No one seemed to have considered these requirements during negotiations, perhaps because there had been so little recent experience with such matters. With the exception of few small deals, the last merger of any size was in 1901 between Manufacturers and Temperance and General. Facing so many unresolved issues, Standard threw up its hands and cancelled the deal.*

Undeterred, Jackson continued to look for other ways to expand. ManuLife bought a 30 percent holding in Canada Trust. "Canada Trust was an exceptional company that was doing well when the banks were in miserable shape," said Jackson. "The banks had done silly things—Dome Petroleum and sovereign country loans where they put their whole capital at risk." When a bidding war developed for Canada Trust, Jackson was prepared only to raise his stake from 30 percent to 51 percent. Genstar of Vancouver, run by expansion-minded co-CEOs Angus MacNaughton and Ross Turner, bid $1.1 billion for the entire company. ManuLife withdrew and made a $150 million profit by selling its shares to Genstar. "In retrospect, I guess we were too much the gentlemen. They were more aggressive," said Jackson.

—◆—

ALTHOUGH THE MANULIFE–STANDARD deal did not go through, it broke the logjam and precipitated other deals that caused less commotion. Mutual Life acquired two small U.S. life companies and an interest in Interior Trust, renamed Mutual Trust. Empire Life merged with Montreal Life. North American Life bought a majority interest in Calvin Bullock, a mutual fund manager. Busiest of all was Trilon

---

*Standard never did sell its Canadian arm. With 1900 employees and 1.3 million clients, it's now the company's largest operation outside the United Kingdom.

Financial, with a growing stable that included London Life and Royal Trust.

As part of the flurry of activity, ManuLife acquired Dominion Life, the eleventh-largest insurance company in Canada with $1.5 billion in assets. That deal put ManuLife into first place, measured by assets, among Canada's 170 life insurance companies. Barely. ManuLife's assets were $13.5 billion; Sun Life's, $13 billion. "I was always frightened of Sun Life," said Jackson. "They were very conservative. I thought if they ever woke up, they'd be really tough competition." Sun Life had been the biggest in Canada since 1908. After almost one hundred years in existence, ManuLife had moved ahead of Sun Life at last. But the Dominion Life deal yielded something else. Just as the task force had accelerated the career of Syd Jackson, the Dominion Life deal produced ManuLife's next leader, Tom Di Giacomo, the last before Dominic D'Alessandro.

FIVE

The Ouster

TOM DI GIACOMO'S FIRST JOB at Manufacturers Life, as a student in 1963, was in the mailroom. He continued to work at the company during the summers while completing his Bachelor of Commerce at the University of Toronto, followed by a Master of Business Administration at the University of Chicago in 1966. Di Giacomo was a prankster who was almost fired for scaring a female colleague with a rubber spider. After a suitable dressing-down, he later admitted, "I became meek and mild for a week."

But he was also smart and quickly came to the attention of the executive. Called in by chairman George Holmes to explain something, Di Giacomo had barely begun when Holmes halted him, saying, "Just hold on. You know more about what you're talking about than I know what I'm talking about, so take your time, we're on the same team." Di Giacomo was named vice president, investments, in 1977, executive vice president and a director in 1984, and then president and chief operating officer in 1985, the first time that title had been used at ManuLife.

In 1984, Dominion Life's American owner, Lincoln National, decided to sell its Canadian subsidiary. Sixty companies expressed interest in buying Dominion, but only those six that actually put in bids showing a dollar range were allowed to question Dominion executives and to take a look at the books. Di Giacomo, named to head ManuLife's takeover team, drove to Kitchener-Waterloo with two other executives. They stayed at the Valhalla Inn to be on time for their early morning meeting at the Dominion Life offices on Westmount Road. With Di Giacomo driving, they left the hotel and immediately got lost. The ten-minute run stretched to twenty before they stopped at a gas station, got directions, and finally arrived half an hour after setting out.

Following that meeting, ManuLife made an offer, one among three firms that took the final step and made a specific bid. A week later Jackson and Di Giacomo were visiting IBM World Trade Corp. headquarters in White Plains, New York. Di Giacomo received a phone call from David Silletto, executive vice president of Lincoln National, telling him that ManuLife's $157.5 million offer had been accepted. Di Giacomo rejoined the lunch meeting with IBM executives and telegraphed the news to Jackson by giving him a thumbs-up. Jackson allowed himself a small smile. In 1986 Di Giacomo and Jackson travelled to Hong Kong, ManuLife's regional chief office for Asia, to attend a board meeting. The trip was a signal of Asia's growing importance as well as proof of Di Giacomo's new place in the upper echelons.

Jackson, who remained chairman, had overseen growth in assets from $2.2 billion to $19.1 billion in fifteen years, but by the time Di Giacomo inherited the CEO role, ManuLife was again in second place behind Sun Life. Jackson acted against expectations and in 1987 chose Di Giacomo rather than Robin Leckie, the chief actuary. "We thought that it was pretty avant-garde to have an investment person as the CEO because it looked as though that part of the business would become increasingly important over time," said director Gail Cook-Bennett.

In 1988, employees in Canadian operations moved into a new head office in Waterloo, a $40-million five-storey building of green glass, spanning three hundred and fifty thousand square feet, with an inner atrium. The staff was an amalgam of 150 Toronto-based employees who moved, about 500 employees from Dominion Life, plus 300 new employees hired after the merger. During the opening ceremonies Di Giacomo was ribbed about his inability to find the Dominion Life office. The new site at Conestoga Parkway and King Street North was easier to locate for visitors from Toronto. Said Di Giacomo, "I didn't authorize construction of this building just so I could find it."

IN 1990, when Di Giacomo bought two small trust companies, Regional Trust and Huronia Trust, he announced a corporate name change to Manulife Financial to more accurately reflect the firm's broadening interests. (The full legal name remained The Manufacturers Life Insurance Company.) That same year, the board appointed Di Giacomo chairman, replacing Syd Jackson, who continued as a director. Di Giacomo now carried all three top titles: president, CEO, and chairman.

The four separate pillars of financial services—banks, insurance companies, brokerage businesses, and trust companies—were becoming more blurred as other jurisdictions followed Jacques Parizeau's lead in Quebec. In 1987, banks were allowed to buy investment dealers; in 1990, trust company rules were also loosened to allow ownership by banks. In 1992, life insurance companies were granted access into banking, and banks were allowed limited entry into insurance. Later that same year, Manulife became the first Canadian life insurance company to take advantage of the new powers by creating Manulife Bank through an amalgamation of several small trust companies that Di Giacomo had acquired. With fourteen branches in Ontario, $900 million in assets, and one hundred thousand customers, Manulife Bank permitted broader distribution of products, such as personal loans and mutual funds.

For Di Giacomo, climbing from the bowels of the mailroom to the burled wood of the executive floor was quite an accomplishment. For the board, giving Di Giacomo three titles over five years offered directors plenty of opportunities to see him in action and be certain they liked what they saw. But somewhere along the way, there was a change in the ambient temperature between the two. Directors and some of the senior officers mingled at dinner the evening before each board meeting. Such events gave board members an opportunity to chat directly to officers and hear first-hand what was happening. For the executives, this command performance was an occasion that confirmed their status.

The dinner held in November 1991, however, was a little different. On that occasion, Di Giacomo borrowed a piece of paper from another member of the executive and jotted down a few speaking points for some comments to the directors. Among the topics he mused about were new capital rules, the probable need to move the U.S. division to the United States or merge with a U.S.-based mutual company, the benefits of rationalizing small territories, such as the United Kingdom and the Caribbean, and eventually, demutualization in order to raise capital.

Some of the directors were disappointed. They were looking for a more specific vision from the CEO. They regarded his speech as little more than ramblings cobbled together at the last minute. Di Giacomo said later he didn't know that directors had such high expectations. "That dinner was not a strategy dinner, it was a blue-skying session. The board just asked me to wax—ineloquently or otherwise," he said. "It was putting the board on notice about issues that were coming down the pike and should not be treated in the usual way. Obviously, I did not have all the answers."

Among the disillusioned was William Blundell, who had just joined the board that year. He had no history with Manulife and no axe to grind against Di Giacomo. But as a former chairman and CEO of GE Canada, he had been through numerous strategic planning sessions. On good boards, he knew that's what directors spent much of their time doing. "It's all about competitive edge [and] how you're going to pursue and achieve that," said Blundell. "Management should come up with a plan and a recommendation. Without such a strategy, you'll have a very restless board."

In March 1992, Di Giacomo received his annual performance review from the board's executive committee. The committee chair was Don McGiverin, governor of the Hudson's Bay Company. At sixty-nine, McGiverin had been a Manulife director since 1974. McGiverin was not one to rock the boat and didn't share Blundell's concerns. Still, Di Giacomo was told to create a long-term strategy. The request was hardly a reprimand, call it constructive criticism, but it marked the first time Di Giacomo had received anything but praise.

ONCE A YEAR, the board met outside Canada. In June 1992, directors gathered in New York for a session held at the Ritz-Carlton Hotel. As part of the program, Di Giacomo arranged presentations by investment bankers Morgan Stanley, as well as insurance consultants Tellinghast, Nelson & Warren. He saw the presentations as helpful background information about international issues, such as demutualization and mergers. When the experts had departed, Di Giacomo asked directors if they had any questions. No one did. Still, rather than see these sessions as helpful, some directors grumbled that Di Giacomo controlled the agenda and restricted discussion.

Directors were, however, pleased to learn that Di Giacomo had created a management strategy committee consisting of the senior officers who reported to him. In the months that followed, however, nothing came of the meetings held at head office, as well as at off-site locations in the Hockley Valley near Orangeville and Langdon Hall in Cambridge. When directors pressed Di Giacomo, he said he didn't want to reveal his thinking until he had consensus.

Di Giacomo's annual performance review in March 1993 was more critical than the previous year's. Three new directors had joined the board: John Cassaday, CEO of CTV Television Network Ltd.;

Arthur Sawchuk, CEO of Du Pont Canada Ltd.; and Paul Tellier, CEO of Canadian National Railways. The new arrivals couldn't comprehend why the board had been so patient with Di Giacomo. "His background was relatively narrow. His experience base was all on the investment side of the business and mostly as a dealmaker. He really had never managed people. He'd never had a real p&l [profit and loss] responsibility," said Sawchuk. "It's a shame. You could argue that it was an injustice to the man to put him into a job for which he was going to ultimately fail."

A CEO can survive a lot of muttering from board members when times are good, but when profits slump, support vanishes. At the annual meeting in April 1993, Di Giacomo announced that net income in 1992 was $76 million, down from $201 million in 1991, the worst performance in ten years. In that same month, Robert Smithen, senior vice president and chief financial officer, announced that after twenty-two years with Manulife he was leaving for a similar role at Canada Life. Such an abrupt departure was significant; in the world of insurance, few senior officers switch to work for a competitor. Some directors conducted an exit interview with Smithen to find out why.

Smithen told them there was no trouble hidden in the books, nor was he dismayed by Di Giacomo's brusque manner. He'd simply become fed up because Di Giacomo either didn't have a clear idea where the company should go or was keeping his plans to himself. For all his talk about the need for consensus, Di Giacomo wasn't a team-builder. Discussions with senior management, Smithen said, tended to be one-on-one with little follow-up.

—◆—

SYD JACKSON, the man who'd picked Di Giacomo to succeed him, decided it was high time to act. In concert with director Gail Cook-Bennett, Jackson pushed for the creation of a powerful new board committee called the Management Resources and Compensation Committee (MRCC). Robert Després, a Quebec City businessman who had been chair of Atomic Energy of Canada and who served on numerous corporate boards, chaired the group; other MRCC members included Blundell, Sawchuk, and Kenneth Whalen, a corporate director from Dorset, Vermont. All the committee members had been CEOs.

In June the MRCC hired Gary Dibb, of Meriden Consulting Group of Toronto, to interview the senior managers who reported to Di Giacomo. Di Giacomo was becoming irritated but pressed on, aiming to deliver his strategic vision in November. Dibb interviewed the six executives for two hours each and found they were split. Half were loyal to Di Giacomo, the others less so. Dibb reported the results to Di Giacomo and the MRCC, but when Di Giacomo asked to speak to the MRCC about the findings, the committee refused. The tide was turning. After wrestling with the matter for two more weeks, the MRCC members decided they would recommend that Di Giacomo be fired when the full board next met on August 19.

The MRCC report to the board meeting focused on three points: Di Giacomo had lost the confidence of senior management, he had lost the confidence of the MRCC, and he had proposed no strategy. Initially, there was some support among directors for Di Giacomo, but after a three-hour discussion, the view to oust him was unanimous. "He was a one-man show. He was very much used to making investment decisions on his own. Most of the senior management and the board were uncomfortable with him. It became a serious issue and we resolved it," said Jackson.

Després and Blundell delivered the verdict to Di Giacomo. "We feel it's best for you and the company to part company. Maybe we should go our separate ways and you should do something different," Després told him. "I didn't put up a squawk," said Di Giacomo. "Even if there were pros and cons, you're going to be caught in the middle of something. Unless you've got support, it's time for a new leader to take the company up to the next stage."

Després called together Manulife's senior managers and told them that Di Giacomo had decided to resign. Jackson would serve as interim chairman with Blundell as interim CEO while the board looked for Di Giacomo's replacement. Blundell gave a brief pep talk about Manulife's strengths and corporate resilience. A terse five-sentence statement was released at mid-afternoon saying that Di Giacomo, who was fifty-one, was leaving to pursue other interests. A friend, unaware of the news, phoned to find that Di Giacomo had gone home, and his secretary was in tears. The war of attrition was over as was Di Giacomo's twenty-five years at Manulife, six of them as CEO.

When I interviewed Di Giacomo three months later he was still struggling to understand what had happened. "We've always been an open company. If there were concerns, I thought they could have been more forthcoming. Nobody ever gave me any real reasons. The road was bumpy, but Jesus, in this environment everybody's got problems. I never got the impression there were differences between me and the board. They were interested in strategy and governance, but those issues were on the table and were being addressed. The only thing that I can figure is that some of them were concerned about the speed and also a lack of cohesion in the management group."

The board asked Robert Swidler to present a short list of candidates by mid-October, with a view to picking a new CEO by year's end. No internal candidate would be considered; the board was looking for new blood, new thinking. "This was a mutual company. And a mutual was like a public utility. It's not hard-bitten. There's a culture that anything acceptable is acceptable," said Arthur Sawchuk. "The inherent nature of a mutual is that it's not a profit-making organization. As long as you pay some little, miserable dividend, it's OK; as long as you cover the capital requirement for the long-term liabilities, everything in life goes on. I knew there had to be somebody who would change the culture to give it a little more business focus." That somebody was Dominic D'Alessandro.

Passport photo when Dominic D'Alessandro, lower right, age three, immigrated to Canada in 1950 with his mother Angelina, and brothers Nicholas, twelve, and Felix, five.

Dominic, right, and Felix dressed for first communion. Angelina is peeking around the door of their house on Rue des Seigneurs.

Dominic, right, with a friend, on the streets of Little Burgundy.

Dominic, fifteen, in calculus class at Loyola with Brother Eugene.

Dominic at graduation from Loyola in 1967.

Dominic with Pearl and his Corvair convertible in 1965.

Dominic in his Beaconsfield home with his mother in 1990.

The D'Alessandro family, from left, Michael, Dominic, Pearl, Anthony, and Katherine, at a nephew's wedding in 2005.

Boardroom portrait of Sir John A. Macdonald, first president of Manufacturers' Life, by Frederick Arthur Verner.

A sampling of the company's logos, used from 1887–1900, 1938–1959, and 1971–1984.

Alf Seedhouse, left, president 1963–1972, and his successor, Syd Jackson, the first president, 1972–1987, of the modern era.

Tom Di Giacomo, chief executive officer 1987–1993, was ousted by the board.

Main door, gardens, and gated entrance of the Toronto head office, erected in 1925.

North Tower and rotunda, opened in 1984, part of Toronto corporate headquarters.

New team at the top, annual report 1993, Chairman William Blundell, left, and D'Alessandro.

D'Alessandro on the October 1994 cover of ROB Magazine.

SIX

New Team at the Top

WHILE MOST of the Manulife directors had never heard of Dominic D'Alessandro, the chair of the search committee, Robert Després, of Quebec City, was an early champion. Després knew that D'Alessandro, during his six years at Laurentian, had doubled the size of Laurentian to $10 billion in assets and topped all of the major banks—except Scotiabank—in return on equity, a key measure of profitability. Després made certain that D'Alessandro was on the short list, along with the four other finalists, who were all from Ontario.

Even after he learned he'd made the cut, D'Alessandro continued to claim he had little interest in the job. "I actually had to fly with Dominic down to Toronto because I was afraid if I didn't sit next to him and take him into the interview that he would bolt. He was really doing this reluctantly. He didn't think he would get selected," said Robert Swidler, who sat in on all the sessions between candidates and directors.

D'Alessandro met three times with the six-member search committee, answering their questions and describing his accomplishments, personal traits, and management style. "I'm not a faddish-type manager. I don't believe that you read a new book and you reinvent yourself. I think it's important to stay abreast of developments, but I think what makes great companies isn't flash. It's hard work, character, commitment, clarity of what you're in business for, and focus."

D'Alessandro chose not to present a detailed vision or specific prescription. "I talked about how those were my values and whatever I did I wanted to be the best at it and that I took great pride in my work. I said it was possible to take a great institution like Manulife and make it perform to the levels of the best in the world. What did that mean? It certainly meant better than a 6 or 7 percent return on equity. It meant getting respect from your peers in the marketplace. It meant being a place where the best minds wanted to come."

For a reluctant candidate, D'Alessandro pitched himself adroitly. "He had a way of describing what the problems were and what his approach would be in layman terms, so that even somebody who was relatively uninitiated could follow him," said Swidler. "There were many board members who were not amongst the most financially literate people I've ever seen. So Dominic had to explain to them what was wrong with the company and how he would go about enhancing its fortunes without in any way making these people feel inferior to him. He succeeded in pulling that off masterfully. They felt that he would not only be the best guy for the job, but that he wouldn't show them up in so doing."

The support of acting CEO Bill Blundell was crucial. He knew Laurentian Group chairman Claude Castonguay as a fellow director of the Conference Board of Canada, so he phoned to hear Castonguay's assessment. "It was a difficult question. I didn't want to see Dominic leave but at the same time I felt it would be unfair to Dominic to give a false or incomplete assessment. So I told [Blundell] as clearly as I could that Dominic was a first-class CEO and that, in my opinion, he could do the job at Manulife," said Castonguay. "He is a very, very determined individual. I'm sure he wanted to put Manulife at the top of the life insurance industry in Canada. I was very sorry to see him leave."

Once Blundell got behind D'Alessandro, support grew until the search committee unanimously recommended D'Alessandro to the full board for approval. "You knew very early on that this was a person who had ideas, who had focus, who knew where to look, who had vision, and could execute. He was a superb communicator around the board table as well," said Gail Cook-Bennett, a director. "When you take a bright person with the right values and the willingness to understand the business—sure, he'd been used to financial services, but insurance is a different beast—he got inside, understood it, managed to motivate an awful lot of people and bring depth to the organization."

D'Alessandro's base salary during his final year at Laurentian had been $431,000, but the real money flowed from the options worth $4 million that he cashed in as he left. Manulife was able to pay him a higher salary, $600,000, but unlike Laurentian, Manulife was not a public company, so compensation could not include stock options. D'Alessandro demanded, and his new employer agreed, to set up something called "phantom equity," which meant that if he took the company public he would receive shares or, if he departed, he would be paid the cash equivalent based on any growth that had taken place.

To figure out the number of phantom shares, Manulife obtained two outside opinions on the company's book value and took the average: it was $2.7 billion. The notional value of D'Alessandro's initial allotment in what was officially called the Long Term Incentive Plan was set at $3 million, the equivalent of owning about 0.001 percent of the company.

———————

WITH THE HIRING of D'Alessandro, the roles of CEO and chairman were split. "New Team at the Top" screamed the 1993 Manulife annual report that was published shortly after D'Alessandro's arrival in January 1994. The cover photo showed CEO D'Alessandro and Chairman Blundell, standing shoulder-to-shoulder, ready for work.

The Manulife D'Alessandro joined at age forty-seven had assets of $39 billion and 6300 employees plus 6000 agents worldwide.

In his first week on the job, D'Alessandro called Felix Chee, who'd been hired as treasurer a few months earlier, and invited him to lunch so he could hear Chee's perspectives as a recently arrived new boy like himself. D'Alessandro was staying in a company apartment at the Manulife Centre a few blocks away and didn't yet have his car, so they went to lunch in Chee's vehicle. As they left Manulife's multi-level parking garage, D'Alessandro said, "My God, we pay people too well here. There are quite a few expensive cars."

When they returned to the garage D'Alessandro was surprised that the space where Chee had previously parked was occupied. Chee told him there were no reserved places. "Not even for the CEO?" asked D'Alessandro. "Do you see any reserved signs?" said Chee, explaining that it was first come, first served. "To his credit, he never reserved a space. He just came in early for the next few weeks and parked in one spot, so he was always the first guy there. After a while, everybody understood that was where Dominic parked, that's where the boss was," said Chee. That self-assurance that he knew best and offered leadership by example would become D'Alessandro's signature style. He would earn his own way and rise or fall based on that performance. Others would do well to follow his lead.

During the first two months, D'Alessandro gave a series of speeches to a total of three thousand employees—almost half the workforce—delivering an upbeat message that recalled his own roots and how he'd been given a chance to prove himself in top-ranked organizations, such as Coopers & Lybrand and the Royal Bank. D'Alessandro told employees that he would not favour anyone simply because they had the right name or the proper background. "We don't care who your parents are or where you came from or even where you went to school. What concerns us is simply: What can you do?"

But Manulife and the other life insurance companies had a systemic problem: Compared with other sectors, the industry was functioning in the paleolithic era. The cover illustration on a story about D'Alessandro in *ROB Magazine* featured a cartoon rendering of him riding a dinosaur. Declared the headline: *Life in the Slow Lane: Can Manulife's Dominic D'Alessandro lead Canada's insurers out of the prehistoric age?* "I was mortified that it would offend, but it didn't," said D'Alessandro. "The story wasn't unsympathetic, but it didn't really give the connotation of an industry that was going anywhere fast or doing anything exciting. It's an industry that was always a little step behind. The trick was to be in step."

As if to underline the revolution in management that had taken place, Manulife ran an ad in *The New York Times* under the slogan "Leadership is the only choice." The ad featured Teddy Roosevelt, noting that Roosevelt was in the second year of his presidency when Manulife "began insuring America's affluent." Affluence was already returning to Manulife. Under interim CEO Bill Blundell, profit in 1993 rose to $187 million—more than double 1992's rock-bottom results of $85 million. Manulife was coming back on course.

Longtime Manulife executives soon saw D'Alessandro's capacity to make quick decisions. "Dominic had ambitious goals for the company in terms of growth and returns and holding people accountable. He was very clear in terms of strategy: Do it well, do it big, or get out of the businesses. He brought a lot of clarity to the company strategically," said Donald Guloien, who was vice president of U.S. individual business. (Guloien is pronounced Guh-loin.)

Under Di Giacomo, for example, a matter involving guarantees in the United States had been discussed for eighteen months without any decision. "I used to find it kind of frustrating. They'd have all the facts, and they'd ask for more. There'd be more and more people involved. We requested a meeting with Dominic and he said, 'It's clearly this way, let's get on with it.' Someone said, 'Do you want another paper?' and he said, 'What more could we have?' He was absolutely stunned, like how long have you guys been working at this?" said Guloien. "He had enough information to make the call. That was a very early sign to me, and to others, that this was going to be a different place."

Guloien was an early beneficiary. As the head of the U.S. individual insurance and annuity business—about 70 percent of Manulife's business in that country—Guloien worked in Toronto but reported to Ken Beaugrand in Boston. Beaugrand wanted Guloien to move to Boston, but Guloien was reluctant, particularly if his stay there was going to be brief. His wife, Irene Boychuk, was head of human resources for Apple Canada, and the couple was thinking about starting a family. Guloien asked D'Alessandro in the summer of 1994 if there was something he could do in Toronto instead of moving to Boston. D'Alessandro offered Guloien the job as head of a new department called business development. Guloien accepted what turned out to be the beginning of many roles that put him at D'Alessandro's right hand.

———

AFTER THE DEPARTURE of Di Giacomo, but prior to D'Alessandro's arrival, the Manulife board retained the Monitor Group, of Cambridge, Massachusetts, to review operations and make recommendations. D'Alessandro feared that the study by the consulting firm, conducted during the first half of 1994, would be an intrusion and a waste of time. "Everyone was wondering what Monitor would say or not say. Did they make a good presentation to Monitor? I thought, 'I've got to get these guys out of here or they'll kill the place,'" said D'Alessandro, who told Michael Bell, the Monitor partner in charge, to wrap up his work as quickly as possible. As a sweetener, D'Alessandro gave Monitor another one-year advisory assignment, which consisted of a $10,000 monthly retainer with no particular responsibilities.

D'Alessandro's attitude reflected what he'd learned at the Royal Bank. "I tell my people, sure, you can get yourself consultants to help you with the strategy, but I might conclude, 'What do I need you for? Isn't that your job?' And it is their jobs and that's why we're successful. It's not been manufactured for us in a binder. I built Manulife without ever spending a nickel on a consultant."

But Monitor's work was almost complete, and D'Alessandro didn't want to defy the board so soon by dismissing the findings. Monitor's 223-page report was a scathing indictment of how Manulife had been managed. Investments, which had lost $1.1 billion during the previous five years, was cited in particular, but all seven key findings were unfavourable: "Manulife does not actively monitor its performance against appropriate metrics. Manulife has lacked the data and process for setting priorities and establishing a strategic architecture. Manulife does not systematically identify and evaluate new opportunities on a company-wide basis. Manulife has undercommitted to developing a highly effective general management team. Disconnect between liability and investment management is the most costly breakdown in Manulife general management. Manulife has missed opportunities for leveraging interrelationships across divisions. Conservative, expense-driven approach to information technology has undermined capability to compete and manage effectively."

In comparison, the new CEO's vision and values were consistent from day one. D'Alessandro had just joined Manulife when Bruce Gordon, vice president, U.S. group and pensions, decided on the spur of the moment to invite his new boss to address some of his U.S.-based account executives and top managers who were attending an awards ceremony in Toronto. When Gordon arrived unannounced at D'Alessandro's office to suggest the idea, the new CEO agreed immediately. The two men went downstairs to the International Room, where D'Alessandro had his picture taken with the group. One of the award winners, Pat Fields, had played college basketball. He was six feet eight inches, so D'Alessandro joined the other winners on the stage while Fields stood on the floor below. That way, all the smiling faces were more or less aligned.

D'Alessandro presented the awards and gave an off-the-cuff speech that offered an early insight into his management style. He said that although he was new to the job and was busy assimilating information, he liked what he saw—but he was going to be watching everyone closely. "He wanted to talk to my people," said Gordon. "He used that to get the message out that he wanted Manulife to be the best in the world in those businesses that we choose to operate in."

———✦———

D'ALESSANDRO CALLED a three-day meeting in June at Toronto's Inn on the Park for the top 125 Manulife officers, everyone from vice president up. Ten-member working groups were assigned designated aspects of the Monitor report for discussion and debate. They then picked a representative who reported their views to a plenary session chaired by D'Alessandro. As each business line or division was scrutinized, the head of that area was given an opportunity to respond.

The Canadian division, said Monitor, had "not cleared the corporate hurdle rate in recent years." The study recommended shifting the corporate culture from just selling life insurance to the new and faster-growth areas of financial planning and savings products. The consultants told Manulife to focus on upper-income clients and resist any temptation to go down-market in search of more prospects.

In the United States, said Monitor, overcapacity and consolidation plagued the entire industry; sales were flat and profit margins declining. Manulife had no particular individual strength, products were higher-priced than average, and the field force was "confused and discontented." One specific comment by a Manulife employee captured the mood of many respondents: "Our products stink!" Manulife needed more customer focus, better communications with the field, and new product ideas.

In the United Kingdom, where Manulife had an inconsequential 0.3 percent of the market share, the company was "very vulnerable" as regulatory pressures increased and new players entered the market. U.K. operations "are unlikely to generate an acceptable return on investment as currently configured." Acquire another company and get bigger or sell the division, said Monitor.

Monitor was more optimistic about the Asia Pacific region as having "the strongest prospects for overall market growth and profitability." The report praised Hong Kong, which was responsible for 78 percent of the company's premiums in the region. Manulife's efforts to establish beachheads in Korea, Taiwan, and Singapore had made little progress. Management was described as short-staffed and ill-equipped, information systems were inadequate, and there had recently been staff departures.

By the time the same group gathered again in September at Queen's Landing in Niagara-on-the-Lake, Ontario, D'Alessandro had considered what he'd heard at the June meeting and was ready to share his vision. His five-point strategy, after only eight months on the job, was simplicity itself. First, give customers value for their money. Second, demonstrate the highest degree of professionalism. Third, make integrity apparent in every activity. Fourth, be the employer of choice by attracting and retaining ambitious, talented individuals. Fifth, follow a vision that he succinctly stated: "Manulife will be the most professional life insurance company in the world, providing the very best financial protection and investment management services tailored to customers in every market where we do business."

In his keynote speech, D'Alessandro reassured officers that among Manulife's great strengths were its underwriting and actuarial capabilities. Indeed, he declared that those professionals had not been sufficiently celebrated. "The importance of these functions has perhaps been overlooked over the very recent past— perhaps because of other challenges that the organization has had to deal with—and there is concern that the depth and strength of our actuarial function is not what it used to be. We must restore our position of having the best actuaries in the industry, by attracting, developing, and retaining superb actuarial talent," he said. Anyone in the actuarial department who disagreed could only keep quiet after hearing such an uplifting challenge.

Moving on to investments, he took the same tack. Pay a compliment, cite criticism, declare that the problems could be fixed, and look to the future. While performance was "acceptable," Manulife had failed to relate investments to liabilities. "This is the famous disconnect between assets and liabilities that the Monitor people and others have commented on. This disconnect has cost us dearly. We have too much real estate. The new money funds had bond portfolios that were not properly matched to the term of the liabilities. These problems can and are being fixed. In the future we will not repeat the mistakes of the past."

Some areas were pronounced a total shambles. "The role of technology within Manulife is not as visible, nor is it afforded the importance that is normally found at other institutions. We appear not to appreciate the potential for technology to be used to improve marketing effectiveness or customer service. The status quo is not a viable situation. We are just falling further behind." A technology conference in June attended by senior systems people from around the world had been a good first step. More such problem-solving sessions would follow.

Innovation was another ingredient that D'Alessandro declared missing in action. "We simply have not made the funds available to finance a proper research and development function. While there are excellent examples of initiatives in several of our divisions, I don't think that most of you would disagree that we need to re-establish our capacity to innovate. It bothers me, for example, to hear that others have better or more responsive products on the market than we do."

Financial services firms, such as Manulife, live or die on their ratings, the measurement by agencies of creditworthy status. The designations not only set pricing to raise capital, but they also reassure clients that the firm will be around in fifty years to pay a death benefit or provide the promised retirement pension. Moody's, one of the top rating agencies, had just given Manulife a rating of AA3. Not only was that three levels below Moody's best rating—embarrassing enough— but it was also two levels below the rating that Moody's assigned to Manulife's major Canadian competitor, Sun Life.

Another agency, Standard and Poor's, said in its report that Manulife was not generating an acceptable level of profitability to receive its top rating, AAA. For that designation, Manulife would have to earn $400 million and show a return on equity of 14 percent, double the current levels. The problem grew worse after the Canadian government seized a competitor, Confederation Life, in August 1994, thereby throwing into disarray the entire insurance sector. At the same time, the federal deficit ballooned, and the ratings agencies downgraded Canada to AA. The agencies have a rule that no company can have a higher rating than its country's, so Manulife was also downgraded to AA. "The place was in dreadful shape. Dominic had his work cut out for him," said Tom Kierans, a Manulife director since 1990. "We took a ratings hit at the same time, which was huge, particularly in the United States. We don't distribute through our own agencies in the U.S. We distribute through a plethora of independent centres. Having the triple A is big league. He assumed the challenge with a degree of buoyancy which was quickly eradicated." Kierans happened to be in Hong Kong with D'Alessandro when they heard the bad news about ratings. "His eyes were unfocused and blank. We were just right at the nadir."

———•≡•———

D'ALESSANDRO COULD DO NOTHING about the federal deficit, but he could begin by improving Manulife's bottom line in order to win back the AAA rating. D'Alessandro declared that his goal was to double annual profits and reach a 14 percent return on equity within two years. The first step was to sell poorly performing assets and get out of unprofitable lines of business. "We can't be all things to all people. I am going to demand very rigorous analysis of what businesses we are in, which are supported by our core competencies and which are not, and demand that we get better and better in those areas where we choose to participate. This is how we will become the best. Great companies benchmark themselves not against last year but against the best in the industry," D'Alessandro said in his Niagara-on-the-Lake speech.

Imagine you were a high mucky-muck sitting in that audience. Some listeners would welcome D'Alessandro's fearless focus, nodding and saying later that it was about time someone took charge. But if this gathering were like most groups in society, many others would be fearful of the changes about to take place. They would worry that their division would be found wanting and that they would be among the first to be fired. Maybe in their heart of hearts they were secretly relieved to think that they'd soon be free to go elsewhere, with a generous severance package in hand.

If that sort of thinking gripped the audience on that September day, then Dominic D'Alessandro had achieved his goal. There's a regime change! Watch out! If you're good, you might be allowed to go forward with us. If you're just a hanger-on, you might as well disembark now. Getting tossed off at high speed might be messy.

SEVEN

Early Acquisitions

DOMINIC D'ALESSANDRO may not have admired Monitor or any other consulting firm, but the study did provide a wealth of useful information. As for assessing the cadre of senior officers he had inherited, he needed no help. "Initially, my reaction wasn't positive about any of the management team. I didn't know whether they would be able to perform at the standards I thought you needed to create a world-class company," said D'Alessandro. But first he had to establish his own credibility. "I'm not going to help the board if I say, 'Look, I've got a management team and I've got to get rid of them all.' That's not very smart. I went about it in a way that I thought was appropriate for the organization, for the individuals, and for everybody, which was sequentially."

The first department to come under his paint-peeling scrutiny was investments. "With an insurance company it's absolutely critical that they manage their investments properly. I can sell a lot of lousy life insurance policies and it'll take a long time for those to bite me in the rear end. But if I'm investing hundreds of millions of dollars every day, I don't need to make too many mistakes and in a very short period of time I can be out of business," said D'Alessandro.

George Neal, head of investments, left in June 1994 and was replaced by two officers: Joe Mounsey, who had been running the U.K. division, and Richard Coles, who had spent thirteen years at Canada Trust in real estate. Coles, D'Alessandro's first executive recruit, went through an exhaustive process of three interviews with D'Alessandro, which included a dinner meeting. "One of the things he wanted to ensure was that he was getting somebody who had a stable family life," said Coles, who fulfilled that criterion. He met his wife at university; they were married in 1972, had three children, and had lived in the same house since 1978. "He thinks that if you have a stable family life, you'll be stable in your business career. There are real stresses by intense business careers put on families," said Coles.

D'Alessandro's main message to all managers was simple: Individual leadership was welcome, but that didn't mean free reign. He wouldn't just check in once a year to see how officers were doing. He'd be quizzing them closely on a weekly, sometimes daily, basis. Over the next seven years, D'Alessandro continued to seek the most suitable leadership for investments. After two years of Mounsey and Coles, he appointed Coles head, naming him general manager. That lasted for two years until the job was upgraded to chief investment officer in 1997 and given to Felix Chee, treasurer since 1993. "When Di Giacomo was there, the investment side was the locus of the company. When Dominic came, the company became more corroborative in the sense that investment wasn't driving everything. There was more glue in the organization. Dominic got things shored up, more focused, a lot more disciplined," said Chee.

Next, D'Alessandro decided to move the investments division away from simply being asset managers and to turn it into a more sophisticated place for marketing and distribution of wealth management products. Chee decided this was not his area of expertise and resigned. "Building distribution really wasn't my forte. I went to Dominic and said it's time I had a change. He agreed. It was a very amicable discussion," said Chee, who went on to run business operations at the University of Toronto and is now in Beijing as special adviser to the president of the China Investment Corp.

In Chee's place, D'Alessandro named Donald Guloien as chief investment officer in 2001 and finally declared himself satisfied with the department. "I have my own team in place now so I don't look at transactions. I trust the people and I know that they will protect the company's interests. That wasn't the case on day one. There were a lot of transactions that were in place that I didn't think were sound from a risk–reward perspective, so we undid them. I have a saying, 'If I'm going to blow my brains out, I'd like to do it myself.' Initially, just about anything in excess of $25 million would end up on my desk. Today, I only see things in the hundreds of millions because we've got much more rigour and processes and the people are very, very sound," said D'Alessandro.

Other departments were also transformed, most on a speedier timetable. Within two years of D'Alessandro's arrival, almost half of the top two-dozen officers had gone, either because they didn't meet his expectations or were due to retire. In addition to George Neal, the dearly departed included Pat Jacobsen, senior vice president, human resources; Kenneth Beaugrand, senior vice president and general manager, U.S. operations; Elvon Harris, senior vice president and general manager, Asia Pacific; Brian Buckles, vice president, operational planning; Stephen Gittins, vice president, information technology; David Bell, vice president, international; and Ross Morton, vice president, reinsurance. "It was an organization that needed shaking up and he shook it up. A lot of people had got complacent. He made changes," said John Richardson, who'd been hired by Tom Di Giacomo in 1992 after working at Canada Trust and was among those who prospered in the new regime. "They would go into his office and try to advocate positions that they hadn't fully thought through and they discovered they couldn't. They could in the past, but they couldn't any more," said Bob Cook, who worked for Manulife in the United Kingdom for the first eighteen months of D'Alessandro's time in office. "But if you'd thought something through, and done your analytical work, you could have a civilized conversation and everything was fine."

When Cook was appointed general manager for Asia and Japan in 2007, D'Alessandro told him, "You're going to want to change some people, but don't do it all at once. It would be too revolutionary and the organization couldn't handle it. I knew all the people I had to change within thirty days, but I didn't do it immediately. It took me three to five years." Those executives who were there when D'Alessandro arrived and made the cut were Felix Chee, Donald Guloien, chief actuary Geoff Guy, John Richardson who ran the U.S. division, and Victor Apps, who was in charge of Asia. Hired by D'Alessandro from the outside were Richard Coles; Peter Rubenovitch, whom D'Alessandro had known at the Royal Bank, as senior vice president and corporate controller; and Roy Firth, with whom D'Alessandro had worked at both Royal and Laurentian, as president of Elliott and Page, the mutual funds arm.

All newly appointed CEOs bring about personnel upheavals. There may be competence problems they are unwilling to put up with, chemistry issues that rub the wrong way, changes in direction that mean former officeholders have the wrong skills, or officers who seize the regime change as the right time to retire. In his day, Syd Jackson had tackled a similar situation. "All of my seniors were fifteen years older, which made it very easy to put in my own people. But it made the board of directors very uneasy for a while. Here I am coming out with all these ideas and there's nobody that they know. 'Is this guy doing the right thing, or is he off his rocker?' So the first year as president wasn't any fun," Jackson told me in 2008. Within three years, he'd replaced all six top executives.

For his part, Tom Di Giacomo had streamlined the structure to reduce by half the number of individuals reporting to him and had brought in outsiders. D'Alessandro, however, took the reorganizational exercise to a whole new high-pressure level by simultaneously getting rid of some executives, hiring new blood, and rewarding a chosen few from the previous administration.

Those executives already at Manulife whom D'Alessandro promoted had to display a certain amount of courage. For example, Donald Guloien was in charge of some U.S. businesses that Monitor didn't like. "I wasn't prepared to lay down because some guys from Boston had come in, the high priests of Harvard. I got into some pretty feisty debates with the lead consultant. I think Dominic realized I wasn't a wimp. I could stand up for myself, articulate arguments, and wasn't afraid to debate with the best of them," said Guloien. "We're number one in the United States now, so it's a damn good thing we didn't shrink or kill that business."

As the newly appointed head of business development, Guloien did not acquire firms, as the title would imply. On D'Alessandro's orders, Guloien sold twenty poorly performing divisions, including group life and health in the United States, insurance and banking in Britain—a country in which Manulife had been operating for seventy-five years—and a dozen retail branches of Manulife Bank. The total capital raised, $3.1 billion, was redeployed to more promising activities.

Monitor had recommended getting out of the U.S. group pension business—particularly the defined contribution 401(k) plans. Profit was marginal, and Manulife was a very small participant in a fragmented market where pricing and profit pressures were likely to increase because of new entrants, such as Fidelity Investments and T. Rowe Price. Bruce Gordon, who was vice president, savings and retirement services, told D'Alessandro in the summer of 1994 that he believed he could create a successful pension business. "It had a thousand participants, it was a little pebble. I was inclined to sell it because it didn't show up on the radar screen. Bruce gave me a song and dance that if I'd just give him a chance, he'd build it into a business. Today, it's a major business," said D'Alessandro. Assets under management in the 401(k) business were about $500 million in 1994. Before being promoted to another role, Gordon turned the business into the fastest-growing small 401(k) provider in the United States, with $10 billion in assets. Today, assets are more than $50 billion.

D'Alessandro's success across a wide variety of fronts produced positive results in his first full year—profits rose to $281 million in 1994 from $187 million in 1993. While that was a record for the company, it did not satisfy D'Alessandro. He pronounced the outcome "reasonable," noting that while return on equity had risen to 9.6 percent, it remained well below his target of 14 percent.

ONE DEPARTMENT that baffled D'Alessandro for years was human resources; he went through three different heads of that department in eight years. Human resources was a "graveyard," admitted D'Alessandro. "The people who were there didn't know the business. It's difficult for them to get credibility with the operating people. I would support them for a year or so, but at the end of the day you have to win your own credibility. Many of those people are just long on process and short on everything else. It's pretty hard to be long on expertise if you don't know the business because no one comes to talk to you or they don't seek your opinion. Then you try to give yourself importance by writing memos and making more complicated forms. So we had some misadventures there."

At root, D'Alessandro did not believe that human resources added much value. "They are necessary to run your compensation program, make sure that your benefits packages are proper and afford-able to both the company and for the employee. They do a lot of the nuts and bolts operations. When it gets to the very high senior-level stuff, Dominic needs to be involved. That's where the conflict comes; he needs to control that himself," said John Richardson.

Finally, in 2002, D'Alessandro installed Manulife veteran Diane Schwartz Bean in the role. Bean, who joined Manulife in 1975, had run both the U.S. and international divisions. Bean had retired in 1997 at fifty, remarried, and moved to Jamaica. She worked part-time on projects for Manulife but became bored and was open to D'Alessandro's offer to become senior vice president, corporate human resources and communications. In an unusual arrangement, she worked three weeks a month in Toronto and spent the fourth week in Jamaica. "HR was never a high-level function to begin with. When Dominic came in, he was designing a professional company firing on all cylinders. He hired some senior people, but they weren't particularly financially oriented and they didn't know our business. He's a very quantitative person and that's a very important intelligence in our company. He was frustrated at having hard questions and getting soft answers," said Bean.

Bean focused human resources on issues such as executive development, hiring and retaining talent, and compensation. "We were no longer dismissed. We were part of the team," she said. "Before there were all kinds of ideas, but they would languish because they could never get up to being heard. We don't over-ask, but we don't get turned down as often."

IN ADDITION TO SELLING assets and hiring new people, D'Alessandro tackled lesser issues like the decor of the executive offices. "He told me it didn't look enough like a bank," said former CEO and chairman Syd Jackson. "I thought it looked pretty good." In fact, Jackson had little to teach D'Alessandro. "I don't think he's ever asked for my advice, and I don't think I've ever given it," said Jackson who retired from the board soon after D'Alessandro arrived.

D'Alessandro was embarrassed by the surroundings he inherited. "This room here," he said, indicating a boardroom that was part of his office suite, "with plastic flowers in it, some faded furniture, dust everywhere. It was incredible. How are you going to get people to think like winners?" Just as he was replacing people, he decided to upgrade the corporate art by creating a museum-quality setting that would inspire performance and celebrate excellence. As a first step, he chose Istvan Nyikos to do a new portrait of Jackson, saying that the one already hanging in the boardroom with the other former presidents made Jackson look too old. D'Alessandro also asked Nyikos to paint a portrait of Tom Di Giacomo. The man might have been fired, but as a former CEO he deserved the same honour.

As for the rest of the art, D'Alessandro found Manulife's collection wanting. "You know, all these paintings, I bought these," he said, waving a hand around his office. "Not to aggrandize me, but how the hell can you have a company that's over a hundred years old and doesn't have a piece of art in the goddamned place? How does that make any sense?" In fact, Manulife owned seven hundred pieces of art, but most held little appeal for D'Alessandro. A four-piece panel in pink and green outside his office was banished to storage as D'Alessandro set out to buy Canadian art that he liked. He established an informal committee, studied sales catalogues, and bid on works at auction, usually paying up to $50,000 apiece.

One particular prize was a collection of eleven paintings that had been assembled by Sam Belzberg, the Calgary-born entrepreneur who, with his two bothers, Hyman and William, built a real estate and financial services empire. Belzberg was forced from his role as chairman and CEO of First City Financial when the firm got into trouble in 1991. The art acquisitions that he had overseen were included in the assets when North American Life bought First City's trust subsidiary in 1992.

When D'Alessandro heard the collection might be for sale, he phoned Brian Moore, CEO of North American Life. D'Alessandro expressed interest in buying all the works, but Moore said they formed part of the assets of North American Life's trust company subsidiary, which was itself up for sale. The paintings couldn't be sold separately.

After Laurentian Bank bought North American Trust in 1995, D'Alessandro bought the paintings from Laurentian. The collection included top Canadian contemporary artists, such as Paul-Émile Borduas, Guido Molinari, Jack Bush, Jean Paul Lemieux, Ivan Eyre, William Kurelek, and Michael Snow. Of the 2000 works of art in the Manulife collection, about 1300 have been added since Dominic D'Alessandro became CEO in 1994. The majority of works were acquired as a result of mergers with North American Life (which included the Monarch Life collection), Commercial Union, and John Hancock (including the Maritime Life collection).

———•———

IN ADDITION to the bare walls that bothered D'Alessandro, the need for better performance throughout the industry was equally self-evident. In August 1994, the month before that meeting in Niagara-on-the-Lake, federal regulators seized Confederation Life Insurance Co., a Manulife neighbour. Thrown into disarray were 300,000 policyholders and annuitants in Canada as well as another 450,000 individuals worldwide, half of them in the United States.

Founded in 1871, Confed had been hijacked by poor management in the form of Pat Burns, named CEO in 1985. Burns, a rough-and-tumble type who'd risen through the ranks and wanted desperately to prove his worth, had taken Confed into new areas where neither he nor anyone else in management had any experience or expertise: commercial real estate, leasing, and the trust business.

For a brief shining moment, annual growth rates of 25 percent were tops in the industry, but when the recession arrived in the early 1990s, Confed charged off the cliff like Wile E. Coyote in the Road Runner cartoons. Confed's real estate holdings amounted to 73.8 percent of assets, twice the level of its most heavily invested competitor (the comparable figure at Manulife was 28.5 percent). Such a concentration meant certain death in an economic downturn in which real estate values fell by as much as 75 percent.

Burns was fired in November 1992 by his board, which brought in Paul Cantor, formerly of the Canadian Imperial Bank of Commerce. (D'Alessandro was on that short list, too. At the time, he was still happy at Laurentian but regarded the opportunity as a way to meet some people in Toronto. Bob Swidler was not involved; Rick Moore of Russell Reynolds Associates conducted the search.) At first Cantor tried to sell Confederation Trust, a division of Confederation Life, only to discover that no one was interested. Shortly after D'Alessandro joined Manulife, Cantor came seeking other solutions. D'Alessandro took the opportunity to ask his fellow former banker for advice. Cantor told D'Alessandro that he would have no trouble understanding the asset side of the business but said that the liability side was more difficult. "I have two pieces of advice," Cantor said. "The first is, hire consulting actuaries. The second is, don't take anyone's advice on the subject of hiring consulting actuaries."

The liability side of the balance sheet (all the promises made to clients) seems counterintuitive. For example, new business puts a strain on the balance sheet because in that first year of a new policy, the selling agent receives a commission that is greater than the premium collected. If an insurance company wants to give a quick boost to short-term profits, all it has to do is stop selling policies. Costs drop dramatically and profits rise.

D'Alessandro worked hard to understand the intricacies of the business. In his first few months on the job, he'd phone Roy Firth, his former colleague at Laurentian, and say, "Insurance is incredibly complex, the types of details, accounting, investments," recalled Firth. "He would be exhausted from absorbing everything. He learned in nine months what other people take twenty-five years to do." Directors such as Tom Kierans, who was president of investment banking firm McLeod, Young, Weir for ten years before joining the Manulife board in 1990, admired D'Alessandro's quick learning curve. "Any arrogant investment banker, and I was an arrogant invest-ment banker in the 1980s, can figure out a business model in three weeks. When I got on the board it took me three years. It didn't take Dominic that long, thank God," said Kierans.

Cantor decided that the only way to save Confed lay in finding a buyer. He met with eighteen life insurance companies, five of which showed interest, but only one—Great-West Life, a subsidiary of publicly traded Power Corp., the financial services conglomerate controlled by the Desmarais family—was prepared to make an offer. Lengthy negotiations led to a tentative deal that did not include a particularly toxic part of Confed's business, $1.1 billion in corporate-owned life insurance (COLI).

In mid-June 1994, Confed's competitors were called in to help save Confed by dealing with the COLI business. Tom Di Giacomo was hired as a facilitator for a consortium of CEOs from the five biggest companies: Manulife's D'Alessandro, Sun Life's John McNeil, Canada Life's David Nield, London Life's Gordon Cunningham, and Mutual Life's Bob Astley. Over the next month, the five agreed to assume the COLI business and share $100 million of Confed's losses.

But the Great-West takeover of Confed, scheduled to close at the end of July, ran into other troubles. Great-West concluded that Confed's financial condition was worse than had previously appeared. Great-West suggested that the five industry CEOs who had agreed on COLI should offer more assistance. At a meeting on Saturday, July 23, 1994, executives from Great-West told D'Alessandro and the other CEOs that Confed needed $300 million in capital. They said that Great-West would invest $75 million if the others would share $225 million. The group was upset to hear that a problem limited to one area of Confed's book of business had spread elsewhere so quickly. Moreover, the CEOs were riled by Great-West's refusal to share any information gleaned from their due diligence of Confed, numbers that would prove the legitimacy of their proposal.

The wrangling continued for ten days. During that time, Great-West's assessment of how much capital was required to save Confed rose, first to $450 million, and then to $600 million, double the amount Great-West had said was needed only days earlier. Representing Great-West were Orest Dackow, Ray McFeetors, and Bill McCallum, all heads of various divisions of Great-West. "I was disappointed with the fact that the original deal didn't get done. We kept thinking we'd found a solution and be told the next day we needed to contribute more. Ray McFeetors was getting his orders from Robert [Gratton, CEO of Power Financial, owners of Great-West]," said D'Alessandro.

At one point, D'Alessandro got angry with McFeetors and said, "Do they pay you enough money to do this?"

"What do you mean?' asked McFeetors.

"Well, you gave us your word on Monday, then you changed on Tuesday, we met that demand, and you gave us your word. Then on Wednesday, Thursday. Do they pay you enough money?" asked

D'Alessandro. "He was pissed off at me for years. I couldn't do that to you. If I gave you my word that something's going to be done, well, it would just be done."

Ratings agencies downgraded Confed's financial status, thereby rendering a bad situation worse. With support from neither the government nor the industry, Confed faced a liquidity crisis—a run on its cash—from policyholders looking for surrender values, investors seeking to flee guaranteed investment certificates, and institutions wanting to dump commercial paper.

On August 11, 1994, the federal government seized Confederation Life. "Confed needn't have happened. I never understood why Great-West Life didn't consummate; they would have acquired the company for nothing, absolutely nothing," said D'Alessandro. "I can't for the life of me imagine, after they'd sweetened the pot to the point where everybody was putting up money to help them buy the thing, why they would keep getting cold feet."

In the end, no one lost money on Confed. Over the next few years, real estate values rose again and the liquidators were able to repay all creditors. The recovery process began immediately. Before the end of August 1994, deals had been struck to sell three of Confed's major divisions to competitors. Great-West bought U.S. group life and health insurance, and Sun Life acquired the British division.

Manulife won the biggest prize of all, paying $100 million for the Canadian group life and health business. When the news of the deal was announced to a gathering of several hundred among the nine hundred Confed employees in that division, a spontaneous cheer erupted, followed by a standing ovation. Much better to join a neighbourhood firm than the Winnipeg-based cheese-paring Great-West, which might slash employment. "That helped us on two fronts. It shored up that business line and it showed us we could be a player. It was a bit of a boost for the morale of the organization," said D'Alessandro.

The Confed deal secured D'Alessandro's place in the insurance firmament. "That was the point when things started to change. It doubled the number of people in the Canadian division, doubled the revenues," said John Richardson, general manager of the Canadian division. "By this time, Dominic had the full support and respect of the board. It changed from trying to get his arms around the thing to actually moving it forward, making some strides and gaining market share."

The deal brought Manulife into the "large-case" group life insurance market, corporate clients with more than five hundred employees. Until then, Manulife had six thousand small-company group clients and received $250 million a year in premiums for a piddling 3 percent of market share. The Confed business added 750 new clients, all large firms, employing a total of 1 million Canadians. Annual premiums jumped to $1.25 billion for a market share of 15 percent.

D'Alessandro told colleague Richard Coles that if he'd just had another three or four months' experience at Manulife, he would have tried to buy all of Confed rather than see it broken up. "He really did have this vision. He knows how to do a deal. He knows the incredible number of moving parts in a big acquisition. It's pretty amazing to see," said Coles.

D'Alessandro's growing confidence and Manulife's newfound strength came none too soon. Manulife's competitors were no longer just sleepy life insurance companies. Financial reforms in 1992 permitted banks into the insurance business. Although the banks could sell insurance only through subsidiaries, not directly via the branches, there was a widespread fear that the Big Five banks would dominate insurance as they did the brokerage business.

D'Alessandro felt better about his prospects, but he knew that the company could flourish only by becoming even bigger. Canadians owned $1.3 trillion worth of insurance, second highest on a per capita basis after Japan. The problem was that there were too many companies all offering similar products to the same small Canadian market. The ten biggest insurance firms had about 80 percent of the business; the others fought over the crumbs. In his view, more consolidation had to occur. The next opportunity didn't take long to combust.

EIGHT

Battling the Board

DOMINIC D'ALESSANDRO is not a morning person. If he's playing golf
on the weekend, he's more likely to tee off at 11 a.m. than at 8 a.m.
Although the D'Alessandros bought a house in the Toronto neighbourhood of Rosedale, they kept their place in the Montreal suburb of
Beaconsfield. Dominic and Pearl preferred Montreal to Toronto and
returned there most weekends. For his first eight years as CEO of
Manulife, D'Alessandro also spent his summer holidays in Montreal,
playing golf daily with old friends. "Toronto is not a very welcoming
city. There's cliques and there's circles that take a long time before you
really break into them," said Roy Firth, who in 1998 moved from
Montreal to work at Manulife at D'Alessandro's invitation. "He would
go back and spend an awful lot of time in Montreal with his close
friends. Montrealers and Torontonians have always had a rivalry. When
you grow up in Montreal, those people who go to Toronto are seen as
traitors." D'Alessandro sold the Beaconsfield house only when their
long-time housekeeper died, eleven years after they moved to Toronto.

And so it was on Saturday, June 24, 1995, that D'Alessandro was
in Beaconsfield, reading the newspapers, and enjoying a leisurely

breakfast of coffee and croissants. Of all the articles he read that morning, the most intriguing was a two-page spread in *The Globe and Mail* by Karen Howlett about North American Life Assurance Co. The devastating story outlined a series of difficulties that the company faced: poor morale among agents, downgrades by ratings agencies, and pressure from regulators to fix the balance sheet.

North American had been trying to find its footing for years. In the 1980s, the firm hired two successive outsiders as CEOs: Drew McCaughey from the Molson Companies Ltd., followed by William Bradford from Bank of Montreal. By the time Brian Moore, a company employee of twenty years, had been appointed CEO in January 1995, North American's condition was dire. The real estate collapse that toppled Confederation Life was also hurting North American Life. Moore had already tried to sell half of a U.S. subsidiary called North American Security Life (NASL). By taking in an investor, NASL would have had access to more capital to cover the costs of growth and commission payments to agents. Manulife, along with other possible buyers, had taken a look at NASL's books but did not make a bid.

In addition to the problems at Confed, there was trouble at U.S. companies, such as Executive Life, New England Life, and Mutual Benefit, so the entire sector was nervous. D'Alessandro knew that financial institutions were all about faith. If policyholders lose confidence, a "run" can cause a firm to founder. "Moore has so far failed to silence the critics," said the *Globe* story. D'Alessandro called Donald Guloien and said, "This is going to be hard for them to recover from."

Brian Moore had already admitted at the North American Life annual meeting in May that the company faced "public doubts about the stability and the future of the Canadian life insurance industry." But he maintained that the company he headed was healthy and he promised more financial disclosure in the next annual report.

After D'Alessandro had spoken with Guloien, the next call he made that Saturday morning from his Beaconsfield kitchen was to Moore. "Have you ever thought of solving your problem for good?" he asked.

"What do you mean?" asked Moore.

D'Alessandro explained that any investment in NASL would be only a Band-aid. "This will alleviate the capital requirement in NASL, but for the rest of the company you're going to need opportunities to grow. The competition is bigger than we are and you are. What would you think about combining your company with us?"

The life insurance business in Canada is like a small town, but even so, D'Alessandro knew Moore better than many of the other CEOs. It was Moore who'd shown D'Alessandro the eleven paintings before Manulife later acquired them. Moore had called on D'Alessandro to raise money for the United Way. "We always had good exchanges," said D'Alessandro. "That's why it was easy for me to suggest to him on a telephone call that he ought to look for a permanent solution. And that's why it was easy for him to say [to his board], 'These are people who will look after the policyholders equitably.' That's what you want. You don't want to look after yourself and leave everybody else in the lurch."

Moore was open to D'Alessandro's proposal. "They were more exposed to real estate than the other life companies. When the real estate market broke in the early nineties, they were hurt. We probably lost about half our capital," said Robin Korthals, named chairman of North American Life in January 1995 after retiring as president of TD Bank, a position he'd held since 1981. "Brian Moore tried to save this company. Various things were explored, including the joint venture [with NASL] but, in the end, events just overtook him. Once we had no other way of bringing capital easily onto our books, he resigned himself to sell the company," said Korthals.

A few days after that Saturday morning call, Moore took a room at the Four Seasons in Toronto. Over coffee, he and D'Alessandro agreed on the broad strokes of a merger. North American approached no other potential buyer. There was no point. Since both companies were mutual life insurance firms, owned by their respective policy-holders, all they had to do in order to consummate a deal was pool their assets. For North American, there was nothing to be gained by finding another interested party or holding an auction. Because Manulife had already studied NASL, they knew the value of at least that part of the company. "We said, 'How about we take a put? If the big deal doesn't close, we will buy your U.S. business at a price that was higher than we thought was market.' We had a fair amount of confidence in this. They wanted a deal. They were under a great deal of pressure," said Guloien.

D'Alessandro and Moore presented the proposed merger to their respective boards for approval. "So much of this is based on interpersonal relations. When the time came that [North American Life chairman] Robin Korthals and Robin's board were going to pull the trigger, Dominic had manoeuvred into the 'Let's do the friendly deal with Manulife,'" said Tom Kierans, who admired D'Alessandro's skill at sizing up companies. "I used to be a specialist in this stuff. The two of us would sit at nine o'clock in the morning to evaluate a corporate takeover candidate given the same portfolio of information. Dominic would come down within 5 percent of the right answer by eleven. It would take me until one."

The rest of the summer was spent conducting due diligence and actuarial valuations on North American Life. The final round of meetings was held at the Inn on the Park in Toronto. After several days of presentations by North American, it was Manulife's turn to describe its financial health. Because Manulife's situation was not in question, chief actuary Geoff Guy's presentation was brief. When he was finished, an actuarial consultant retained by North American Life declared that Manulife's reserves were too large and that the firm was too conservative. As Guy began to respond, Manulife corporate controller Peter Rubenovitch decided enough was enough and interrupted to declare that the due diligence process was over.

The two CEOs announced the merger between Manulife and North American Life at a news conference on September 7, 1995. When the deal came into effect on January 1, 1996, the combined operation had $47 billion in assets ($6 billion of which came from NAL), creating the largest insurance firm in Canada with a 13 percent market share. Manulife cemented its standing as the largest group life and health carrier in Canada, the largest in individual annuities in Canada with a 22 percent market share, and the second-largest seller of individual insurance in Canada with a 10 percent market share. North American Life also brought to the table its leading position in the United States as a provider of variable annuities. (Variable annuities allow people to set up their own pension plan by investing money in return for monthly payments upon retirement.)

Several North American Life senior officers were given top roles in the merged firm: Jim Boyle became executive vice president of U.S. operations, Peter Hutchison was named senior vice president, corporate tax. There was another young comer, John DesPrez III, thirty-eight years old, a securities lawyer who'd joined North American Security Life in 1991. He ended up running Manulife's U.S. business and would later be a candidate to replace D'Alessandro. (DesPrez is pronounced De-pray.)

Manulife also inherited a car and driver from North American Life, a perk that D'Alessandro had not previously permitted. He did not, however, commandeer the newly acquired company car. "I don't want the driver at my house in the morning, waiting and polluting the air, because I never know if I'm going to be fifteen minutes late." He drove his BMW 7 Series to work himself. He set up a pool arrangement to share the car and driver among a number of senior officers. His frugal ways also meant he didn't stay in hotel suites, although he did not stop other executives from doing so, hoping that his example was enough.

Brian Moore moved into the office beside D'Alessandro and lasted two years as the head of Manulife's Canadian division. "I don't think he was ever entirely comfortable with the team he inherited or they with him," said D'Alessandro. "Given my age at the time, he found it too frustrating and chose to avail himself of his entitlements." (Moore continued to work in the industry but is now retired and lives in Ireland.) As part of the merger agreement, the name North American Life disappeared. Boardroom furniture, a bronze elevator door, and portraits of previous leaders were moved into a conference room, a sure sign that North American Life was gone for good.

———•———

WHEN D'ALESSANDRO JOINED Manulife in 1994, the firm was Canada's most global life insurance company, with 60 percent of revenue coming from outside Canada, but it was not a leader in any business in Canada. By acquiring Confed's life and health business and merging with North American Life, D'Alessandro pushed Manulife to the forefront in both group and individual insurance. Selling poorly performing businesses also reduced the drag on profits.

As a result, in 1995 profits reached $481 million, up from $281 million the previous year. In 1996 Manulife was the first Canadian insurance firm to pass the $500 million mark in profit, a level that put the company among the most profitable mutual companies in North America. Return on equity was 12.4 percent, still short of D'Alessandro's 14 percent target.

Another benefit of the North American deal was gaining ownership of two mutual fund distribution companies: Elliott and Page, with its $2 billion in assets in Canada, and Wood Logan in the United States. "One of the things Wood Logan brought to the organization was professionalism and a style that was quite a notch above what you normally see. They take these guys to finishing school: how you eat, what you use this implement for, what you say, how you dress, how you look. They worked at it, and I think some of that rubbed off on the rest of the organization," said D'Alessandro, who had come some distance from his hand-me-down roots and admired any systemic effort to improve appearance and performance.

At the time of the merger with North American Life, Wood Logan had about 25 agents who acted as wholesalers. Now there are 145, each covering a specific region, dealing with numerous institutions, such as UBS and Citibank, as well as with financial planners like Linsco Private Ledger. "That type of sales culture gets pushed down into the other businesses—our 401(k) unit, mutual funds, and life insurance. People see the success that they have," said Hugh McHaffie, executive vice president, U.S. wealth management.

In an effort to buttress Elliott and Page and Wood Logan in the growing business of wealth management, D'Alessandro set out to exercise more control over Manulife's interest in Altamira Management Ltd. of Toronto, a mutual fund manager. Manulife's relationship with Altamira began in 1991 under Tom Di Giacomo, when Manulife invested $1.75 million and gave Altamira $900 million of Manulife's money to manage.

By 1996, ownership of Altamira was split among four groups: Ronald Meade and other co-founders (11 percent); management and employees headed by Frank Mersch (28 percent); Almiria Capital, made up of more than two dozen pension funds and institutional investors (30.5 percent); and Manulife (30.5 percent). At the time, Altamira had become the "hot shop." Its mutual funds, run by Mersch, had outstanding results, and were sold on a "no load" basis, thereby reducing costs to investors. D'Alessandro was unhappy with the original transaction because Manulife seemed to earn less than the other investors. "I still get emotional about that transaction. What everybody misses in all of that is that they had no assets and we gave them assets to manage. I don't know whether it's the Italian in me but, when you roll the clock forward, they're managing $1 billion for me and $100 million for third parties. My returns are 9 percent on the $1 billion; on the $100 million they're making 12 percent," said D'Alessandro. "If we wanted to know what the heck was going on, we had to make an appointment. I'd ask, 'Why are the funds you're managing for me earning so much less than the funds you're managing for somebody else?' They'd tell me to 'Get stuffed.'"

Relations between D'Alessandro and Altamira chairman Ron Meade became strained. The two sides eventually ended up in court, so their version of events differs. What is not in contention is that Meade began looking for a buyer and struck an agreement to sell

Altamira to TD Bank in June 1996 for $765 million. TD then changed its mind and the deal collapsed.

Shortly after, D'Alessandro decided to take control. Manulife offered $32 a share, a bid that valued the firm at $660 million. Media reports at the time knocked Manulife in general and D'Alessandro in particular. Typical was a story in *The Globe and Mail* on October 14, 1996, which said that in all his recent deals "there has never been public criticism of Mr. D'Alessandro that comes near matching what has been levelled by Almiria directors. The Manulife CEO has been accused of blocking a $765 million bid for Altamira by Toronto-Dominion Bank and scooping up the mutual fund company with a low-ball offer."

Meade lobbied Manulife directors, urging them in turn to encourage D'Alessandro to increase his bid. Some of the directors became convinced that Manulife should follow Meade's advice, add an extra $60 million to the Altamira acquisition price, and put the situation—including the bad publicity—behind them. Said D'Alessandro, "How could you have that situation? What confidence would the markets have had in us to allow us to go forward and do the other things we did?"

D'Alessandro refused to be stampeded by either Meade or the Manulife board. "I think it was one of my finest moments. I said 'If you want to sit here [in my chair], we'll take the high road. If I'm sitting here, I'm going to do what I think is the right thing. It's not you who they are denigrating in the newspaper every day. It's not you whose character they're slamming and depicting. As long as I'm CEO of the company, this is what we're going to do.' That was the end of the discussion about taking the high road and paying them more money."

The directors learned their lesson. "First of all, we were wrong. Second, we did not then have the appreciation for Dominic that we do now. This is before we knew he was going to become the superstar that he did. Third, the perception on the street was that Manulife wasn't very smart or very strong and could be pushed around.

Dominic just drew that line in the sand," said Manulife director Tom Kierans. "It turned out well because it was one of the building blocks that established his ascendancy over the street."

The dispute between Meade and Manulife went to court, but before the judge could rule, in 1997 venture capital company TA Associates Inc. of Boston came in as a white knight and bought Altamira. Manulife happily sold its interest to TA Associates for $38 a share or $255 million, a prodigious return on Manulife's original investment of less than $2 million six years earlier. "It was a big win," said D'Alessandro, but it came at a personal cost. "It was very nasty. It left a lot of bitterness with me. I don't think I've ever been involved in a business transaction quite as unpleasant and distasteful."

Altamira's market pre-eminence soon waned. Frank Mersch, Altamira's star manager, left the company in 1998. By 2002, when National Bank of Canada bought Altamira, TA Associates had lost money on its investment. "Dominic thinks of it as dodging a bullet," said Donald Guloien. D'Alessandro regularly reminded directors that if he had done what the board wanted to him do, which was bury the problem by buying Altamira, the deal would have destroyed Manulife.

SOME CEOs HAVE their boards in their pocket because the CEO has appointed all the directors. The relationship between D'Alessandro and the Manulife board was quite different. "The board is very separate from me. These are not my friends who I appointed to the board. They hired me; I didn't hire them. I've been very, very respectful of the prerogative of the board to pick their own. I haven't stuffed the nominating committee. If a good candidate comes along, I'll speak up for him. They also understand that their job is not to run the company, their job is to oversee things to make sure that I do," said D'Alessandro.

D'Alessandro has, however, successfully put forward a few names. His suggestions for director have included Pierre Ducros, a

Montreal-based technology executive who was appointed in 1999, and Scott Hand, a golfing partner and former CEO of Inco, who was named in 2007. "He doesn't bring stupid ideas. The likelihood we'd approve them was good," said Arthur Sawchuk, chairman of the board from 1998 to 2008. "Dominic has a presence about him, and he has the respect of everybody on the board. It was a very good working relationship. Dominic kept them very well informed. There were never any surprises. I think they appreciated that," said John Richardson, a director from 1999 to 2002 and the only member of management—other than D'Alessandro—ever appointed to the board.

Top-quality directors, such as Tom d'Aquino, were drawn to serve on the board by D'Alessandro's formidable presence. D'Aquino worked for Prime Minister Pierre Trudeau as a policy adviser and speechwriter. A lawyer, author, and educator, in 1981 he became CEO of the Business Council on National Issues, now the Canadian Council of Chief Executives, a group comprising Canada's top 150 CEOs. In 2005, d'Aquino ended a self-imposed rule against serving on outside boards. He decided to limit himself to three boards, received nine offers, and accepted Manulife first. (The other two boards he joined were technology firm CGI Group Inc., and Coril Holdings Ltd., the private family holding company of Alberta entrepreneur Ron Mannix.) "The fact that Manulife was the most successful of our financial institutions globally made it very attractive. Dominic was the CEO; I held him in high regard. I knew him to be an extremely hard worker, smart, very dedicated, very passionate, and also very committed to growing the business beyond the borders of Canada," said d'Aquino.

Senior executives attend the four-hour Manulife board meetings that include presentations from officers who run business units. "I always walked away saying to myself, 'Is there one individual who knows more about all of this in detail than anyone else in the company? Yes, it's Dominic.' That I find, in a corporation the size and complexity of Manulife, highly, highly unusual," said d'Aquino. "I'm only a director, I go to eight or nine meetings a year. But I go to bed knowing that this guy, twenty-four hours a day, Saturdays and Sundays, is leading the business and really knows it well. That is the most exceptional thing about Dominic D'Alessandro. That's the thing that speaks most clearly to his success."

The directors also spend an hour in camera with D'Alessandro at each board meeting. "Directors wear a number of different hats, and they need to be reminded of context and what is at stake. He is able to do that with punch and clarity. He talks and is open to questions. Those are stunningly useful sessions. You know what's on his mind. It's a mini-strategic-cum-risk sort of approach to the business, focusing on what has happened since we last met," said Gail Cook-Bennett.

Manulife directors don't hold an annual retreat at a golf resort in a sunny clime to plot strategy, as do some other boards. "They take their spouses, and they get a whole lot of presentations pulled together, and it looks like a strategic retreat, but nothing really strategic is happening," said Sawchuk. "The notion that strategy is once a year is a goddamned joke. The fact is that you have a strategy. It's there in the business plan. What you need to be doing is getting those issues on the table monthly, or at every meeting, and jig your strategy, and ask if any of them are so life-threatening that you need to radically change your strategy, then you'll enter into that. We came to the idea that strategy was a perpetual process, not an episodic event."

In fact, D'Alessandro alone plotted much of the strategy. In speeches to senior managers, he'd say, "The business strategy is right here," and tap his head. "When you need to know, I'll tell you." "Dominic doesn't impose his strategy on a lot of people. He expects people to come forward with strategies. He's a little bit like a conductor of an orchestra. He doesn't have to know how to play the oboe to be able to know when the oboe sounds proper," said Roy Firth, who has worked with D'Alessandro since his days at the Royal Bank and is now executive vice president, individual wealth management.

D'Alessandro expected the board to give advice, not directives. "You have somebody to go and talk to every six weeks and tell them what you're doing and what you're planning to do and justify actions. They make sure that I pay attention to all aspects of being a CEO, not just aspects that I'm particularly enamoured of. We all have preferences. I'd much rather spend time talking about a financing technique, a product, an analysis or a risk, and less on some other aspects of the business that are every bit as important, whether it's personnel matters, process, compliance, or legal," said D'Alessandro.

Although he is a member of the board, D'Alessandro does not see himself as being *of* the board. He runs the place; directors provide counsel. "Absent some crisis, they're not there every day making decisions, being responsible for a whole bunch of people's successes or failures. I'm always one of these guys who has personalized. I've never been incented by money. My reputation has been my incentive. I'd rather die than let you down."

NINE

The Asian Strategy

MANULIFE'S EARLIEST FORAY to China occurred in 1897, when Alfred Ellis was sent to Shanghai. His first sale was a fifteen-year $2000 (Hong Kong dollars) endowment policy to a thirty-one-year-old Chinese man, with an annual premium of HK$151.60. Directors were fretful. Manufacturers' had no experience with Chinese clients and no mortality figures on which to base life expectancy, the key to profitable sales. On June 27, 1900, the board passed a resolution that "No further business be accepted from the Chinese Empire without approval of the Board."

In an attempt to learn more about that market, head office made inquiries into local practices, including the smoking of opium. A reply from John Anderson, dated October 1, 1902, was unlikely to allay their fears. "Your question for my opinion of how much opium a Chinese man may smoke and yet be an acceptable risk, is a difficult one. It depends on his manner and nature of life and what he daily works and exercises himself at," wrote Anderson. "My feeling would be that if a man did not go beyond 8 pipes per day, he might then be called a moderate smoker."

Manulife had been operating in ten cities in China when the company was tossed out of the country in 1941, along with all other foreign insurers, and it wanted back in. By 1994, when D'Alessandro joined Manulife, the only foreign firm operating in China was American International Group (AIG) led by CEO Maurice "Hank" Greenberg, who first visited Beijing in 1975, established a representative office in 1980, and finally won the first insurance licence awarded by China in 1992.

Manulife's efforts to return to China began before D'Alessandro's appointment. In 1991 Manulife established a training program in Hong Kong for the People's Insurance Company of China. In 1992, Manulife was the first Canadian insurance company to open a representative office in China, in Beijing. Manulife set up an actuarial exam centre in Tainjain, the only one in China, the following year. In 1993, Manulife launched a training program in Canada for the People's Bank of China (PBOC), so that annually four PBOC employees could study the insurance business. By 1994 Manulife had added representative offices in Shenzhen, Shanghai, Chengdu, and Guangzhou.

As a member of the Team Canada trade mission to the People's Republic of China led by Prime Minister Jean Chrétien in November 1994, D'Alessandro met mayors, party secretaries, and provincial governors. In Beijing, he held talks with the deputy general secretary of the Communist Party, Yan Mingfu, as well as Wu Yi, the minister responsible for China's Ministry for Foreign Trade and Economic Co-operation.

When the members of the Team Canada mission attended a meeting of the Canada China Business Council with Vice-Premier Zhu Rongji, D'Alessandro rose to ask a question. He began by introducing himself, saying, "I'm Dominic D'Alessandro and I'm from Manulife." The vice-premier interjected, "I know your question. The next company will be Canadian."

Once the vice-premier had made his promise, Manulife redoubled its efforts. Forty insurance companies were vying for market access. They included other Canadian insurers that might also try to ride on the reverence for Norman Bethune, a Canadian surgeon who'd lived in China in the 1930s. Bethune gained heroic status after Mao Tse-tung wrote about Bethune's devotion in an essay that was required reading during the Cultural Revolution.

D'Alessandro had a hero, too: Hank Greenberg, who had built AIG from scratch into one of the world's top financial institutions. "Dominic loved to talk about AIG. He was fascinated by Greenberg," said Mickey Cohen, a friend of D'Alessandro's and an AIG director from 1993 until he retired in 2008. "Dominic's a very similar story: a modest background, ran the company with an iron fist, had hugely winning instincts. Greenberg was an iconic figure to Dominic and maybe he saw himself in that mould."

On his next trip, in 1995, D'Alessandro met Siao Yang, one of the early believers in an open China as governor of Szechuan province, the largest province in China, with a population of 125 million. He saw Yan Mingfu again, along with his wife, Wu Ke Liang, general secretary of the Soong Chi ling Foundation. Both had been translators for Chairman Mao. Mingfu spoke Russian and Chinese, so his wife translated for him and D'Alessandro. She and D'Alessandro spoke in English and French until he mentioned that he'd grown up in Montreal. She expressed surprise, saying, "Isn't that an Italian name?" When D'Alessandro said that it was, she switched into Italian.

The breakthrough came in the spring of 1995, when the People's Bank told Manulife to apply for a licence. Marc Sterling, an American lawyer based in Taiwan who was hired by Manulife in 1993 as executive vice president for Asia, met with Di Wei Ping, head of the Insurance Commission. Sterling showed him the forms Manulife had filed in the past and asked if he should use the same forms again. "I don't know," Ping replied. "I wouldn't have read that. You weren't going to get a licence." A new form was devised, and only then did Manulife learn there was a next step—to find a Chinese joint-venture partner. Sterling drew up a list of five possibilities, including Sinochem, a conglomerate.

In October 1995, Premier Li Peng visited Canada. D'Alessandro hosted a table at a banquet and was asked to include an unnamed Chinese guest who turned out to be Sui Hui, an official with the Ministry of Foreign Trade and Economic Co-operation. She had obtained her Master of Business Administration at the Université du Québec à Montréal through a co-op arrangement with the Canadian government and called herself a member of "the Canadian mafia" inside the Chinese system. Hui was curious about Manulife's progress and asked D'Alessandro if he'd thought about having Sinochem as a partner. D'Alessandro said he had but added that Manulife had been unable to meet anyone at a sufficiently high level in the company.

"Would you like to meet Sinochem's CEO?" Hui asked. When D'Alessandro said yes, she disappeared across the room and returned with Zheng Dunxun, chairman and CEO of Sinochem. A joint-venture deal was concluded a few months later. Manulife was granted a licence in 1996, the second foreign insurer to be approved. "There was no law for a joint venture to exist. There was no law on shareholding—all those things had to be negotiated. In those days I used to visit Beijing almost fifty times a year, and we would genuinely negotiate every point," said Sterling, chairman of Manulife-Sinochem, the joint-venture firm.

At a Canada China Business Council meeting in Shanghai in November 1996, D'Alessandro chaired a panel on the Chinese economy. Among the panelists was Sui Hui, who spoke about her role as a matchmaker. She said that one of Manulife's competitors had approached her after the Manulife-Sinochem joint venture was announced to say they, too, were a big North American insurer and asked why Manulife had been given the go-ahead and not them.

"It is not important to be big or the biggest. It is important to be first. And Manulife was first," she replied. "You have to set up the friendship first. You have to have good relations first for mutual trust."

PREMIER LI PENG and Prime Minister Jean Chrétien were scheduled to attend the grand opening in November 1996 of Manulife's first office in Shanghai, but it wasn't until 6 A.M. on the day of the ceremony when Manulife officials were certain that Li Peng would actually be on hand. When word came he would appear, all the other participants were told to be standing in their designated places by 9 A.M., well in advance of the noon arrival of the two leaders.

Once the ribbon had been snipped and the official photos taken, the protocol dictating departures for the banquet at another location was equally rigorous as that for the arrivals. "They leave the room, they get in their cars, we can't leave the room until they're gone," said Sterling. "There were a bunch of Manulife executives tearing down flights of stairs to get in the buses to go and chase after them." The cost to Manulife to obtain that first licence was $20 million over the five years of effort.

Once the Shanghai office was open, it took another six years, until 2002, for the second licence to be granted for Guangzhou. Today, Manulife is licensed in thirty-five cities in China—twice as many as AIG—and has nine hundred employees. Most of the cities are huge. Of the ten cities where Manulife was granted a licence in 2007, eight have populations greater than Toronto's three million.

Operations in Shanghai, a city of fifteen million, broke even after five years; the profits are used to pay for startups in other locations. Only the Shanghai office is at full strength, with three thousand agents. To build a staff of that size requires thousands of applicants. In each new location, the number of agents grows slowly as new hires undergo training. Only 40 percent of the inductees make it through the first year. After five years, only 15 percent of the original group remains, the rest have fallen by the wayside. Manulife now has ten thousand agents, four hundred thousand customers, and annual sales of $150 million in China.

The goal is to be in one hundred cities with thirty thousand agents by 2015, at which time China should be profitable. That profitability will be aided by the fact that commissions paid to agents are 35 percent of the first year's premium, far lower than in Canada where commissions, with bonuses, can be twice as much as the first year's premium paid by the client.

Although there is corruption in China, Manulife refused to make any under-the-table payments to win the licences. "The first time the first dollar comes out of your pocket, they'll all be there. It's like flies, you open the screen door, you allow corruption in, that's it, they're all in," said Sterling. "At the senior levels in the Chinese government, we had good connections. Corruption in most markets is at the other levels."

———

WHILE MANULIFE WAS ABLE to avoid corruption in China, Indonesia was a much different experience. In 1985 when Manulife launched a new business in Indonesia, a crescent-shaped swath of seventeen thousand islands spread over an area three times the size of Texas, it looked like the ideal market. Population was 230 million, annual growth rates ran to 20 percent, savings rates were twice North American levels, but the insurance policy penetration rate was a minuscule 0.2 percent.

Manulife formed a joint venture, as required by law, with Dharmala Group, a conglomerate with wide economic interests. Manulife held 51 percent and Dharmala 40 percent, with 9 percent owned by the International Finance Corp., the private sector arm of the World Bank and a major source of developmental aid to Indonesia. The business was profitable in the fourth year. "Dharmala were very good local partners for many, many years. They took a positive interest in a business they didn't really understand. They were an investor. The relationship between ourselves and them was very cordial," said Philip Hampden-Smith, who was put in charge of Indonesia in 1998 and is now based in Singapore as general manager, Southeast Asia operations.

By 2000 Manulife was by far the largest foreign insurer in Indonesia, with more than seventy branches in thirty-three cities, three thousand employees and agents, and four hundred thousand policyholders. While Manulife continued to prosper during the Asian economic crisis of 1997 to 1998, Dharmala did not. "What happened to Dharmala happened to many financial institutions: the dramatic weakening of the rupiah, the fact that many people were unhedged. A lot of people had liabilities in one currency being covered by assets in another currency. There was a liquidity crisis. The government, in an effort to keep the banking industry afloat, loaned money to the various banking institutions, including Dharmala's own bank. It just wasn't enough and they went into liquidation," said Hampden-Smith.

Unable to pay debts owed to more than two dozen creditors, including Manulife, Dharmala declared bankruptcy before the Indonesian Commercial Court in 1998. The new court, established at the express wish of the International Monetary Fund and the World Bank at the time of Indonesian president Suharto's resignation in May 1998, was supposed to be more competent and less prone to corruption than Indonesia's traditional judicial system.

In the case of Dharmala, the new arrangement seemed to work. In June 2000 Dharmala was placed under court protection and its various holdings were put up for sale. Manulife had the right of first refusal to buy Dharmala's joint-venture stake. Manulife offered US$18.1 million, the value listed by Dharmala in the court filings. "The reality was that it was very hard for anyone to buy the company because there was literally no cash in Indonesia. McDonald's weren't even selling their burgers. They were selling a rice packet, rice with an egg on top, because people couldn't afford burgers," said Hampden-Smith.

Even though Manulife was the only interested party, the Indonesian Finance Ministry declared that Dharmala's 40 percent interest should be sold at auction. A few days before the sale date in October, someone approached Manulife claiming that Dharmala's stake had already been sold to Roman Gold Assets, a company based in the British Virgin Islands. The source claimed that there had been a deal in Singapore ten days earlier, which had involved a complicated trail through a vendor called Highmead Ltd., a company registered in Western Samoa. Highmead had apparently bought the 40 percent interest from a Hong Kong firm, Harvest Hero, which in turn had been pledged the ownership stake as collateral for a loan in 1996. Manulife knew such a sale was impossible and the government agreed. The auction, run by a judge and a curator, proceeded and Manulife bought out Dharmala.

————

AS MANULIFE'S LAWYER tried to leave Jakarta and return to Hong Kong, he was stopped at the airport and questioned by police. Three days later, police arrested and jailed Adi Purnomo, a Manulife Indonesia vice president, on suspicion of fraud. "Indonesia is the kind of place where the rule of law basically disappears. If a local company wants to apply pressure to a foreign entity, they apply pressure physically to people in situ. One of the ways of doing that is to pay the police to incarcerate members of that company and use them as hostages to fortune," said Hampden-Smith, whose wife was also subject to harassment. Two men on motorbikes stopped her car, and one of them held a knife to her throat in front of her young son; the men then fled, mission accomplished. An Islamic group distributed pamphlets in Jakarta claiming that Hampden-Smith was a spy.

Clearly, powerful forces did not want the Manulife deal to go through. The preferred owner was the mysterious Roman Gold, whose sole director just happened to be based in Surabaya, the hometown of the Dharmala president, Suyanto Gondokusumo. A journalist digging into the so-called sale found that the address of Harvest Hero's Indonesian director was the Salty Chicken Shop. The proprietor, who had been in business at that location for a year, had never heard of Harvest Hero. Still, the court froze Manulife's payment; the deal was in limbo.

Two weeks after the auction, an individual claiming to represent Roman Gold approached Manulife. He said Manulife could end the legal wrangle by paying Roman Gold US$40.8 million. Manulife officials met with the party in Singapore, secretly videotaped the meeting, and rejected the deal. "We'd effectively pay twice. They'd have their money, the government would have their money, and we'd have no money. That was in their very simplistic mind a good deal," said Hampden-Smith.

These sorts of shenanigans were familiar to Hampden-Smith, who was born to British parents in Japan, grew up in Pakistan, and has lived in Sri Lanka and Hong Kong. "I'd seen all this in some way, shape, or form before, but I was always optimistic and I knew we were right." Manulife rejected the attempted extortion and appealed to the Indonesian government for help in halting it and the ownership standoff—but to no avail.

Rather than knuckle under, Manulife turned to Prime Minister Chrétien, who wrote to Indonesian president Abdurrahman Wahid. As a result, Purnomo, the Manulife official, was freed after twenty days in jail. For a time, it looked as if Indonesia would not bend any further; the Attorney General said he was sympathetic but unable to help. "The Indonesian minister of economy and the Attorney General openly admitted that the police's behavior towards Manulife was impossible to justify but implied that they were powerless to bring the police to heel. An official close to the minister was quoted as saying: 'Money talks ... It is not as though Rizal [the minister] is not committed to finding a solution. He is very frustrated, but it all comes down to trying to find a way to break the fortress,'" said the authors of a 2002 case study done for INSEAD, the international graduate business school with campuses in France and Singapore.

Manulife next enlisted help from the World Bank and the International Monetary Fund. The organizations pressured the Indonesian government, saying that foreign aid would be cut off if such corruption did not end. That tipped the balance. On May 21, 2001, Indonesian president Wahid announced that Manulife had been wronged. "We have to handle this Manulife issue because it has disturbed the relationship between the two countries and Indonesia's relationship with the IMF," he said. In November, Harvest Hero's

Hong Kong representative pleaded guilty to backdating documents relating to the alleged sale.

The battle was not yet over. Dharmala launched more than a dozen lawsuits against Manulife. Among the allegations, Dharmala claimed that it had not received dividends from the joint venture. In June 2000, a panel of three judges ruled that Manulife's Indonesian business was bankrupt—despite having assets of US$400 million and a profit the previous year of US$9 million.

D'Alessandro was irate and complained that Manulife was the victim of a "public mugging." Manulife released the videotape of the extortion attempt by Roman Gold, saying the firm was simply a front for Dharmala. Manulife also charged that the judges who ruled on Manulife's "bankruptcy" had "received significant financial entice-ment." Manulife appealed the lower court decision and in July the Supreme Court overturned the bankruptcy ruling. The three lower court judges were suspended. "This is one of the most astounding cases in Canadian business, where essentially an attempt was made to steal our company, with the sanction of the courts," said D'Alessandro. "We were able to defend ourselves. It cost us an enormous amount of money to hire lawyers and investigators and everything else. The Canadian government went flat out for us, but in the end, it was the World Bank and IMF that did it for us."

The World Bank and the IMF used Manulife's situation to push for judicial reform. "I'm very proud of the fact that, in a small way, my company is contributing to the development of Indonesia. Not just through the provision of insurance services, but because we stood up the way we did and were able to bring the spotlight on these abuses. Everybody knows there's judicial corruption in Indonesia, but there was never anything that compelled them to do anything about it. Now they've started," said D'Alessandro.

In the end, the Dharmala imbroglio benefited Manulife. "I used to get a lot of calls from Indonesian business leaders saying, 'Look, we can't publicly support you, because of the nationalistic sentiment around, but we do want you to fight this because if we were in the same position as you, we wouldn't be able to fight it. We couldn't muster the resources that you can muster,'" said Hampden-Smith. "Our name awareness in Indonesia went through the roof. We went from single-digit name awareness to incredible name awareness because everybody knew it was a scam. During all the fights we lost almost no customers, no staff. Most people recognized what was going on for what it was."

The halo continues. In Indonesia, Manulife has 25 percent of the market share and more than one million policyholders—up from two hundred thousand in 1998. Clients have more than $1 billion invested in mutual funds. "To this day, I'll have people come up to me in Asia who say, 'Well done,'" said Hampden-Smith. "We helped publicize a problem that was endemic. It hasn't totally been cured, but I think it did make a lot of people more aware of how bankrupt the legal system was."

———◆———

MANULIFE'S SORTIE into Japan was equally convoluted and not without brinksmanship that almost ended the deal. In Japan, where Manufacturers had been doing business since 1902, there were 8500 policies in force by 1923. After the conquest by Japan of Manchuria in 1931, the company began to wind down its operations. When Japan attacked Pearl Harbor in 1941, the government seized the business, including the statutory deposit.

Supervision of activities so far from head office had been time-consuming. Ken McNab, who started in the underwriting department in 1927, began travelling in 1930 and spent the next three decades on the move. "I first went out to the Orient in 1930, and from that date through the next twenty-six years there was rarely a year in which I didn't make an international trip," he said. In 1940, a company publication said this about a recent journey, "After dining in Johannesburg on Friday, in Nairobi on Saturday, in Cairo on Sunday and breakfasting the next morning in Malta, Mr. McNab reached England on Monday afternoon."

As the twentieth century came to an end, Manulife was established and doing business in nine Asian countries and territories—but not in Japan. In 1999 Manulife set out to enter Japan through a two-step process by spending $1 billion to buy Daihyaku Mutual Life Insurance Company, the largest investment ever by any Canadian company in Japan. The deal bought 1.4 million customers, $2 billion in premiums, $17 billion in assets, and a market share of 2.1 percent in the world's best insurance market, where per capita ownership of life insurance is at levels that are twice as high as in the United States. Although Donald Guloien led the negotiations in Japan, Dominic D'Alessandro was the driving force behind the deal and travelled to Japan each month. "Dominic wanted to get into Japan for a long time. The company has a significant Asian operation and not to be in the biggest market of all was glaring, something missing from our portfolio," said Craig Bromley, CEO of Manulife Japan. In order to conclude the deal, Manulife sent a team of sixty actuaries, lawyers, and finance personnel to Japan. "They talked every night for hours at a time about tactics and strategies. Dominic ran the strategy of the deal. He was very involved," said Bromley.

Unlike transactions in North America, which can be concluded in a matter of days or weeks, negotiations took eighteen months. "It's like a thousand separate transactions. You're buying each piece of real estate and each painting on the wall rather than buying the whole corporate shell," said Bromley. "If you didn't get it onto a piece of paper, you didn't own it."

The two-step deal almost fell apart at the last minute. Under the first step the sales force and the goodwill were acquired and put into a new corporate entity. The "old" Daihyaku was to be gradually liquidated by the Japanese insurance industry. A year later, the consortium shut down that company, an action that they had promised not to take, and put the assets up for sale. Manulife was the obvious buyer, and after lengthy negotiations an agreement was reached.

On December 13, 2000, the day the deal was to be signed, the industry consortium demanded another 45.3 billion yen ($50 million).

D'Alessandro immediately wrote a letter saying, "In all my years of negotiating complex transactions around the world, I have never seen anything so devoid of good faith." He rejected what he called the "insulting" demand and said that Manulife was pulling out of the deal.

The next day, the request for more money was withdrawn, and the agreement was successfully concluded. "You should never negotiate with a gang. They all hide behind each other," said D'Alessandro, who prides himself on his deal-making ability. "I think about it all the time. Every time you think, you see something new. When I do a deal, there are no loose ends."

THE ACQUISITION INCLUDED a distribution system that would have otherwise taken Manulife years to build: four hundred and fifty offices and six thousand agents. "It turned out to be a very good deal because it's very hard to get into Japan. You go to Japan, you don't see any foreign names except Starbucks and McDonald's. All the cars are Japanese, all the equipment and elevators are Japanese, all the companies are Japanese," said Bromley.

Distribution was given a further boost when Manulife signed an alliance in 2004 with Bank of Tokyo-Mitsubishi that included an investment in Manulife Japan. "They were the biggest bank in Japan and that really cemented our credibility in the minds of the public and dramatically improved our sales," said Bromley. In all, Manulife now has sales agreements with about three dozen banks and securities firms, makes about $300 million a year in Japan, sells more than $4 billion in variable annuities, and in 2008 moved ahead of The Hartford, the former leader in the annuities, in new business.

The Asia and Japan division now accounts for about one-quarter of all earnings and is the company's fastest-growing region. To achieve such growth in Japan, Manulife added new products, such as universal life and variable annuities, that had not previously been available. "The universal life product that was sold in Japan not long after we cut the deal was the Canadian model slimmed down with the front end, the underwriting, and the back end, customer service, done in Japan, and the rest done in Waterloo. The variable annuity is from the U.S., made appropriate for Japan," said Bruce Gordon, former senior vice president, Canadian operations. "We have exported Canadian knowledge, know-how, and management centres of excellence around the world. Manulife is the best example of free trade that has never been written up."

TEN

Going Public

IN 1997, when London Life Insurance was shopped around the insurance industry to see who was interested, Dominic D'Alessandro salivated at the prospect but was unable to make a bid. "I didn't have $2 billion lying around, and I didn't have the leadership team here I thought I needed to do an acquisition that size," he said. Great-West Life, the same company that had flummoxed the industry leaders on Confed, paid $3 billion for London Life, beating out a bid by Royal Bank. Great-West's parent, Power Financial, was a public company and so had the ability to raise such funds—a step that a mutual company like Manulife could not take.

As a first response, D'Alessandro beefed up Manulife's Canadian division. In 1998 he brought in Roy Firth to run Elliott and Page, hired Trevor Matthews from National Australia Bank to head Manulife Canada, and transferred Bruce Gordon from the U.S. division. As for the second part, access to capital, the only way Manulife would ever have enough capital to acquire rivals would be to demutualize. To do so, Manulife would have to reverse the 1958 process in which stock companies owned by shareholders had been turned into mutual companies owned by policyholders. In 1956, the Gooderham family trust had decided to sell its 45 percent controlling stake. Manufacturers worried that a U.S. investment banker, Lazard Frères, was advising interested Americans. Such sniffing around was not the first foreign pursuit of a Canadian life insurance company. Harold Allen, a New York financier, had taken a run at Sun Life that began in 1950 and lasted until 1956 when, unable to corral more than 15 percent of the shares, he finally gave up.

Mutualization, the practice by which policyholders replaced shareholders as owners, was seen as the best way to guarantee Canadian ownership. In December 1957 the newly elected government of John Diefenbaker passed enabling legislation. A shareholders meeting on July 30, 1958, approved mutualization of Manufacturers; the company paid $275 a share for all of the Gooderham trust's 150,000 shares. The family received $18.7 million of the $41.3 million that the entire company was worth, the equivalent of $800 million today. At the same time Sun, Confederation, Canada Life, and Equitable were also mutualized.

During the next four decades when Manulife was owned by policyholders, management answered to no one. Many mutual companies regarded themselves as more akin to organized religion than bottom-line enterprises. By 1998, however, demutualization was a growing trend in Australia and Britain. After a year of consultations, white papers, and hearings in Canada, in March 1999 the federal government passed the necessary legislation allowing demutualization.

The decision transformed the insurance industry. In addition to providing the ability to raise money through capital markets, demutualization meant companies could attract top talent by being able to offer stock options. Companies would also become more focused on profits because analysts would be scrutinizing financial results while shareholders sought investments that paid off through dividends and rising share prices.

When word about demutualization came in the form of a letter from Manulife, most policyholders were likely surprised to discover that they had been owners all along. For those hardy souls who kept reading, they learned they were about to receive a windfall of shares— at no charge. The toll-free number offering more information about the giveaway was flooded with callers. The most-often asked question: "What's the catch?" There was none; they would receive a payment in the form of cash or shares for their ownership position and retain their insurance coverage.

Initially, however, the rules laid down by Ottawa meant that insurance executives could not hold options or own shares in their own companies. An irate D'Alessandro phoned Finance Minister Paul Martin and said, "How the hell does that make any sense? I'm telling everybody they should invest in Manulife stock and I can't own any myself, which I would buy with my own money?" Martin changed his mind. D'Alessandro invested $5 million and bought 280,000 shares. (Options were permitted a year later.) D'Alessandro has used that block of shares for charitable donations. Manulife shares split two-for-one in 2006; this holding is now 514,000 shares.

Under the legislation, the government also permitted some industry consolidation. Companies with a market capitalization (the number of shares times the share price) of less than $5 billion could be acquired after two years of being public. As a result, Clarica and Canada Life were available for purchase, but Manulife and Sun Life were not. In the case of those last two companies, they had to remain widely held with no single shareholder owning more than 20 percent. Add the Big Five banks and the government's policy created what became known as "the seven tall trees."

Deciding how many shares each policyholder received was a complicated task. "We divided the demutualization benefits into two components. A vote is a vote is a vote. Whether you had a $1 million policy or a $100 million policy, you had one vote. So, every policy got a fixed amount for the vote—$4000. The variable component was a function of how many years, the size of your policy, and its cash surrender value. It was an algorithm. We spent a long time to satisfy everybody. We called in experts from the U.S., from the U.K., from Australia. We finally found satisfaction," said D'Alessandro.

Each eligible policyholder received 186 shares, regardless of whether he or she had one policy or a dozen. That basic designation covered one-quarter of the shares distributed, with the other 75 percent based on the algorithm that took into account the policy's cash value, the face value, and the time held. Policyholders approved the manna from heaven at a special meeting held at head office on July 29, 1999, forty-one years minus a day since mutualization had been approved at the same location on July 30, 1958.

Fred Simons, a Manulife officer noted for his organizational skills, was brought out of retirement to oversee the project, for which two hundred employees were seconded. The regulators wanted Manulife to disclose so many facts that the weight of the information package threatened to exceed postal delivery limits. Simons found a vegetable ink that reduced the weight and mailing costs. The two documents sent to policyholders in 124 countries totalled 388 pages and were printed in English, French, Spanish, and Cantonese. If they'd all been piled up, the documents would have created a stack five miles high. Policyholders chose among three options: cash, shares in Manulife Financial, or a fifty–fifty combination. Those who did not respond received shares. The average payout to each Manulife policyholder was $13,000.

The final, tricky pieces of the puzzle were share price and timing. Manulife hired three investment-banking firms: Merrill Lynch, Credit Suisse First Boston, and ScotiaMcLeod. In any such deal, the company wants the highest price possible to produce the greatest amount of money. The investment bankers want the share price set low enough that shares fly off the shelves and rise in price once trading begins. That way, initial investors make money and are happy with the investment bankers' advice.

The two sides eventually settled on $18, the low end of the $18 to $24 range originally announced. "We wanted to make sure that our clients got the best price they could because many of them were unsophisticated; they probably would sell them off, not realizing what they've gotten. In those circumstances, you're almost in the position of trust where you've got to do the best you can for your clients," said John Richardson, who as senior executive vice president and a director was part of the group from Manulife that travelled the globe to explain the new offering to brokers and potential investors.

The first day of trading in Toronto was September 24, 1999, followed by Hong Kong and the Philippines on September 27, and New York on October 21. In the Philippines, fifty thousand policyholders received cash and shares worth 8 billion pesos, a transaction so large that it had to be backstopped by that country's central bank for fear that the currency transactions that followed could affect the peso's value.

Manulife's demutualization raised $2.5 billion and was the largest initial public offering (IPO) in Canadian history. This transaction was different from a conventional IPO, where the money raised is used for various corporate purposes. In this case, the full $2.5 billion in proceeds was used to pay those policyholders who wanted cash rather than shares. When the deal was complete, Manulife, with operations in 15 countries and territories, 28,000 employees and agents, revenues of $14 billion and $112 billion in assets under management, was a public company with 450,000 shareholders.*

At the time of demutualization, the more than 500 million shares issued meant that Manulife's market capitalization was $9 billion. Coincident with demutualization, Manulife's return on equity finally hit 14 percent, D'Alessandro's stated goal five years earlier when he was named CEO. He immediately raised the target to 15 percent, and then blew past it, reaching 16.1 percent in 2000. At that point, Manulife had a market cap of $11 billion—four times more than the book value of $2.7 billion when D'Alessandro had joined—and was among the dozen biggest publicly owned firms in Canada.

---

*Manulife operated in Canada, the United States, the United Kingdom, China, Hong Kong, Macao, Japan, the Philippines, Indonesia, Singapore, Taiwan, Vietnam, Germany, Bermuda, and Barbados.

For a company that had been modernizing since the days of Syd Jackson, demutualization was a huge leap. "Demutualization was a big cultural shift because all of a sudden you were accountable to more than your board and your policyholders. You were accountable to shareholders, so we became far more focused on quarterly reporting," said Diane Bean, who joined Manulife in 1975 and worked for three CEOs. "The sense of having to achieve more demanding targets came from Dominic, who set very clear goals about what had to be achieved."

Demutualization was a personal bonanza for D'Alessandro. When he joined Manulife in 1994, the board approved a Long Term Incentive Plan (LTIP) that was meant to mirror the kind of rewards received by executives at public companies through stock options. (All Manulife executives from vice president up participated in the LTIP.) The notional value of D'Alessandro's phantom equity account was set at $3 million. In 2000, when a stock option arrangement replaced the LTIP, D'Alessandro received $11 million in the form of cash and restricted shares that could not be sold until retirement, a separate grant of $5.5 million in restricted shares, and 1.4 million options—all on top of his annual salary of $1,075,000 and a bonus that year of $3 million.

D'Alessandro's payment prize by far exceeded anyone else's. Second place went to John Richardson, senior executive vice president, who received an LTIP payout of $1.1 million, restricted shares worth $3.5 million, and 158,200 options on top of a salary and bonus of $1.3 million. D'Alessandro also bettered Gord Nixon, who in 2001 had replaced John Cleghorn as CEO of the Royal Bank. Nixon's total compensation that year was $7.3 million compared with D'Alessandro's $9.6 million—not counting the one-time $11 million LTIP payout.

In the months that followed Manulife's listing on global stock exchanges, there was little demand for the shares of any insurance company. The price was further depressed by poor economic conditions in Asia, where many of the new shareholders sold their shares to raise cash. During October, the first month Manulife's shares were on the market, the price dipped to $17. In a speech delivered that month to a meeting of the Life Insurance and Market Research Association in Toronto, D'Alessandro admitted there were moments when he wondered if he'd made the right career choice. "When I first reviewed the research for this speech, I wanted to rush out and slash my wrists. How in heaven had I gotten myself into an industry that had unfavourable demographics, a skeptical client base, a hostile regulator, and new and formidable competition [the banks] on the horizon?"

In all, five firms demutualized: Clarica was first on July 21, 1999, followed by Manulife on September 25, then Canada Life on November 5, Industrial-Alliance on February 10, 2000, and Sun Life on March 23. Demutualization represented the single largest distribution of wealth in Canadian history—$10 billion to two million citizens, for an average of $5000 each, compared with Manulife's payout per policyholder of $13,000. More importantly, the new Manulife shareholders saw share price improve. After a year, Manulife share price was $32, up more than 75 percent.

———

NOW THAT MANULIFE was a public company, with the ability to forge a merger using the currency of a share exchange with another public company, a bank beckoned. Early in 2002, John Hunkin, CEO of Canadian Imperial Bank of Commerce, approached D'Alessandro. Would Manulife care to talk about a merger with CIBC? Initially, D'Alessandro declined. He was dubious that Ottawa would approve a deal, given that two previous proposals for bank mergers in 1998 had been denied. Politicians saw no gain in such deals; Canadian voters did not favour bigger banks and fewer players. What anyone might think about a cross-pillar deal, in which a bank and an insurance company merged, was less clear, but D'Alessandro wasn't certain he wanted to waste time finding out.

CIBC needed the boost a merger might bring more than did Manulife. Of all the Canadian banks, CIBC had so often been a hapless victim that it came to be called, "The bank most likely to walk into a sharp object." CIBC had been a lender to every deadbeat major corporate borrower in the last three decades, from Massey-Ferguson through Dome Petroleum, Olympia & York, and Enron right up to subprime mortgages. "That's what happens when you have a franchise run by very nice people, well educated, well born, well introduced," said D'Alessandro. "[Businessman and former lieutenant-governor of Ontario] Hal Jackman says it the best. He says when we got out of school, all of them got jobs, they got the best jobs. Today, you wouldn't get a job."

After being spurned initially, CIBC's Hunkin persisted and was able to convince D'Alessandro to discuss the cross-pillar merger. For the next several months, the two CEOs made no attempt to hide their meetings, openly visiting each other's offices. No one ever twigged to what was happening until Janet McFarland broke the story in *The Globe and Mail* in January 2003, long after events had concluded with no deal.

What kept D'Alessandro intrigued was Hunkin's tantalizing offer that D'Alessandro would be CEO of the merged firm. D'Alessandro concluded that Hunkin was more interested in finding a successor than participating in the creation and running of a global financial services giant. "John's very likeable, he's a real gentleman. He never told me this, but he may well have been eager to just move on to the next phase of his life," said D'Alessandro. "Initially, I said it's an interesting idea but we'd have two problems. One is to convince the market. A company like ours would be spending the first year of this thing just going out and briefing our shareholder base or quietening them down." The second problem, said D'Alessandro, was that such cross-pillar mergers as Citibank-Travelers and Allianz-Dresdner Bank hadn't worked. "Over time, he brought me around. The values got to a level where it was compelling," said D'Alessandro.

Even though both men knew that Ottawa had no appetite for mergers between banks, they hoped that a cross-pillar merger between a bank and an insurance company might be less troublesome because the number of banks was not reduced—competition would not be affected. "I never took Ottawa's view for granted. That was always a risk," said Donald Guloien, Manulife's chief investment officer, who was brought into the talks by D'Alessandro. The real question in this case, Guloien said, was: "How will this play on the Main Street of Brampton?" CIBC had conducted research and public opinion surveys about a cross-pillar merger and found there would be no public outcry.

Manulife had assets under administration of $142 billion; CIBC was twice as big, with assets of $291 billion. Negotiations got far enough along that the two men agreed to a share exchange, an easier arrangement than a cash transaction. D'Alessandro met with the top half-dozen CIBC executives in order to gauge the bank's bench strength. There were also gatherings involving the two management teams, but they never got as far as deciding on a name for the new institution.

Nor did D'Alessandro ever put the question of a merger with CIBC directly to his board. "It was more in the nature of a strategic discussion: Would it be a good idea, wouldn't it be a good idea, what are the pros and cons? I don't think there was a consensus. There was a mixed view," said Manulife board chairman Arthur Sawchuk. "Generally speaking we've been happy with strategies that tend to stick to the nature of our business, which is the insurance business. Diversifying away from that is a little more risky in that you're focusing the company's energy in another business."

———————

BUT D'ALESSANDRO WAS NOT to be denied. He wanted to know Ottawa's view. In the summer of 2002, D'Alessandro and Hunkin flew to Ottawa on the CIBC corporate jet to meet with Finance Minister John Manley. Manley had recently replaced Paul Martin, who had resigned not only from his position as finance minister but also from the Jean Chrétien Cabinet, in order to prepare his leadership bid. Despite his brief tenure at finance, Manley had previously been minister of industry and so was familiar with commercial issues.

Sitting in with Manley was Kevin Lynch, who had been deputy minister of finance for two years and deputy minister of industry for five years before that.

D'Alessandro and Hunkin brought no documents and made no PowerPoint presentation. Instead, they described their merger proposal orally. Because neither Manley nor Lynch was at finance when bank mergers had been derailed, they said they wanted to take a closer look at the government's policy before responding. "We certainly didn't say no. They'd presented a very good case for their institutions, why this would be a beneficial thing," said Manley. D'Alessandro and Hunkin came away from the meeting feeling elated about what they regarded as Manley's positive view. "He was very excited about it. Both of us left the meeting thinking it was a done deal because it broke the logjam of this sterile policy we have now, which means no one can do anything," said D'Alessandro.

When Lynch looked into the matter, he discovered that cross-pillar mergers were covered neither in the statutes nor by regulations. The policy was simply the result of a ministerial statement prohibiting cross-pillar mergers. That meant the current minister could revamp the cross-pillar policy without having to bother with Parliament, just by making another announcement.

Manley wasn't prepared to take such a step without further study. "We gave it thought and decided that there was a pretty good rationale for opening up the possibility of cross-pillar mergers," he said. "The rationale for preventing it that had previously existed, namely the fear of acquisition during a demutualization phase, was clearly over, so it should be re-examined."

Manley obtained Prime Minister Jean Chrétien's approval to announce a policy review. He would call for submissions from interested parties and aimed to declare the government's view on cross-pillar mergers before he brought down the budget in February 2003. "We could do it all on a fairly fast track because we were conscious that there were some commercial realities," said Manley. "You can only keep these things alive for so long."

About the same time, two banks—Bank of Montreal (BMO) and Scotiabank—approached Ottawa with a merger in mind. Chrétien was opposed to bank mergers, but there was an established process for the banks to lay out their rationale in public. "I told them, if you make the case well enough, I'm prepared to be favourably disposed," said Manley, "but understand that on an issue like this, the guy in the corner office is going to have to be convinced as well. After a lot of tossing and turning, they decided they just didn't want to take the chance. BMO had been through it once and it's too disruptive to the institution to announce something like that and then not be able to complete it."

Lynch called D'Alessandro to explain the steps the government had in mind when reviewing the question of cross-pillar mergers. When he heard the plans, D'Alessandro became impatient; he could not wait the months it would take to carry out such a study. "That's not what I want—I don't want you to change the policy, I want an exception to the policy," he said.

Given D'Alessandro's response, Manley saw no point in launching a review. "I wasn't going to go down that road if the advocates for it didn't want it. So it was just a dead end," said Manley. With no change in the policy, and no exception permitted, Manulife and CIBC did not merge. D'Alessandro was unhappy with the outcome, saying, "The industry in Canada can't rationalize the way we probably should." (After he left politics, Manley became a member of the CIBC board of directors in 2005.)

In 2008 D'Alessandro was back in the picture with CIBC when the bank wrote down billions of dollars that had been invested in asset-backed paper and subprime mortgages. Needing capital, CIBC raised $3 billion in equity. Among the investors was Manulife, which bought $500 million worth of CIBC shares, a 5 percent stake in the beleaguered bank. Bay Street analyst John Aiken of Dundee Securities raised the possibility of a cross-pillar merger to rescue the ailing CIBC, with Manulife as the most likely candidate.

D'Alessandro has said the investment in CIBC was just that, an investment, not a prelude to a deal. "I never wanted the job. John

[Hunkin] had to convince me that this was thing to do. There's this myth that somehow I want to go back and be a banker. That's not the case. My company today is twice the size of the CIBC and twice the size of BMO. At the end of the day, I didn't go home crying that the government didn't turn on the green lights. I had other avenues to pursue." The street kid from Little Burgundy had his eye on another prize—south of the border.

ELEVEN

Left at the Station

DURING THE TIME Dominic D'Alessandro was in talks with CIBC's John Hunkin, he was also negotiating with David D'Alessandro, chief executive officer of Boston-based John Hancock Mutual Life Insurance. It was almost as if D'Alessandro believed if he got busy with two unlikely deals, one of them was bound to pay off. Just as no one had previously brought a cross-pillar deal to Ottawa, no Canadian financial services institution had ever proposed, let alone pulled off, the purchase of an American financial giant.

The first contact between the two D'Alessandros occurred in the spring of 1997, when Dominic saw that someone with the same name had been appointed president of Hancock. On May 9, Dominic sent David a congratulatory letter. "What a remarkable coincidence that two fine, long-established mutual insurance companies such as ours should be led by individuals with the same, rather unusual surname," he wrote. "I look forward to meeting you in the not-too-distant future. We could compare backgrounds; who knows, there might be a common ancestor!" He enclosed a copy of the Manulife annual report and told David if he ever came to Toronto, they should meet.

David replied on May 20, noting other uncanny connections. "Coincidentally, my father's first name was Dominic and, as I am sure you know, so was the star first baseman of the 1950s-era Chicago Cubs." David went on to say that he knew Michael Bell, who had led the Monitor Group study of Manulife at the time of Dominic's arrival in 1994, and that Bell spoke highly of Dominic. David agreed the two D'Alessandros should get together, either in Boston or Toronto.

Nothing came of the exchange until May 2000. Dominic was headed for Boston, where Manulife had established its U.S. national sales and marketing office in 1995, so he contacted David and they met for dinner at Morton's. "We commiserated about how difficult it was to be a CEO and how no one felt sorry for us," said David. "We commiserated about how difficult it was taking the company public during the dot-com craze. The dot-coms were everyone's favourite. We were running around trying to sell a mutual company's stock when we looked like a dinosaur and they all looked like rocket ships."

They were surprised to discover other similarities. Both men were the same height, five feet seven inches, both were precocious children, and both had done well in spite of adversity when young. David was descended from Italian immigrants who operated a grocery store in Utica, New York. Born in 1951, David grew up speaking Italian and English, acting as an interpreter for his grandfather.

At four, David became involved in the family business. He'd inherited his grandmother's ability to tell if meat was going bad. Meat hanging in cold lockers has no smell. The family talent was being able to identify bad meat by licking it because bad meat made the tongue tingle. After his grandmother died, David's grandfather would take him to the slaughterhouse on twice-weekly visits. His reward was a hot dog, but David's taste buds couldn't save the business in the next generation. His father was a compulsive racetrack gambler who lost the store and the family home while David was in college.

In the case of both Dominic and David, their mother was the dominant parent. Dominic's father died early; David's father hardly participated in home life. His mother, Rosemary, gave up trying to keep her husband on the straight and narrow, and decided instead to protect the three children from their father's addiction by lavishing all her attention on them.

The two companies, Manulife and John Hancock, were just as well matched as the two men. "Of all the scans we'd done, this was the company most like us, in terms of pedigree, history, establishment in the community, reputation, brand. It had got a little tarnished in the credit cycle, they lost a lot of money, but otherwise it would be a company that we'd be proud to be associated with," said Dominic. "It wasn't so big that it was impossible. We both knew the Boston community and the regulators."

WHEN THE FOUNDERS of a new life insurance company in Boston presented their plans to the state legislature in 1862, they chose to name the firm after an illustrious scientist and inventor, Benjamin Franklin. The name was rejected, just as the first offering by Manufacturers' had been denied. The revised choice was John Hancock, president of the Continental Congress and the first to sign the Declaration of Independence in 1776. His distinctive signature came to mean any signature—as in, "Put your John Hancock here." On April 21, 1862, a charter was granted to the John Hancock Mutual Life Insurance Company.

The first Hancock office was modest, a single room in the back of a building at 41 State Street. The first president was George P. Sanger. Like John A. Macdonald, he kept his day job, in his case as district attorney, until his term was up in 1869, when he began devoting himself full-time to the company. Within three years the company had expanded to nine other states, including distant Minnesota. In 1879 Hancock was the first mutual insurance company to sell "industrial insurance" to factory workers as they left work at the end of a shift. Agents collected premiums weekly. By 1929 the company was operating in thirty-seven states and jurisdictions, including the District of Columbia and Hawaii. Even in the depths of the Great Depression in 1932, Hancock was strong and distributed $348,000 every business day. In 1934, total payments to policyholders since the firm's founding reached $1 billion; Hancock was the eighth-largest life insurance company in the United States.

Growth meant new office buildings in Boston's Back Bay area: an eight-storey building on Clarendon Street, built in 1922, with Corinthian pilasters and an atrium; a twenty-six-storey tower on 200 Berkeley Street, built in 1949, that included the 1100-seat John Hancock Hall, complete with stage, orchestra pit, and two Steinway pianos; and the sixty-storey Hancock Tower, designed by architect I.M. Pei. Construction of the tower began in 1968 and was delayed because of soil conditions, followed by trouble with windows that popped out and crashed to the street. All were eventually replaced and the building was officially opened in 1976.

Hancock's first Canadian connection came in 1969 when Hancock bought Maritime Life, a tiny company based in Halifax with only $30 million in assets compared with Hancock's US$10 billion. As Harry Bruce wrote in his corporate history of Maritime Life, *Never Content: How Mavericks and Outsiders Made a Surprise Winner of Maritime Life*, Hancock's eighty-one vice presidents outnumbered the entire Maritime Life staff. Because ownership by foreigners was prohibited at the time, the $6.8-million deal required special approvals by provincial and federal authorities.

Hancock left Maritime Life alone, allowing the firm to retain its name and run its own business. By 1986, Maritime Life's assets had mushroomed to $1.7 billion and the firm had become Hancock's most profitable subsidiary. Maritime continued to grow by acquiring a division of Confederation Life in 1995, Aetna Canada in 1999, and Royal & Sun Alliance Life Insurance Company in 2001. In 2004, Maritime Life had two thousand employees and was the seventh-largest life insurance company in Canada.

WHEN DAVID D'ALESSANDRO arrived at Hancock in 1984 as vice president, corporate communications, he realized that life insurance was, in his words, "vaporware ... as insubstantial as any service peddled by the airiest dot-com company." All Hancock had, like any life insurance company, was its reputation. "If ever there were a brand-based business, life insurance is it," he said in his book, *Brand Warfare*, published in 2001.

D'Alessandro's background was in advertising, and it didn't take long for a marketing opportunity to appear. In 1985, the Boston Marathon was in disarray, losing the best runners to other contests that offered more prize money. The event organizers, the Boston Athletic Association, desperately needed help. D'Alessandro said Hancock would sponsor the race for fifteen years at $1 million a year, so the Marathon could raise its profile and pay substantial prizes.

Sports branding was further escalated in 1994, when Hancock became one of the dozen corporate sponsors of the Olympics. Hancock also became a sponsor of Major League Baseball, college football, and the Champions on Ice figure skating tour. David D'Alessandro was considered such an expert that he was listed by *Sporting News* as one of the one hundred most powerful people in sports.

In June 2000, at forty-nine, D'Alessandro became the youngest president and CEO in the history of Hancock. In office, he spoke out against bribes paid to Olympics officials and wrote an opinion piece in *The Boston Globe* on child abuse by Catholic priests, in which he demanded the resignation of Cardinal Bernard Law. David also wrote two books, including *Career Warfare*, which set out a plan to manage your boss, told how to create an impressive personality, and advised up-and-comers to be ruthless.

SOON AFTER HANCOCK had demutualized in 2000, the firm fell into financial difficulty. One-third of the company's profits came from guaranteed income contracts (GICs) sold to pension funds that sought guaranteed annual growth. It's not unusual for an insurance company to have 10 percent of its business in GICs, but Hancock had 33 percent. All of the money Hancock received from clients buying GICs had to be reinvested at higher interest rates, usually in private placements. "The private placement world was starting to dry up and we were starting to take too much risk, airline risk, farm risk. We simply had too high a proportion of that business on our books," said David. Rating agencies were pushing Hancock to reduce its reliance on GICs and threatened to downgrade the firm. "If you go from a double A to a single A, you can no longer sell GICs because pension funds don't buy single-A GICs," said David. "You also have a problem on the life insurance side, what I call the mother's milk of the business, because you're selling against some high-grade companies like Met, Prudential, or New York Life—who are double-A companies."

Between 1999 and 2003, Hancock reduced the proportion of revenue earned by GICs from 33 percent to 28 percent, but the downgrade threats continued. After demutualizing at $17 a share in 2000 and seeing share prices rise to the low $40s in 2001, Hancock then saw the price settle to around $32.

In addition to the GICs, Hancock had another problem. About 8 percent of Hancock's portfolio was in holdings that were below investment grade, a proportion of stinkers that was more than twice as high as at competing firms. "It's not that the Hancock was going to go down in flames, but we were definitely going to suffer, in our opinion, a 30 to 40 percent hit to the stock. My job was to find value for the investor," said David D'Alessandro.

In 2002, when Dominic was talking about a merger with either CIBC or Hancock, David was looking at buying Jefferson Pilot Life Insurance Co., of Greensboro, North Carolina, as well as a couple of annuity companies in the Midwest. He also flirted with FleetBoston Financial, a Boston-based bank. Dominic believed he was making progress with Hancock, but in fact David was having trouble convincing his board that a deal with a Canadian firm would work as well as a merger with a U.S. company. In the case of a cross-border deal, the potential existed for "flowback" if Hancock shareholders decided to sell rather than hold the Manulife shares they received in exchange for their Hancock shares, a frequent event when a foreign company buys an American firm.

On November 25, 2002, David flew to Toronto, checked into the Four Seasons, and waited for Dominic to pick up him up for dinner at the York Club. After the two were seated in the Card Room, one of the club's private rooms, David told Dominic that he was calling a halt to the possibility of a merger with Manulife. Hancock was entering into exclusive negotiations with a U.S. insurance firm that he did not name. "He was disappointed and, I would say, displeased," recalled David. "He thought we were moving along. He already had an operation based in Boston, he had an operation in the Far East where we did, we both had Canadian operations of size. He saw the potential of it. I liked him enormously. We got along. We trusted each other, which is part of it all. Not a small part of it, I might add."

That trust had vanished. "I was pissed. I'd waited around for the right deal," said Dominic. "He left me at the altar. It was a monumental transaction that would have completely transformed our company. You get yourself emotionally committed."

⸻•⸻

WITH CIBC AND HANCOCK both going nowhere, Dominic D'Alessandro was falling behind as the rest of the industry consolidated. Manulife's recent acquisitions had all been small deals. In 2001 and 2002, Manulife bought Commercial Union's Canadian life insurance operations, which added $1 billion to funds under management. D'Alessandro also bought the group business of Zurich Life Insurance with two hundred thousand policyholders.

But those purchases were chickenfeed compared with what was going on in the industry. Aetna Life bought Financial Life and Excelsior Life and then was in turn acquired by Maritime Life. Canada Life bought Crown Life, New York Life, and CNA Life. Sun

Alliance was bought by Royal Life, and Imperial Life by Desjardins Financial. Mutual Life bought the Canadian arm of Metropolitan Life. The banks were busy, too. Royal bought Mutual of Omaha and The Bank of Nova Scotia acquired Glacier National Life.

With big deals like CIBC and Hancock off the table, D'Alessandro set his sights on something a little closer to home: Canada Life. Surely he could pull off this deal. He and Canada Life CEO David Nield were friends. For several years they had enjoyed dinners together with their wives, Pearl and Clare. A year before demutualization, D'Alessandro and Nield had talked about merging their two companies, but Nield had been unable to convince his board. Now was the hour. Or so D'Alessandro thought.

On Friday, December 6, 2002, D'Alessandro called Nield and asked to see him. Nield invited D'Alessandro to his home that evening. They sat at Nield's kitchen table while D'Alessandro drank a Diet Coke and his host sipped ice water. D'Alessandro presented a letter to Nield offering to buy Canada Life at $38 a share. As he watched his friend read the offer, he knew there was trouble: Nield fell silent and began shaking.

"What would you like the offer to be? How could we take this forward?" asked D'Alessandro.

"It's going to take a long time. I have to consult with the board," replied Nield.

"We've started a sequence here. We don't have a long time," said D'Alessandro. "There's some room to negotiate, but not infinite room. What deal would fly?"

"The market's going to decide," said Nield.

D'Alessandro told Nield if he could point out values that Manulife had failed to identify, he'd be prepared to raise his offer. After thirty minutes, D'Alessandro left, feeling a bit shaken himself. He'd expected things to go more smoothly.

In addition to Nield's unhappiness with D'Alessandro's price, there was a fundamental misunderstanding as to whether or not something had happened. "David was of the view that Dominic's approach was so sketchy that it didn't signal anything. I think he got legal advice to that effect," said Donald Guloien. "Our legal advice was that if you talk, even in the general terms that we had, we have to signal a change in intent. David probably came to the conclusion—incorrectly—that we were trying to pressure him and that wasn't the case at all."

The bid had become hostile, an uncommon situation in Canadian business, although D'Alessandro preferred to use the term "unsolicited." Nield's reluctance upset D'Alessandro, who took the rejection personally. "He would become resentful when people turned down his proposal. It's like, 'How could you go for anything else?' He likes people sharing his point of view," said Roy Firth.

The bid could not have come as a surprise to Nield. Manulife had acquired 9.1 percent of Canada Life shortly after Canada Life had demutualized, making Manulife a prime candidate to buy Canada Life or prosper from a bidding war, if there were one. Canada Life, like Clarica, had been protected against a takeover for two years following demutualization in 1999, but that period had expired. Sun Life had already bought Clarica earlier that year, so Canada Life was next in line. With the Clarica deal, Sun wrested top spot among Canadian insurers away from Manulife. CEOs claim such standings don't matter, but they do. Other than Avis Rent A Car, with its "We try harder" ad campaign, no one ever celebrated being number two, least of all Dominic D'Alessandro.

ON SATURDAY, D'ALESSANDRO met with Guloien, other Manulife officers, and legal advisers to debrief them on his meeting the night before with Nield. The group worried that Canada Life would leak the offer to the media. When investors saw that Canada Life was "in play," the sudden interest would drive share price higher, perhaps beyond Manulife's reach. D'Alessandro phoned Nield and said, "I'm prepared to improve the offer to $40. Will that give you comfort so we can start talking about an arrangement?"

Nield repeated what had become his mantra. "The market has to decide. I can't tell you the price."

D'Alessandro pleaded for some indication of value. "Well, can't you tell me, is it $50, is it $60, is it $42, so I know whether I can make an offer?" Nield did not respond.

Matters had taken a terrible turn. Because D'Alessandro knew Nield well, and counted him as a friend, he'd expected an amiable conversation and maybe even a handshake deal. "It ended up being a little bit more acrimonious than Dominic ever expected. We had to fire our arrows at each other because that's what you do. So it ends up being publicly hostile," said Craig Bromley, who was part of the Manulife deal team. "Dominic had a very good relationship with David Nield and truly admired David as an individual. He had the belief that they fully understood that if we made an offer, it would have to be made public very quickly and things would have to move along. They felt that we were putting a gun to their head," said Guloien.

On Monday, December 9, D'Alessandro went public with his improved offer for Canada Life of $40 a share, a total of $6.3 billion—a 30 percent premium on Canada Life's Friday closing price. If successful, the merger would create the largest insurance company in Canada and the fourth-largest life insurer in North America. The new company would dominate the Canadian market with the largest market share in group life and health, individual life insurance, and individual fixed annuities. In the United States, the combination would be the biggest in new 401(k) defined contribution pension plans.

After meeting with his board, Nield rejected Manulife's bid as too low and signalled that he was open to offers from other companies. On February 17, 2003, Great-West Life bid $44.50 per share, a total of $7.3 billion, $1 billion more than Manulife. The prize was too rich for D'Alessandro to chase. Great-West won.

Manulife sold its 14.7 million shares of Canada Life to Great-West for $654 million. (Manulife also bought shares in Clarica and

Sun when they went public and made sizeable gains on those two as well. The precise amounts have never been revealed, but D'Alessandro said the total earned from holdings in all three companies was "in the billions.") For his part, D'Alessandro felt he'd not only failed but had also lost a friend in the process. "Dominic had a great deal of respect for David. Dominic was deeply aggrieved, felt disloyal, and said at one stage, 'I wish I'd never started this,'" said Guloien.

It's an endearing thought, how D'Alessandro felt so personally tortured by Nield's rejection. But this was not the same situation as had occurred with Brian Moore and North American Life, where the two mutual companies simply pooled their assets. Unlike North American Life, Canada Life was robust. Moreover, Canada Life had become a public company and was widely known to be available for sale. David Nield had worked hard to push the share price as high as possible in order to position himself for a bidding war that would benefit his shareholders.

Did D'Alessandro really expect that Nield would recommend a Manulife offer to his board without first testing the waters to see if there was a higher bid? In fact, it was Nield's fiduciary duty to go looking for another bidder. Journalists went so far as to describe D'Alessandro as depressed about his lack of success. "I keep reading about myself and how disappointed I was. If I was as disappointed as I was portrayed, I would have been suicidal and I don't think I was," he told reporters.

Maybe he wasn't suicidal, but the success he so avidly sought was certainly eluding him at every turn. In a single year, D'Alessandro had lost out on four possible acquisitions. He'd missed the sale of Clarica, refused to increase his offer when Great-West outbid him for Canada Life, and spent fruitless months in talks with two potential partners, CIBC and John Hancock. A succession of consolidation trains had left the station. Dominic D'Alessandro remained standing on the platform with nothing but fervent hopes and a battered suitcase, the immigrant lad still looking for a way to a better future.

TWELVE

Passion and Performance

SOME SAD SOULS claim to be the smartest in the room and think they have to prove it, and then there are others, like Dominic D'Alessandro, whose prowess is readily apparent. Pick a timely topic and D'Alessandro will have an opinion, facts to back it up, a relevant book he's recently read that he can summarize in a few deft sentences, and a prodigious capacity to summon arguments to convince any skeptic.

Don't have a subject? He'll make a quick judgment about you and eagerly supply some thoughts about life, world affairs, or the economy that he appears to be revealing for the first time, honouring your ears with his ideas, seeking a response, testing your mettle against his, going through some mental gymnastics to give his grey matter a workout, and discover a bit about who you are, too. As a boy he was smaller than his chums, and because he was twice pushed ahead a grade, he was always in classes with older kids. Sports were out, he could not excel physically, so his mind became his means of finding a way to joust with others and win a place at the head of the pack. All of this can mean that he sometimes seems to have a chip on his shoulder, and why not? D'Alessandro came from nowhere to rise to the top. It irritates him to see others propelled forward by their breeding and background rather than their drive and determination.

———•———

IF I HAD A DOLLAR for every time someone told me a CEO I was writing about "doesn't suffer fools gladly," I'd be a wealthy man. In the case of D'Alessandro, the oft-repeated phrase happens to be true. He cares passionately about everything, but particularly about doing well. That attitude also means that he wants others to work as hard and achieve as much as he can. He is relentless in his efforts to spur colleagues to greater heights as he searches for kindred souls with ambition and self-confidence, team players who know their stuff. "He pursues excellence. He wants to do a really good job, better than anybody else and make a difference," said chief financial officer Peter Rubenovitch. "He has very high standards and he thinks if you're blocking and tackling that you're in a position to put yourself in the way of opportunity. If you do a really good job, take care of your business, things will happen."

The downside of that personality trait, however, is that he can lose his temper when confronted by incompetence or if he has probed for an answer that's not forthcoming. This capacity for anger was something D'Alessandro himself eventually acknowledged. In a 2004 speech when he received the Loyola Medal from his alma mater, he reflected on life lessons and mentors who'd helped him along the way. "The other day I was telling some of my colleagues at Manulife that I could not recall a single instance in my career when someone I worked for got impatient or angry with me," he said. "I was quickly told that, regrettably, this was one area where I hadn't quite mastered my lessons."

D'Alessandro made an equally telling reference in his speech to the 2008 Manulife annual meeting. In thanking Arthur Sawchuk for his services on the occasion of the chairman's pending retirement, D'Alessandro complimented him by saying he "so skilfully managed my moods and helped me deal with all of the many stresses that are an inevitable part of running a large company."

Sawchuk's office as chairman was beside D'Alessandro's, so there were many occasions when the CEO charged through Sawchuk's door like a badass cowboy entering a saloon, guns a-blazing. "Dominic can be very intense. Every now and then he needs to blow off a little steam. I'm his pressure relief valve," said Sawchuk, a Manulife director since 1993 and board chairman from 1998 to 2008. "I don't compound it, I find a way to calm it down and bring it to a steadier state and then move forward with some advice. Sometimes he just wants somebody to talk to about the subject, so I'm the sounding board. As he once said to me, 'Arthur you're not saying no, but I think I know from your body language that you mean no,' so he's learned to read me, too."

For D'Alessandro, talking to Sawchuk was therapeutic. "He's like a shrink. I've become very fond of him. It's hard to get mad at Arthur. He's so well-meaning. All my management team love him. They see him as a big teddy bear. He shuffles around, he's nice to everybody. He puts on no airs."

In recent years, D'Alessandro's tirades have become fewer and less explosive. "A lot of comments people have made to you about his emotional toughness are more probably to do with his first five years than the last five. I think he's mellowed out. He's matured substantially in the best sense of the word," said Sawchuk. "He's much calmer about things but, still, if there's a bad piece of work, you're going to hear about it, which you should. Everyone should. The worst thing in any organization is when people don't get regular performance assessments. They don't know where they stand. This organization is never confused about where it has to go."

On the way to mellow, D'Alessandro regularly administered tongue-lashings. Most members of management suffered his verbal abuse. "He's kind of a volatile character. Sometimes I'd get the lashings on behalf of others. If something went wrong in one of the divisions, I'd be called in and he'd vent his spleen on me," said John

Richardson, who worked for D'Alessandro for eight years before retiring in 2002. "When it was all over, he felt much better. I never took it personally. When I got it, I deserved it."

Richardson and Richard Coles both worked in the 1980s at Canada Trust under CEO Merv Lahn, who was regarded at the time as one of the toughest bosses in Canada. Richardson once told Coles that D'Alessandro was "Merv Lahn squared." Said Coles, "Dominic's incredibly tough. He wants performance. He doesn't want excuses, he doesn't BS, he wants the right answers, he wants people to understand what the questions should be ahead of time. He's very, very challenging."

Coles claims he never suffered a reprimand from D'Alessandro but witnessed his scoldings at the weekly Friday meetings of the executive committee. Once a month, those meetings were expanded through videoconferencing to become the management committee— the executive committee, plus the next fifteen officers in the world- wide pecking order—an organizational concept D'Alessandro began at Laurentian and transplanted to Manulife. "You were expected to understand your business. You talk about the good things, but you were expected to bring up the challenges, and if the challenges didn't get brought up before they started to show up in the financials, that was pretty serious," said Coles.

In D'Alessandro's view, any failings should be addressed immedi- ately, whatever the venue. "He believed that you challenge people in front of their peers and everybody understands that maybe they've got to also work hard and pull up their socks," said Coles. D'Alessandro did not shout or pound the desk. Instead, his face blackened, his body seethed, and his voice became acerbic. Everyone else went heads- down and waited out the storm. "It's worse than anger, he can be incredibly cutting and biting and humiliating. He also views that he was the leader and people paid attention. Some people grow from it, other people don't," said Coles, who retired in 2001 but retained close connections to Manulife as a director of three different entities: Manulife Bank, Seabrook Asset Management, a Halifax-based firm in which Manulife has an ownership position, and Elliott and Page, one of Manulife's mutual fund managers.

Others who worked at Manulife agree that D'Alessandro was an equal opportunity employer when it came to scathing admonishments. "It happened to all of us. That's just the nature of the man," said Felix Chee, who spent seven years at Manulife. "There's positive stuff and there's negative stuff, and at the end of the day you have to weigh everything up and say, 'Do I still want to be here? Do I still think that there's meaningful things for me to do and do I still enjoy doing it?' Everybody has to come to his own calibration on that."

Even knowing the right time to present an idea to D'Alessandro was a learned skill. "There are times to approach on certain issues and times not. He gives all decent proposals a good hearing, but you need to pick your moment. An even worse thing is presenting something that's wrong," said Diane Bean. "He has a huge capacity to forgive a mistake, but he cannot forgive people who won't admit they made a mistake. That drives him nuts. It's all part of this accountability culture. He doesn't like anybody who dodges accountability. He likes people to own up, move on, and he can forgive that."

Of the two-dozen executive officers at Manulife when D'Alessandro arrived, only four lasted through his full tenure: Diane Bean, Bob Cook, Donald Guloien, and Bruce Gordon. Some of the others who arrived during D'Alessandro's time learned how to gain his confidence. "If Dominic trusts you and thinks you know what you're doing, he doesn't meddle very much. After a period of time you learn what he wants to know about and what he doesn't," said John DesPrez. Once, when DesPrez hadn't heard from D'Alessandro for a while, he asked about the silence. Replied D'Alessandro, "If I have to talk to you a lot, it's a really bad sign, because then I don't need you. If you don't hear from me, that means all is well."

D'Alessandro sometimes went so far as to put his own executives on the spot during quarterly conference calls with analysts that are broadcast so anyone can listen. "Somebody would ask a question and one of the other people might answer, and then Dominic will follow up with another question, along the lines of 'What about this, and what about that?'" said Michael Goldberg, a financial services analyst for thirty-five years. Most CEOs would never put a colleague on the spot by asking a supplementary question in such circumstances; queries posed by analysts are usually rigorous enough. "It's unique. It reflects his deep sincerity to really communicate and do the right thing. I guess the way I've thought about people working at Manulife—if they're good at what they do, it would be like paradise because they will get recognized. If they're not good at what they do, it would probably be like hell on earth."

Even in his daily dealings with management, D'Alessandro used pointed comments to keep underlings on a short leash. When Donald Guloien was appointed chief investment officer, he told D'Alessandro he wanted to expand his role beyond merely managing Manulife's investments in the general account. Guloien said he could increase fee income by also managing assets for other investors. "You can pursue that ambition, but don't, whatever you do, mess up my general account," D'Alessandro said. As he recalled the conversation, Guloien said, "I guess you could call it encouraging with a little bit of an edge." Guloien did expand those third-party assets from about $10 billion to $100 billion; the general account grew, too.

D'Alessandro is well aware of the impact of his powerful personality. "Not everybody thrives in such an organization, likes to have their judgments questioned or be asked to explain their opinions. That's the way I run the company. The degree to which I question things, many times I'm just doing it to see how well you know your stuff," said D'Alessandro. "If I get the idea that I can ask you more questions in five minutes than you've actually thought of, then you've got a problem. I think it sets a tone in the organization that people are expected to be proficient and diligent and do their work."

FOR ALL HIS REPUTATION as a tough boss, D'Alessandro continues to retain the respect of many executives who worked for him and then left under a variety of circumstances. He still regularly sees for lunch former colleagues, such as Richard Coles and Felix Chee. "He wasn't the easiest guy to work with because he was tough. But I respected him and he was smart. I enjoyed my time working there," said Chee.

There were also occasions when poor performance did not arouse the ire of D'Alessandro—as long as there was a good explanation. During the dot-com boom, Paul Rooney, now CEO of the Canadian division, recommended to D'Alessandro that Manulife spend $10 million to develop an internet business so customers could buy life insurance online. D'Alessandro agreed, and in 1999 Rooney set up an operation so different from the rest of the company that the office space featured pinball machines for employee entertainment.

Rooney created a website called Manulife Direct, learned how to draw online traffic, built a needs calculator using software so that potential clients could figure out their net worth, and sold the first policy online—all within three months. But the fast start soon fizzled; there were too few buyers. "They wanted an agent to make sure they were doing all the right things before they closed the deal. We burned through $8 million of the $10 million," said Rooney. Some of his colleagues thought they could make it work, but not Rooney. "There was no way I could see a viable business model that would turn into a profitable business."

When Rooney told D'Alessandro that he'd blown $8 million and urged that the business be shut down, D'Alessandro was sanguine. "This is exactly the right thing to do. The only mistake you could have made was coming in here and telling me that we needed to spend another $10 million, good money after bad," said D'Alessandro. The needs calculator survived; a version is still used in agent presentations. "Manulife's a meritocracy. Results matter, but you can fail around here and still do well. You just can't make a habit of it," said Rooney.

Colleagues in good odour with D'Alessandro can sometimes josh him out of one of his moods. CFO Peter Rubenovitch and D'Alessandro were to play golf with a group at Rocky Crest on Lake Joseph in Muskoka. Delayed at a business meeting, they were running late. D'Alessandro was driving and Rubenovitch was navigating, but he missed a road he should have told D'Alessandro to take and it was a while before they realized the mistake.

D'Alessandro turned the car around, gunned the engine to make up for lost time, and was stopped for speeding. The fine was $200; D'Alessandro was furious. Later that day when all the golfers gathered for dinner, D'Alessandro was still going on about the incident and how it was Rubenovitch's fault. Rubenovitch went to an ATM, withdrew ten $20 bills, gave the money to D'Alessandro, and said, "I don't want to hear any more about it."

Because of D'Alessandro's outbursts, all the members of the executive team always knew exactly where they stood. "Dominic is very passionate and demanding. [He'd say] 'You've got a big business and you've got to run it. If you can't, I'll find somebody else to run it.' That's what you expect from a driven CEO," said Bruce Gordon, who joined Manulife in 1988 and ran several divisions in the United States and Canada. "He's a voracious reader, so if you send him stuff and give him the right amount of time to prepare, he'll have read it, he'll be knowledgeable with his questions, and push you on the strategic side. He has the ability to scan through the numbers and say, 'This one really looks funny,' and start to press. If you don't give a good answer or he doesn't like the answer, he'll drive down into more and more detail. Once the strategy is approved, he'll leave you to implement it and do the correct operational things," said Gordon.

That probing could be tough on some people. "If something went wrong he tore a strip off you. If you can't take that, and maybe some people couldn't, they chose to go somewhere else. But if you want financial excitement and bright people around you, an international scene you can play in if you wish, this was the place to be," said Gordon. "So, demanding? Yes. Passionate? Yes. Demeaning? No. Within closed walls for the executive committee, yeah, you were going to hear it if something wasn't going right. But if you want to be world-class and successful, I think that's what comes with it."

Outside the workplace, D'Alessandro could also be caring, as Bruce Gordon discovered in 2005 when his son, David, died of cancer at thirty-three. D'Alessandro attended the memorial service, had tears in his eyes as he gave Gordon a consoling hug, and told him to take as much time off as he wanted.

Through it all, D'Alessandro had no artifice. "He can be very charming and he can be very, very tough, but he doesn't lie, he doesn't cheat, he doesn't dissemble. I'm not sure there's much to know that isn't there, isn't visible," said Diane Bean. "What he does or what he says is always consistent with who you know he is and what he's trying to accomplish. I can't say to you what he's going to do next week, but when he does something next week I would not be surprised at it. It wouldn't ever be out of character."

NO ISSUE DEMONSTRATES that inner core of consistency and integrity better than D'Alessandro's decision on a hedge fund called Portus Alternative Asset Management. D'Alessandro never concerned himself much with advertising or branding, but he was willing to spend money to preserve the company's reputation. On February 2, 2005, the Ontario Securities Commission halted the opening of new Portus accounts, effectively freezing activity. Portus had promised many things that in retrospect appeared impossible but had made for a winning sales pitch: steady returns, low volatility, minimal tax, and full protection on the amount invested.

Before the OSC acted, neither D'Alessandro nor anyone else in upper management at Manulife had ever heard of Portus. It was just another among the myriad of investment choices offered by hundreds of financial advisers. D'Alessandro was heading to Asia for a two-week visit, so he asked general counsel Jean-Paul Bisnaire to look into the matter. D'Alessandro returned from Asia on a Saturday; Bisnaire reported his findings to D'Alessandro on the Sunday. Portus was a referral deal. Manulife advisers gave the names of potential clients to Portus and received a 5 percent fee of any amount invested. "It looked like it could be fraud. It looked like our clients were referred into a situation that wasn't what it was purported to be. There appeared to be a fair bit of misrepresentation as to what Portus was," said Bisnaire. "I reported all of that to Dominic and he quickly came to the conclusion that we should be keeping our clients whole." On March 3, the day before the OSC put Portus into receivership, Manulife released a letter signed by D'Alessandro saying that the firm would guarantee the full amount its clients had invested in Portus, about $260 million.

There was no legal obligation; D'Alessandro just decided that was the right course. "Our clients want to know the status of their investment and we don't think they should have to wait for the investigations into Portus to be completed before they get an answer," D'Alessandro wrote. "Whatever the outcome of the investigation, Manulife Financial guarantees that you will recover 100 percent of the principal amount you invested with Portus. We will, in effect, 'stand in your shoes' and aggressively pursue all avenues to secure and recover invested funds."

In a follow-up letter, D'Alessandro offered clients three options: a principal-protected note backed by a portfolio of mutual funds, a guaranteed investment certificate (GIC), or a cash payment equal to their original investment. He apologized to clients and also promised that they would share in any excess payment to Manulife as the company pursued the matter through the courts. No other firm followed D'Alessandro on that high road. The best anyone else did was to refund the commission collected by the financial adviser involved.

KPMG, the accounting firm appointed as receivers, found that after only two years in business, Portus—Latin for "harbour"—had $662 million in assets but more than $1 billion in liabilities. Canadians had invested about $750 million, with one-third of that coming from Manulife clients. The co-founders of Portus, Boaz Manor and Michael Mendelson, were charged with various crimes, including money laundering and fraud. Manor was scheduled to have a preliminary hearing in March 2009; Mendelson pleaded guilty to one count of fraud and was sentenced to two years in prison. At Manulife Securities, three people involved in approving Portus for referral business were fired.

Other Manulife employees were not surprised by D'Alessandro's actions. When the OSC first announced the problem in February, a panicky investor phoned his friend, Warren Thomson, a Boston-based Manulife executive. Thomson had never heard of Portus and had not talked to D'Alessandro but told his friend not to worry. "Dominic used almost the same phrase I'd told my friend—that this was an inappropriate product to have sold to Canadian retail customers and we're going to 'step into our customer's shoes,'" said Thomson. "He doesn't need lawyers to tell him that we have a probability of hanging people up in courts for years. [He asks] what's the right thing to do?"

D'Alessandro knows he acted responsibly, even though legally there was no reason to do so. "I'm very proud of that. We didn't know what it was going to cost us. We didn't know whether we were going to be on the hook for $260 million or zero. When we looked at all the facts, it was clear that we hadn't done the kind of job that I would be proud of."

That kind of action created a culture at Manulife of learning from mistakes rather than simply suffering punishment in silence. "Like all companies we have areas of weakness, but sometimes our weaknesses are our strength. There is a culture here that says, 'If you criticize everybody as being wrong all the time, you never do anything.' People are expected to learn by their mistakes. The Portus situation is a great example where we took a negative and turned it into a positive," said Philip Hampden-Smith, who is in charge of Southeast Asia. "It's like a bungee: if you have top-down you also get some bottom-up. If you apply a common-sense approach from the top-down, people from the bottom-up begin to see the benefits because they realize that it works."

In 2007 Manulife launched a class action suit against Société Générale (Canada), which had backed some of the Portus products.

The lawsuit was on behalf of all investors in Portus, not just Manulife clients, and Manulife paid all the legal costs. "We wanted to benefit everybody who had invested in Portus. Other people wouldn't have the resources to put in a claim," said Jean-Paul Bisnaire. Under D'Alessandro's initial estimate, if Manulife won the lawsuit, the company's loss would be about $45 million of the $260 million that Manulife had already repaid to clients. "In the scheme of Manulife, it's not very much," said D'Alessandro. "That's the worst-case scenario. It's not bad." The two sides reached a settlement in November 2008 before the class action was certified. Société Générale denied all allegations but agreed to pay an amount that meant non-Manulife investors received 94 percent of their money back. Manulife investors, of course, had previously received 100 percent. In the end, the cost to Manulife was only about $15 million to preserve a reputation that was priceless.

THIRTEEN

The Other Game

FIGHTS SUCH AS THE ONE with Portus are not necessarily about winning admiration for the man himself. Dominic D'Alessandro claims he doesn't need either praise from his peers or national adulation. While some CEOs have egos that require constant feeding through public acclaim and podium appearances, D'Alessandro chooses his speaking engagements carefully and only accepts an invitation when he has something to say. At annual meetings, he is far more frank than other CEOs, who tend to be mundane, even milquetoast. At the Manulife annual meeting in May 2007, D'Alessandro denounced the "hollowing out" of Canada with the departure of so many head offices. "I sometimes worry that we may all wake up one day and find that as a nation, we have lost control of our affairs," said D'Alessandro. "I believe that ownership matters a lot. It matters not only for economic reasons but, more importantly in my opinion, for our own sense of self-esteem and pride in our country."

In the run-up to every annual meeting, colleagues suggested topics for his remarks to shareholders or urged him to hire a professional speechwriter, but D'Alessandro always followed his own counsel on content and wrote his own material. Over the years he penned some zingers. In 2002, for example, in the midst of the Enron debacle, D'Alessandro said, "Imprisonment of those convicted of serious offences, together with forfeiture of all ill-gotten gains, will do more to stop future Enrons than any number of new regulations ever could."

Or he might debunk conventional wisdom about worshipping at the altar of corporate vision. "There is a great similarity between the strategies of most institutions in the financial services sector. What really distinguishes competitors from each other is the effectiveness with which they pursue these strategies in the face of constant change," he told the 2003 annual meeting. "Execution is the vital difference." He called for the designation of Quebec as a distinct society in 1996, a step no politician would take until 2006, when Prime Minister Stephen Harper declared that Quebec was "a nation within a united Canada."

D'Alessandro rarely sprinkles quotes from other people into his talks. In all of his speeches over the years, he has cited famous names only a handful of times. There are no French philosophers or American poets, just a very few select business leaders, such as Jack Welch, retired CEO of General Electric, and Sir John Bond, former chairman of Hongkong and Shanghai Bank. For the most part, D'Alessandro has been happy to let his own words stand without any buttressing by others as he tackled topics ranging from bank mergers to the brain drain.

While D'Alessandro wants respect, he does not go out of his way to seek media coverage and gives fewer interviews than many CEOs. "I have more attention than I should get," he once said. That's not to say he doesn't carefully take note of what's written about him, because he has also said to colleagues, with pleasure, "My press has gotten better since I stopped giving interviews."

JUST AS HE does not curry favour with the press, D'Alessandro cares not a whit for prestigious international organizations, such as the

Bilderberg Group or the Trilateral Commission, which executives join in order to run with the in-crowd. "I'm not a be-seen kind of guy. I'm a quiet person. I'm not meaning to disparage, that's just not my style," he said. A must-attend event for many CEOs is the World Economic Forum held annually in Davos, Switzerland. On the one occasion D'Alessandro was scheduled to go, he was supposed to be there with his fellow members of the advisory board of Schroders, the London-based asset managers. At the last minute he said to his wife, "Why don't we go to Italy instead?" Rather than swan around Davos, he and Pearl stole away to Rome for a few days, stayed at the Lord Byron near Villa Borghese, walked the city, and savoured the food.

Other than Schroders and a similar advisory board role at investment banker Lazard Frères, D'Alessandro limited his outside work to serving on two other boards, Hudson's Bay Co. and TransCanada PipeLines. He resigned from all four boards several years ago, saying that he already had a full-time job. Although he had good relations with the Liberal governments of Jean Chrétien and Paul Martin, he was able to make the transition to Stephen Harper, who appointed him to the Advisory Committee on the Public Service of Canada as well as to the North American Competitiveness Council, a group of thirty-three business leaders from Canada, the United States, and Mexico. He has never been politically active beyond modest financial contributions to individual candidates from all three parties.

D'Alessandro is also chair of the Toronto Region Immigrant Employment Council (TRIEC), an organization that tries to deal with the problem of underutilization of skilled immigrants' education, talent, and experience. "That's the kind of poster-child role that he is very effective at and doesn't take much of his time. He just has to write a couple of letters to the prime minister and show up once in a while," said Diane Bean, who is co-chair of TRIEC. D'Alessandro has also led fundraising campaigns for the Salvation Army, the United Way, and the Corporate Fund for Breast Cancer Research.

Helping the right cause matters to D'Alessandro, but often being asked by the right person is the propellant. Warren Chippindale, who hired D'Alessandro as a young student accountant, phoned D'Alessandro in 2007, wearing his hat as chairman of the board of the Montreal Neurological Institute. Chippindale had already recruited Jacques Bougie, former CEO of Alcan, as co-chair of a $40-million campaign and he wanted a co-chair from Toronto. D'Alessandro declined, saying he'd just finished two fundraising campaigns and was all tapped out.

Chippindale asked D'Alessandro at least to take a tour of the facilities. If D'Alessandro still didn't want the role, Chippindale promised to back off and not bother him any more. D'Alessandro took the tour, guided by Bougie, who then accompanied him to the airport. En route to his flight home, D'Alessandro agreed to help. The campaign raised $60 million, including $1 million from Manulife and $500,000 from D'Alessandro, who jokingly told people, "Warren forced me to go down there. I got there and I fell in love." D'Alessandro has also personally given $1 million to the United Way of Toronto, $1 million to Concordia, and $500,000 to both St. Michael's Hospital in Toronto and the Art Gallery of Ontario.

Through a program called the Executive Flexible Spending Account, Manulife pays an annual sum to every officer from vice president and up that's equivalent to 10 to 12 percent of base salary. Recipients can do whatever they want with the money: lease a car, join a golf club, or pay school fees for their children. D'Alessandro donates his bonus to charity. In the three years from 2005 to 2007, he collected $398,224 and passed the money on to a variety of causes.

FOR ALL HIS STUDIED lack of interest in his image, however, D'Alessandro does relish winning awards, perhaps because the circumstances are more controllable than a media interview. In 2001, when he won the CEO Award of Excellence in Public Relations, D'Alessandro opened his speech with a rare citation, in this case from Prime Minister John Diefenbaker, who said, "There's no amount of flattery I could ever find excessive." In addition to receiving the

Business Leader Award from the Ivey School of Business in 2008, he was named Distinguished Entrepreneur by the University of Manitoba in 2007, Canada's Most Respected CEO in 2004, and Canada's Outstanding CEO of the Year in 2002. He received the Order of Canada in 2003 and has been awarded honorary degrees from the University of Ottawa, Ryerson University, McGill University, the University of Toronto, and York University.

Even Pearl gets dragged into his need for praise. In his remarks at the Art Gallery of Ontario dinner on the occasion of being named CEO of the Year, he said, "I was told that I should keep it a secret for a while but that I could share it with my wife. So, I rushed home and told Pearl the news. She was very surprised ... in fact she showed more surprise than I thought was necessary ... I think it was when she said, 'You must be kidding,' for the fourth time that I got a little testy!" In D'Alessandro's mind, however, all of those accolades pale beside the Horatio Alger Award he received in April 2005. Founded in 1947, the Horatio Alger Association, based in Alexandria, Virginia, was named after the nineteenth-century author who wrote numerous books for boys, all of which follow the same rags-to-riches formula about the impoverished lad who started as a bootblack or some other hardscrabble job, conquered insurmountable obstacles, and then rose to heights of success by dint of his own hard work and entrepreneurial nature.

The group wraps itself in a flag of convenience that combines patriotism with overcoming adversity to achieve great goals. At a spring ceremony in Washington, D.C., that lasts three days, the Horatio Alger Association hands out college scholarships and names ten Distinguished Americans, a list that's usually dominated by business leaders, such as Howard Schultz, chairman of Starbucks; Boone Pickens, chairman of BP Capital Management; and Sherry Lansing, former CEO of Paramount Pictures.

Winners can also come from outside commerce. Recipients have included actors Tom Selleck and James Earl Jones; baseball great Hank Aaron; TV personalities Carol Burnett, Lou Dobbs, and Oprah Winfrey; astronaut Buzz Aldrin; and Senator Chuck Hagel, the two-term Republican from Nebraska; as well as some folks who have since fallen upon hard times, such as 1997 winner Alan "Ace" Greenberg, chairman of Bear Stearns, the investment banking firm rescued from bankruptcy in 2008 by competitor J.P. Morgan.

In 2004 the Horatio Alger Association added an international designation. The first recipient was Jim Pattison, the Vancouver entrepreneur with interests in media, packaging, and automotive. Pattison in turn nominated D'Alessandro, who was uneasy when Pattison called on him to tell him what he had in mind. "Jimmy, is it going to cost me any money? Because I don't want to get involved in an award where people expect you to pay them tons of money. I wouldn't do that with my shareholders' money."

"Oh no, only if you want to," said Pattison. "This is because of your achievements. They want to celebrate people like you." D'Alessandro agreed to let his name stand as a candidate. The organization, which does not approve all nominees, welcomed D'Alessandro into the club as only the second individual outside the United States to be so ordained. In the end, Manulife donated US$100,000 to the Horatio Alger organization. "In the United States, to have one of these awards, if you look at the people involved, there's an enormous cachet. You run into these people all over the place," said D'Alessandro.* He returned to Toronto pumped by the occasion, and loves to talk about the induction ceremony held in the chambers of the U.S. Supreme Court, lunch at the State Department, and the moment during the dinner at the Daughters of the American Revolution Constitution Hall when a bald eagle was released and flew above the tables of awestruck guests.

Even being asked to accept an honour is something to be cherished. During one of our several interviews, D'Alessandro suddenly rose from his chair and led me across his office to a stand-up

---

*Other Canadians honoured since include David Ritchie, chairman, Ritchie Bros. Auctioneers, of Richmond, British Columbia; Wallace McCain, vice-chairman of Maple Leaf Foods Inc., of Toronto; and Rebecca MacDonald, founder, Energy Savings Income Fund, of Toronto.

desk. There lay a large, blue, hard-sided folder containing a multi-page letter from an organization saying it wanted to fete him at a special dinner on a specific date a few months away. "Look at this for a beautiful presentation case," he said. "Isn't that something?"

The invitation had arrived without warning; I was surprised that the group just assumed he would agree without sending out some sort of feeler in advance. But the way D'Alessandro talked about this offer, there was little doubt he would accept. For a guy who claims he doesn't care what the world thinks about him, he delights in the adulation that flows from any such occasion in his honour.

FOR ALL HIS WEALTH—and at $15 million a year he was among the highest-paid executives in Canada from 2005 to 2007—D'Alessandro is not a conspicuous consumer. The townhouse where he lives is modest by CEO standards. "I have a well-developed sense of who I am. I try not to be arrogant. I'm intellectually arrogant, business arrogant, but I have other redeeming qualities. My wife thinks it's ridiculous, but if someone takes advantage of me, I get upset. I just don't like a plumber charging me three times what they charge the guy next door."

Although he did not play sports as a youth, D'Alessandro golfs regularly and is good at the game. He belongs to Beacon Hall, a top-ranked eighteen-hole course in Aurora, Ontario, about thirty minutes north of Toronto, which is limited to 250 members and has an initiation fee of $100,000. D'Alessandro hits a long ball and usually plays in a foursome, depending on who's available, that includes Mickey Cohen, a former deputy minister in the federal government who worked at Olympia & York and Molson's; Cohen's wife, Judith; Scott Hand, former CEO of Inco and a Manulife director; and Bill Birchall, vice chairman at Barrick Gold.

The golf course is the only arena where D'Alessandro appears to bend the rules a bit in his favour. All golfers have an index, which is a measure of their playing ability. Once called handicaps, they used to be set with the guidance and oversight of the course pro. Nowadays, software has taken over. Players enter the results of every round into a computer system that calculates a precise index that can easily be converted into a specific handicap for a particular course. It's a method that's meant to be fair and put all golfers, no matter the level of difficulty of their regular home course or which tee box they use, on an even footing.

D'Alessandro doesn't bother with such niceties. "The fact that he's been an eighteen handicap in golf for all the time I've known him is a bit unusual. Usually golf handicaps move up and down but he just keeps insisting on taking a few bucks out of my pocket," said Bob Cook, Manulife senior executive vice president and general manager for Asia, whose own handicap is in the mid-teens. "I forget what year I was playing with him and I was playing his club, Beacon Hall. I probably got the local pro in trouble because I asked, 'When was the last time Mr. D'Alessandro posted his score?' It was like four years earlier. This is not the way the handicapping system is supposed to work. You're supposed to keep it up to date," said Cook.

This lack of rigour seems unusual for a man who doesn't like to see poor golfing etiquette in others. "He often measures people by their attitude on the golf course. He'll often tell stories about a particular person who will cheat, have that extra ball in the pocket, drop it, and say 'Oh, I found it.' He uses various interesting ways to take the measure of a man or a woman. Some of those people might not be here any more," said Jean-Paul Bisnaire, Manulife general counsel. "I wouldn't say that he fired somebody for that, I'm saying he takes the measure of a man, or the measure of a person, in a number of ways. And one of the ways is how he comports himself on a golf course."

D'Alessandro's drive off the tee usually travels a solid 260 yards, although he can get into funks where he sprays the ball. "He's a fun guy to be with on the golf course. He's got a natural golf swing. He's got the patience that his heritage would suggest, in other words he's hit the ball before he realizes he hasn't taken a practice swing. I've always told him if he ever put his mind to it, he would be a very good golfer and he could get his handicap down to single digits," said Mike Wilson, who golfed with D'Alessandro during his eleven years on the Manulife board before resigning in 2006 to become Canada's ambassador to Washington. "He's a very competitive guy. You hit a great shot and he's really conflicted because he knows you hit a great shot and you beat him—but he's bloody mad that you beat him."

Mickey Cohen, who probably plays more golf with D'Alessandro than anyone else, has a very different view. As far as he's concerned, D'Alessandro is not a seriously competitive golfer. In fact, the two men have devised their own way of keeping score. A par on a hole means one point, a birdie two points. There is no penalty for a bogey, so if a hole is going badly because a shot went awry, their rules allow hitting a second ball or even a third. "Winning the hole with a bogey or a double bogey is no joy for either of us. Most people torture themselves over golf. They have to play it perfectly and they keep tight scores. We don't have to be miserable. We invented this game so we can enjoy ourselves," said Cohen. They keep a points tally for the full season, but no money changes hands. "He loves the game. He loves bragging rights, but he loves to practise as much as he loves to play. He'll go out there and just hit golf balls."

D'Alessandro, whose best handicap was an eleven a number of years ago, doesn't bother putting his score into the index because so many of his rounds are with Cohen and include those "mulligans," or opportunities to take a shot again. "I haven't really kept score for ten years. I don't even know how the new system works. I register as an eighteen and when people ask me what my handicap is I say eighteen. Usually I'm not embarrassing myself. I can go on a streak and make six, seven pars in a row and then collapse. It's just to get out there and walk and not have anything on your mind but hitting that little ball."

In the last three years, Cohen has worked hard to improve his game and has reduced his handicap from sixteen to ten. "Everybody noticed my game was getting better, but nobody took more pleasure than Dominic. He doesn't care that much about his handicap. He never plays tournaments. For him, golf is an extreme pleasure. He wants to enjoy the golf and that couple of hours of friendship."

That friendship was put to the test in August 2008. While playing together at Beacon Hall, Cohen was driving the golf cart with D'Alessandro as a passenger. They were close to a green, so Cohen took his wedge and a putter from his bag and said he'd walk on ahead, leaving D'Alessandro in charge of the cart. D'Alessandro remained in the passenger seat, reached over and took the steering wheel with his left hand and pressed the accelerator with an outstretched left leg, but he wasn't watching where he was going and ran over Cohen. The cart ended up on top of Cohen, who was calling, "Dominic, Dominic, what are you doing?" D'Alessandro backed the cart off Cohen, who suffered a broken right leg and crushed bones in his foot. Cohen's golf was over for the season; he walked with crutches and then a cane for four months. "He behaved with such graciousness and equanimity. He's been more worried about how I felt than the fact that I took a season of golf from him," said D'Alessandro. The incident gave rise to a joke on Bay Street: Which would you rather do, go hunting with Dick Cheney or golfing with Dominic D'Alessandro?

———————

IN ADDITION TO GOLF, D'Alessandro's other most obvious pleasures are smoking and his daily intake of half a dozen cans of Diet Coke. He's unsuccessfully tried to quit smoking for years. In a typical month, he'll smoke for a week and then chew Nicorette gum for the other three weeks. Socializing, especially the superficial kind, has no appeal. Some CEOs spend several nights a week on the black-tie circuit, believing that their attendance adds lustre to any occasion. Not D'Alessandro. "Dominic hates the social scene. He doesn't want to smile at everybody. He loves Pearl, he loves his family, he likes being home. He's not a party boy," said Cohen. "In business, he's eminently self-confident. Put him in front of a prime minister who says, 'What should I do with the economy?' and he'll tell you. But in a social setting, with strange people, he may be shy. Either he's shy or he doesn't want to waste his time with strangers. Take your pick."

The homebody D'Alessandro prefers dinner with family, an evening reading business documents he's lugged home in his briefcase, or watching old movies—maybe a 1930s Busby Berkeley musical, *Champion* starring Kirk Douglas as boxer Midge Kelly, *To Kill a Mockingbird*, or for the umpteenth time, his all-time favourites, *The Godfather*, Parts One and Two.

His idea of fun is not heading out with several other couples on one of those bicycle tours through wine country, when the Type A CEOs race each other to the next stop. He'd rather holiday with Pearl at their condo in Naples, Florida, moving among his three balconies that face east, south, and west so that he can follow the sun all day, reading a good book. His choice of titles is eclectic and ranges from *The Black Swan* by Nassim Nicholas Taleb, with its thesis about unexpected events, to Cormac McCarthy's *No Country for Old Men*, the grim tale of a serial killer. Although he had three siblings, it's almost as if Dominic D'Alessandro grew up as an only child who is so self-reliant that he needs no one. For him, his own company is the best company of all.

———◆———

THAT SELF-RELIANCE goes back to his youth, when D'Alessandro had to figure things out for himself in a household led by a busy single mother with little time for the joys of parenting, such as reading a bedtime story. His upbringing meant that he was a standoffish parent who expected a lot from his three children, Anthony, Michael, and Katherine. Growing up with a successful father like D'Alessandro cast a long shadow in their lives. In Montreal, when he was a senior officer at Royal Bank and then CEO of Laurentian, people everywhere treated D'Alessandro with a certain deference. "I guess they felt they had a big burden to try to live up to. It's been tough for them, not because I brutalized them by beating them up because they didn't deliver triple-A marks, I think it was self-imposed." There was also the added pressure of relatives saying to them, "Are you as smart as your father?"

D'Alessandro owns two 40-unit apartment buildings in Toronto that his sons manage. He has also purchased a building lot for commercial redevelopment by them. Katherine wants to be a writer and is working for a communications and publishing firm. In 2008, when Michael was married, "I put a big disc on the calendar, circled it in red, and said, 'I want to mark this day. It's the first day in a long time that all three of our kids are happy at the same time.' They've all had issues. We've had our share of challenges. This is why I've encouraged them to do other things and I'm helping them. You know, I never expected them to do what they can't do. I'll take care of my kids, but I'm also a strong believer that they should earn what they have. Because they're my kids, they shouldn't stop having aspirations, stop having desires, stop having responsibilities," said D'Alessandro.

His regrets are typical of any hard-driving parent who has spent too much time at the office. "If I could turn back the clock, there are a few things of a personal nature with my kids that I would've done differently. I would have spent more time with them, especially the boys," he said. "I grew up without that type of tending. I sorted things out for myself. Far, far more important to me were my actions than the words. My kids would see how much I cared for them simply because of how attentive I was to their needs. The fact that I wasn't there to tuck them into bed [or] I was impatient and didn't read them bedtime stories, what does that mean? No one ever read to me."

FOURTEEN

The Hancock Merger

WHEN HANCOCK'S DAVID D'ALESSANDRO abruptly ended talks with Manulife in November 2002, he did so to work on a merger with Prudential Insurance Co. of America that would have created the largest insurer in the United States. Negotiations got very specific. Life insurance would be handled by Hancock in Boston and investments out of Prudential headquarters in Newark, New Jersey. Total employment in those two offices would remain constant, but individual departments as small as a dozen people were told how many employees they would have to cut in order to find the savings that would help sell the deal to shareholders. In the end, the two sides could not agree on price. Prudential was willing to pay only 5 percent more than the market price, not enough of a premium to satisfy David D'Alessandro. Talks collapsed in April 2003.

Next, Hancock sent out feelers to other firms. "Principal [Financial Group] weren't interested. We looked at demutualizing Massachusetts Mutual Company and merging with them with us being the dominant player, but none of those had the potential of the Manulife deal—so I called Dominic."

Dominic's patience had paid off. On May 5, David flew to Toronto, checked into the Four Seasons Hotel, and met Dominic for dinner at a nearby restaurant, Prego.

"The deal fell through," said David.

"I knew Met wouldn't buy you," said Dominic, referring to Metropolitan Life Insurance Co. "I knew the deal wouldn't work with Met."

"It was never Met."

"Who was it, then?"

"It was Pru," said David. David sketched out the deal he'd been talking about with Prudential, described how it had fallen apart, and then declared his interest in reactivating the idea of a merger with Manulife. The two sides signed confidentiality agreements and agreed they would never use the word *synergy*, a descriptive that shows up in far too many mergers as if such arrangements were scientific and aimed only at finding ways to save money, mostly by reducing employment. "This is a revenue discussion, not an expense discussion," they said.

David was well aware from his conversations with Dominic that, this time, he could not back out. "Dominic was particularly sensitive to not wanting another deal to bail publicly. He had talked to his board about the potential of a Hancock deal after we spoke a few times. There was no fire sale going on. If the price was right, we thought we would find safe haven and miss the downgrades. But we weren't about to do something for less than a proper price and for the proper fit. We knew that what had to happen had to have a chance of being a well-consolidated company," said David. They set up due diligence committees that included teams for investments, insurance, budgets, and the like. They established a three-month deadline, with both men receiving regular reports, to see if the two sides could strike a deal.

By the time Dominic, David, and John DesPrez, president of Manulife USA, met on August 4 at Morton's in the Back Bay area of Boston, there had been a lot of discussion, but no firm deal. At one point during the evening, David floated the idea that the John Hancock name should replace Manulife everywhere in the world. As far as Dominic and DesPrez were concerned, such a notion was a nonstarter. They'd keep the Hancock name in the United States, where it was well known—they'd be foolish not to—but after more than a century of use they were not about to give up the Manulife name in Canada and Fields Abroad.

The three men settled one other substantive matter that night. Earlier that year, Hancock had sold its head office complex—the Hancock Tower, the Stephen L. Brown Building at 197 Clarendon Street, and the Berkeley Building at 200 Berkeley Street—to Beacon Capital Partners of Boston for US$910 million. (The one hundred–floor Hancock Tower in Boston had been sold in 1998.) Hancock leased back the space where employees already worked from the new owners. The injection of cash from the deal made Hancock's first quarter numbers look far better than they otherwise would have.

Shortly thereafter, Hancock admitted that it could lose as much as $750 million in its investment portfolio. To offset that pending loss, Hancock said it planned to sell the mutual funds division in order to prop up corporate health in the second quarter. Dominic asked David not to proceed with that sale. Dominic didn't want Hancock dumping prized assets just ahead of a merger. David agreed to abandon his plans and retain mutual funds so he could deliver as much as possible of Hancock's well-known and highly regarded brand.

IN ORDER TO PUT Dominic D'Alessandro's idea to acquire John Hancock into an appropriate context, let's take a look at what Canadian banks and life insurance companies had been doing along those lines during the previous 150 years. The short answer is not much. In addition to following the population growth in Canada, Canadian banks tracked north–south trade routes, so they opened branches in the Caribbean during the nineteenth century to finance the flow of molasses and rum. Most Canadian banks also had outposts in New York and London. As corporate clients opened mines in South America or won cable TV licences in the United States, Canadian banks provided financing. But as far as banks acquiring assets with physical facilities in the United States, the deals were few and far between.

Some Canadian banks that happened to gain a foothold in the United States did little with it. When CIBC acquired Bank of British Columbia in 1901, the booty included branches in San Francisco, Seattle, and Portland. What could have been a stepping-off point for U.S. expansion was seen as nothing more than a nuisance, what with the need for a separate board of directors, a different management team, and onerous reporting requirements. CIBC added a few branches in California over the years but never tried to reach any real scale.

As the American and Canadian economies grew in the 1950s and 1960s, Canadian bankers worried about disturbing the U.S. elephant. If they bought a bank in the United States, would the American banks demand reciprocity and want freedom to buy a Canadian bank? Foreign competition! What a fearful thought! And, given the fragmented regulatory oversight in the United States, even if a Canadian bank did buy something, that would only give access to one state, so why bother? U.S. competitors might bulldoze their way north and end up with a national franchise.

In fact, for many years, foreign banks—including U.S. banks—had little interest in Canada. But beginning in the 1960s, "briefcase bankers" began operating from hotel rooms in Canada, looking to skim off profitable corporate deals. Canadian law was finally changed to admit foreign banks officially; the Bank of Tokyo was the first, arriving in 1981. Within fifteen years there were fifty-two subsidiaries of foreign banks operating in Canada, with $65 billion in assets.

Even with all that foreign activity in Canada, most Canadian bankers were still reluctant to move into global markets. William Nicks, who headed The Bank of Nova Scotia until his death in

1972, led all Canadian banks into blue-collar consumer loans in the 1960s, but he also enjoyed the company of the King of Greece and was the only Canadian banker with a truly international perspective. Much of Scotiabank's foreign strength today was built on the base Nicks created, but the growth was gradual, not done with a single mega-deal.

Manufacturers' opened its first office in the United States, in Detroit, in 1903. The agent in charge, Robert Campbell, of Lindsay, Ontario, knew he had a difficult task. "He is well aware that Canada stands like a ragged sparrow beside the great American eagle. He admitted that Canadian financial institutions, in fact most things Canadian, are virtually unknown below the line," said an official company history. The ragged sparrow flew. Ellen B. Sheehy, the dean of the company's female representatives, started in Detroit in 1916 and sold policies for more than thirty years. By 1947, the company had $65 million worth of insurance in force in Michigan alone. In the United States, insurance is regulated by each state, so Manufacturers' opened agencies in Pennsylvania in 1908, Ohio in 1909, Washington and Oregon in 1924, California in 1927, and Illinois in 1933.

For the longest time, the sole Canadian bank to complete a multi-million dollar acquisition in the United States, and thereby have physical locations, was Bank of Montreal (BMO). In 1984, CEO Bill Mulholland, an American citizen himself, bought Harris Bankcorp Inc. of Chicago. As recently as 1998, when the Royal and BMO were hoping to merge, senior officers at the Royal saw Harris as the trophy they were most looking to possess. To that point, Royal had conducted no such parallel activity in the United States, Canada's largest trading partner.

Although Canadian insurance companies have sold millions of policies in the United States, they have not been very acquisitive either. In 1982 Sun Life bought Massachusetts Financial Services, a Boston-based investment management and mutual fund company, and struggled for years to make the deal work. Confederation Life had a large regional office in Atlanta until the company went bust in

1994. Other major Canadian players, such as London Life and Mutual Life, had little or no U.S. presence.

More recently, TD and Royal have begun buying small regional banks in the United States. From 2000 to 2004 Royal Bank paid US$5.5 billion for a dozen relatively small U.S. acquisitions, including Centura, headquartered in Rocky Mount, North Carolina. If you drive Highway 70 in North Carolina from the Raleigh-Durham area to the Outer Banks, you'll see a few branches bearing the blue-and-gold RBC Centura signage. But there are half a dozen other players; no one bank dominates. TD has a higher profile in Boston, where the Celtics and the Bruins play in TD Banknorth Garden, named after a bank that TD acquired in 2005. In 2008, TD acquired Commerce Bancorp for US$8.5 billion, giving TD 1100 branches in the United States—about the same as the number of TD branches in Canada.

Such activity is modest compared with that of banks based in countries such as Spain and the Netherlands. Even so, all the Canadian banks were huge compared with the Canadian insurance companies. Until Dominic D'Alessandro. After he lost out on Canada Life and CIBC, he turned his acquisitive sights onto the Boston-based Hancock. If D'Alessandro could pull off this deal, Manulife would rival Royal Bank, his former employer.

——◆——

AFTER THE DINNER at Morton's, Dominic and David met in David's office the next day to hear the result of due diligence being conducted on each other with the help of external attorneys and actuarial advisers at the Hyatt Harborside near Boston's Logan Airport. Each side had about 175 people working on the deal. Hancock chief financial officer Tom Moloney declared there would be no Sunday sessions. For him, as an Irish Catholic, the Sabbath was sacrosanct. Some meetings were also held in Toronto and Montreal—to keep the negotiations secret from the outside world, so as not to drive up Hancock's share price and make any eventual takeover more expensive.

Officials from Manulife were pleased to find very little overlap in the distribution side of the business. For example, Hancock brought to the table a brokerage relationship that Manulife did not have—M Group, the biggest seller of high-end insurance in the United States. "The only business we were both in to a significant degree was personal life insurance," said DesPrez. "The only other one that overlapped was variable annuities (VA). But their VA was this big"— and here DesPrez put his thumb and finger almost together—"ours was this big"—placing his hands wide apart. "They had really got nowhere in that business. Manulife was in 401(k), Hancock wasn't; they were in long-term care and we weren't; they were in mutual funds, we weren't."

Dominic and David had drinks and dinner with the Manulife board in Toronto on September 2, met the following day, and again in Toronto from September 15 to 16. During those sessions they agreed that Dominic, fifty-six, would be CEO of the merged company. David, fifty-two, would be chief operating officer, handle integration of the two companies, and become president a year after the deal closed.

Getting-to-know-you meetings were held in Boston and Toronto for senior executives from both sides. According to Bob Cook, then Manulife senior vice president, U.S. insurance, a facilitator was hired to help each side understand the corporate culture of the merging partner. The facilitator first asked those present from Manulife, "'Top of mind, what are these people at Hancock all about? What drives their decision-making?' All of us said, 'They're a marketing company. The brand is everything.' They all nodded and said, 'You got that right.' Then he turned to the Hancock people and said, 'What about these Manulife guys?' 'Financial discipline. Every decision they make has got a financial angle to it. There's a cost-benefit analysis, a long-term assessment of the financial impact.' And we all said, "Yeah, we're OK with that. That's kind of the way we see ourselves.'"

Price, the last major hurdle, was negotiated in a matter of minutes. David said, "I've got to have a premium, my shareholders will kill me if I don't have a premium." The numbers each had in mind were a mere 50 cents apart. They settled on US$37.60, an 18.5 percent premium on share price that day, Wednesday, September 24. Hancock shareholders would receive 1.1853 shares of Manulife for each share of Hancock held.

Dominic had one final gut-check. On Saturday he called John DesPrez on his cellphone while DesPrez was driving with his son after a football game. "Dominic was obviously sitting there fretting. He asked me, 'Are you sure we can run this thing if all the top guys leave?' We were getting the sense that these guys really wanted to cash out. I said, 'Well, obviously that would be the optimal way for this to play down, but yeah, we could do it. It'll work,'" said DesPrez.

In fact, there wasn't much choice but to proceed, and fast. Word of the merger had begun to spread. "By talking so long and so openly about selling the company, Hancock chief executive David D'Alessandro has all but invited bids. The leading contender to buy Hancock: Manulife Financial Corp.," said an article in *The Boston Globe* on Friday. "The Hancock brand would be just the ticket for Manulife's stated goal of a major expansion into the United States. Trading yesterday in Hancock's stock was about triple its usual volume, suggesting that word of the new round of discussions was beginning to leak." There was no time to waste; the deal was announced by press release on Sunday. Manulife would acquire Hancock in a $15-billion deal, the largest-ever cross-border transaction by a Canadian firm.

———— ◆ ————

ON MONDAY, SEPTEMBER 29, the two D'Alessandros met the media at news conferences in both Toronto and Boston, where they "entered a packed conference room here to near rock-star treatment ... with flash bulbs popping and a half-dozen television crews jousting for position," according to Scott Bernard Nelson in *The Boston Globe*.

"Manulife's acquisition of one of America's most recognizable brands was big news north of the border, where Canadians tend to feel overshadowed by their larger, richer neighbor," wrote Nelson. Said Dominic, "In Canada, this creates a global champion. Canada is a small country, and it needs companies like this, deals like this." By happy coincidence, Manulife had sold its first policy in the United States one hundred years earlier.

The merged firm had twenty-one thousand employees and $333 billion in funds under management. While they might not have used the word *synergy*, merging the two would yield $350 million in savings because such departments as information technology and other back-office services could be combined. Hancock shareholders who'd hung on since demutualization in January 2000 enjoyed a 121 percent increase in the value of their holdings.

Under the terms of the deal, the name Manulife would continue on all products outside the United States, but everything in the United States would go under the Hancock name. "Hancock has a storied brand in the U.S.," Dominic told the media. "We don't have anything like it. The notion of operating under the Hancock brand is not in the least offensive to us. Just the opposite."

In Canada, the combination of Manulife and Maritime Life put Manulife either first or second among all insurance companies in almost every product area. In Asia, the merger meant that Manulife was in new markets, such as Malaysia and Thailand, and it added to business already conducted in Singapore, Indonesia, and the Philippines. In the United States, Manulife moved from fifth to third place in overall market share, as well as into first spot in universal life, survivorship life, 401(k) sales to small business, and into second place in variable life, long-term care insurance, and total life insurance sales. "The Hancock deal has been a game changer for the company. It has put them in a very strong position in the United States, which was the biggest market and now is far and away the biggest market. This puts them in a very strong position to grow the company further," said former Manulife director Mike Wilson, Canada's ambassador to the United States.

There was only one irksome matter: salaries. In 2002, David was paid US$21.7 million, tops in the U.S. insurance industry. By contrast, Dominic, who at one point had castigated executives who were "corrupted by outsized rewards," earned a measly $3.6 million. Said Dominic, "Executive compensation is one issue we're going to have to face up with. Some reconciliation of the two compensation systems is going to take place. David and I are keen at avoiding friction. We are going to give it our best shot."

An editorial in *The Boston Globe* the day after the news conferences had an air of resignation. "Corporate mergers and acquisitions are everyday realities now, but shifts in status for iconic companies such as John Hancock Financial Services still unsettle the city's emotional landscape. For some Bostonians who suffer a second-city complex anyway, every new takeover feels like another inexorable step toward becoming a back-office town."

In the long run, the merger was embraced. The city of Boston also lost through acquisition the head offices of FleetBoston Financial Corp. in 2003 and Gillette Co. in 2005 without any apparent negative impact. "I'm doing better today than I was doing before. Gillette is a much better partner for the city today. John Hancock has been a much better partner in recent years," Boston mayor Thomas Menino told a local business group in April 2008. "There's too much emphasis put on headquarters." The Boston Foundation's Paul Grogan, often a critic of Menino, agreed. "There was a series of fears that thus far have proved groundless. I know I sound like a member of the administration, but the mayor is right about this."

Although the deal was cheap compared with previous takeovers, no other bidder topped Manulife's offer. Analysts calculated that the price Manulife paid was 1.6 times Hancock's book value, much lower than the average multiple of 2.4 paid in the dozen insurance industry deals during the previous year. In retrospect, losing out on Canada Life in February 2003 had been a blessing in disguise. "That enabled us to go on and do the John

Hancock deal. You couldn't create a playbook more favourable by design," said Guloien. "I was not at all disappointed. From my perspective, as head of the U.S., Canada Life's operations in the U.S. were just dribs and drabs," said John DesPrez. "We would have wasted a lot of time unloading most of it. And it was clear if we did it, then it was going to mean we couldn't do anything else for two or three years. I didn't like the opportunity costs of that equation. CIBC—I was not a fan either. There's not a big history around the world of bank–insurance company operations working. I've always been a big believer that companies should focus on what they know how to do. Dominic's a banker and he thought it was a fantastic financial trade. And it would have been, but the question is: How would you operate that company? It was a shot. It didn't work out. I think all for the better because if we'd done that, we wouldn't have been able to do the Hancock. There's only so much bandwidth."

DAVID D'ALESSANDRO, who was in charge of the Integration Planning Group, set the tone for assimilation at the first post-merger meeting attended by executives from both firms. "There's already been some discussions between Manulife and John Hancock with regards to how we're going to merge things and who's better at what and which system is going to prevail," he said in his opening comments. "Are we going to do it the Hancock way or the Manulife way? I would encourage everybody to work together to try and find the best answer to those questions. Let me be absolutely clear to the Hancock people. If in doubt, if we're at loggerheads here about what to do, Manulife wins. Manulife bought John Hancock. They paid a premium. Full stop."

Taking such a position so early in merger proceedings is unusual. Everyone knows there's a winner and a loser, but there's often a lot of grandstanding anyway. "I think it shocked the Hancock people quite a bit. I think it shocked the Manulife people even more," said David.

"It wasn't about graciousness, it was about making the deal work." Manulife's centralized purchasing, for example, was adopted over Hancock's departmental authority, as was Manulife's more rigorous financial discipline when it came to investment philosophy.

Marketing was a different matter. "We were better marketers than they were. That was one of the reasons we had a better brand. We knew what we were doing in branding," said David. "But how to organize certain departments, how much control personnel had, what level of authorities are given for making deals, those are all somewhat subjective, but you know, Manulife does things a certain way, why wouldn't we do it that way?"

While David was nominally in charge, Manulife executive vice president John Mather and Hancock chief financial officer Tom Moloney did the heavy lifting, aided by hundreds of employees from both companies. In addition to being approved by Hancock share-holders in February 2004, the deal was also scrutinized by 160 different regulators and government agencies, including the Delaware Insurance Department, the U.S. Federal Reserve Board, the Securities and Exchange Commission, and Canada's Office of the Superintendent of Financial Institutions. The Massachusetts Insurance Commissioner approved the acquisition only after Manulife agreed to keep its U.S. headquarters in Boston, maintain employment of 4200 in the state, keep community and charitable donations at least at current annual levels of US$7.5 million, and continue sponsoring the Boston Marathon through 2018.

Just as the North American takeover had brought Manulife a car and driver, the Hancock deal that closed on April 28, 2004, offered Dominic D'Alessandro the pleasure of corporate jets, a luxury he had previously eschewed. Hancock owned a fractional share in several corporate jets, an arrangement by which Hancock had access to aircraft in return for an annual fee, monthly mainte-nance payments, and a per-hour charge. Hancock executives were allotted a certain number of hours for business and personal use. D'Alessandro ordered an end to the arrangement. "I thought it was a little excessive. It certainly wasn't our style. I just think that it's inconsistent with the message that I give people about treating shareholder money as your own." Bragging rights, however, were something else. Those were his and his alone.

D'Alessandro in the Manulife boardroom, 1994.

D'Alessandro and North American Life CEO Brian Moore announce their amalgamation, September 1995.

At the 1996 opening of the Shanghai office, from left, D'Alessandro, Prime Minister Jean Chrétien, Chinese Premier Li Peng, and Zheng Dunxun, CEO of Sinochem.

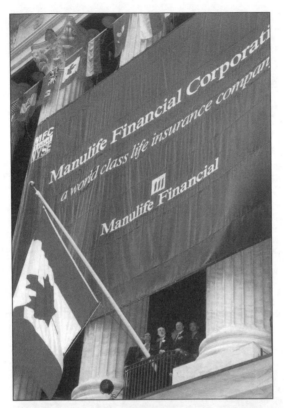

Exterior of the New York Stock Exchange, top; Chairman Arthur Sawchuk and Manulife officers at the first day of trading, October 21, 1999.

Last Tango in Halifax

WITH TODAY'S FINAL FLIGHT, AIR CANADA'S DISCOUNT BRAND TO BECOME A FARE CLASS, B4

REPORT ON BUSINESS

CANADA'S BUSINESS NEWSPAPER ■ FOUNDED 1962 ■ GLOBEANDMAIL.COM ■ TUESDAY, SEPTEMBER 30, 2005

▲ S&P/TSX comp.	▲ S&P/TSX 60	▲ S&P/TSX-VEN	▲ DJ Industrial	▲ S&P 500	▲ Nasdaq comp.	▲ Gold (NY, US$)	▲ Crude (NY, US$)	▼ Dollar (US¢)	▼ Euro (C$ buys)	▲ US 10-yr bond	▲ Cdn 30-yr bond
7,445.82	417.90	1,383.28	9,380.24	1006.58	1,824.56	$382.40	$26.40	73.91	0.6373	4.06%	5.22%
+12.54	+1.08	+0.10	+67.16	+9.73	+32.49	+1.80	+0.24	-0.01	-0.0070	+7 pts.	+5 pts

INTERNATIONAL

Tyco trial opens

Jury selection began yesterday in the fraud trial of former Tyco executives Dennis Kozlowski, above, and Mark Swartz, who are accused of looting the conglomerate of more than $600-million (U.S.) to finance lavish lifestyles. **B16**

Sun revises results

Troubled computer maker Sun Microsystems revised its fiscal fourth-quarter results, taking a $1.05-billion (U.S.) charge after realizing its first-quarter loss will be greater than expected. **B2**

Spam on rise

Spam will account for 66 per cent of all e-mail traffic by the middle of next year, rising from half this year and threatening efforts of legitimate marketers to reach potential customers, market researcher Gartner Inc. says. **B16**

NATIONAL

Alcan deal proceeds

Alcan's $6.2-billion takeover bid for French rival Pechiney has received key clearances from regulators in the United States and in Europe, clearing the way for the deal to go to shareholders for a final verdict. **B4**

Denim chain eyes merger

Money-losing denim retailer Pantorama is looking at a possible merger, sale or acquisition to turn itself around. **B9**

Alaska favours subsidies

U.S. subsidies for the proposed $20-billion (U.S.) Alaska natural gas pipeline are very much on the political table, Alaska Governor Frank Murkowski says. **B10**

Gas plant proposed

Access Northeast Energy is promoting a scheme to build a $500-million liquefied natural gas processing plant in Port Hawkesbury, N.S. **B12**

MONEY & MARKETS

Procyon shares soar

Shares of Procyon Biopharma hit a 52-week high after the Montreal-based drug developer reported that its flagship prostate cancer drug safely reduced the spread of tumours in patients who had failed traditional treatment. **B22**

Greenback slides

The U.S. dollar tumbled against the euro and the yen in New York trading yesterday. **B22**

The first look at today's market action globeandmail.com

Merger chiefs herald a 'transforming' deal

John Hancock's David D'Alessandro, left, and Manulife's Dominic D'Alessandro addressed a news conference yesterday in Toronto.

Say Manulife, John Hancock agreement could trigger a number of other mergers

BY SINCLAIR STEWART

Manulife Financial Corp.'s proposed $15-billion takeover of John Hancock Financial Services Inc. is a "transforming" deal that could redraw the boundaries of the North American life insurance sector by triggering a number of other mergers, executives of the two companies predicted yesterday.

With more than 20,000 employees around the world and a market capitalization of nearly $35-billion, the merged company would immediately put pressure on smaller rivals to pursue acquisitions in order to remain competitive, said David D'Alessandro, chairman and chief executive officer of Hancock.

If the deal succeeds, Manulife will become the No. 2 life insurer in Toronto during a morning conference call. "And I think this transaction, because it will be successful, will cause much of the industry to take a much harder look at itself and see that in order to compete with companies like this, they're

start looking around and saying, 'Hey, we're mid-size, what are we going to do?'" he told analysts in going to have to do something."

D'Alessandro is slated to become chief operating officer of the merged company, and add the title of president one year after the transaction closes. He will report to Manulife CEO Dominic D'Alessandro, who is no relation.

As was widely expected, Manulife shares tumbled in the first day of trading since the deal was announced and closed at $38.41, down $1.44. Hancock shares also fell to $33.82 (U.S.) on the news, a drop of 48 cents, which may suggest some investors are not pleased with the takeover's value.

See TAKEOVER on page B8

Manulife's U.S. foray

Eric Reguly, B2
Maritime Life employees wait. B5
Manulife and sports. B7
Analysts predict pressure. B21

Canadian executives regain their urge to merge

BY ANDREW WILLIS

Across Corporate Canada, there's a new hunger for cross-border takeovers, as the likes of Manulife Financial Corp. chief executive officer Dominic D'Alessandro strive to build world-beating companies.

The appetite for doing big deals reflects a drive for growth among Canadian executives and boards of directors who have regained confidence in the prospects for their sectors and find it easy to raise money. These same executives see few takeover opportunities in the mature home market. The urge to merge is felt most keenly at companies in highly regulated sectors such as financial services, railways and utilities.

See MERGERS on page B8

Big investor threatens to vote against Manulife takeover

BY SHAWN McCARTHY, NEW YORK

One of the largest institutional shareholders in John Hancock Financial Inc. is threatening to vote against the merger offer from Toronto-based Manulife Financial Corp., saying the takeover price is simply too low.

"I think the price doesn't make much sense, frankly," said James Barrow, president of Dallas-based Barrow Hanley Mewhinney & Strauss, an investment manager that owns 10.75 million shares in Hancock.

No individual shareholder owns more than 5 per cent of Hancock stock. Barrow Hanley is Hancock's second-largest shareholder, with 3.7 per cent of the shares outstanding.

In a telephone interview, Mr. Barrow said the Manulife offer represents only 1.3 times the Boston-based insurer's book value and, at that rate, the company is worth more as a going concern.

"You ought to be able to generate more than that out of it," he said.

See PRICE on page B9

Ottawa shuffles $1-billion within budget

But most cash ends up where it began

BY HEATHER SCOFFIELD, OTTAWA

The federal government has finally said how it will shift $1-billion from low-priority expenditures to higher ones — as promised in last February's budget — but much of the money has ended up in the departments where it started.

"It could be a question of smoke and mirrors," said one senior federal government source.

Treasury Board Secretary Lucienne Robillard released details yesterday about how the government will reallocate $1-billion to pay for unexpected costs such as the SARS outbreak and the extra overmud-cow-disease, and also pay for new programs in areas such as health, environment and community development.

According to the Treasury Board announcement, the Department of National Defence had to give up $200-million as part of the cost-shifting exercise, the biggest contribution towards the $1-billion total reallocation.

But the money never actually left National Defence, said Randy Mylyk, spokesman for Defence Minister John McCallum.

And at the same time, the department received a total of $1.1-billion in extra funding this year, Mr. Mylyk said.

"We're getting extra, extra, extra," he said.

See BUDGET on page B14

Air Canada, union at odds over pension

BY KEITH McARTHUR, TRANSPORTATION REPORTER

A dispute over how to deal with a $1.5-billion deficiency in Air Canada's pension plans is threatening to unravel hundreds of millions of dollars in labour concessions agreed to in June, union lawyers warned yesterday.

"The entire June labour process is on the verge of collapse because of brinksmanship. It strikes me that if this happens, we've got a very serious problem all around," said Sean Dewart, a lawyer for the Canadian Auto Workers union, which represents customer sales and service workers.

The issue of how to deal with the unfunded liability in the pension plans has been simmering ever since Air Canada filed for protection under the Companies' Creditors Arrangement Act on April 1.

See AIR CANADA on page B14

Community, *a sculpture by Kirk Newman, at Toronto head office.*

Canadian division head office in Waterloo, Ontario, opened in 1988.

Weather beacon and annual Fourth of July flag on John Hancock premises at 200 Berkeley Street in Boston.

The John Hancock sign at Fenway Park, with the Hancock Tower on the skyline.

U.S. headquarters at 601 Congress Street in Boston's Seaport District.

Donald Guloien, left, and John DesPrez III, below, contestants for D'Alessandro's CEO role.

FIFTEEN

Largest in the Land

THE DAY AFTER the Hancock deal closed, at Manulife's annual meeting in Toronto, Dominic D'Alessandro was riding high. "By market capitalization, Manulife Financial will be the largest insurer in Canada, and after AIG, the second biggest in North America," he told shareholders. "It is also, as we speak, the largest public company in Canada. Who would have thought it possible?"

Who indeed? Manulife was even larger than the Royal Bank, the long-time Canadian market cap leader and the very company that had rejected D'Alessandro's hopes for top spot. Rather than sink into despair or reconcile himself to a boring career mired in the banking hierarchy, he'd gone out and reinvented himself. Call it spite, call it determination—the motivation didn't matter; he'd achieved a goal few others would ever have set for themselves, let alone achieved. "Hancock established Manulife as one of the world's most successful insurance companies," said Gord Nixon, who replaced John Cleghorn as Royal Bank CEO in 2001. "Hancock and Asia are his legacies."

However, the Hancock merger did hurt return on equity (ROE), the performance measure that D'Alessandro most admired. From a high of 17.7 percent in 2003, ROE tumbled to 13.7 percent in 2004, a reflection of the capital base that more than doubled in the merged firm. ROE did not return to pre-merger days until 2007, when it set a new record of 18.4 percent. However, fears of "flowback" were never realized. Most U.S. Hancock shareholders retained the Manulife shares that they'd received in exchange. Manulife did not have to spend anywhere near the $3 billion set aside to buy its own shares and prop up prices.

The merger also improved the quality of Hancock's investments by cutting the number of poor performers from 8 percent of the portfolio at Hancock to 6.9 percent in the merged company, a ratio that was lowered to 4.8 percent by 2008. That improvement over time was the result of a single conversation between Donald Guloien and John DesPrez, when they talked about the future of guaranteed income contracts (GICs) that had pulled down the performance of Hancock's portfolio. "My people on the asset side were saying we can't intelligently invest those funds. John then said, 'Why would I raise them?' We quickly curtailed that business," said Guloien.

Directors could see Guloien's leadership savvy. "Don was one of the first guys I really noticed after I got on the board. He knows his stuff; he's a good operator. Since I was an investment guy, I probably had some insights. I've always been impressed by his capacity to manage that side of the business," said Mike Wilson, who joined the board in 1995 after a Bay Street career and seven years as finance minister in the Brian Mulroney government. "Dominic led the charge on getting the asset side of Hancock more aligned with the way that Manulife did things. While Dominic set the strategy, clearly it was Donald Guloien who rolled his sleeves up and made it happen. He did that very effectively and in a very short period of time without taking a bunch of losses," said Wilson.

In addition to GICs, other types of investments were also halted. "Dominic was of the view that the funding agreement business was just one that we couldn't sustain. We couldn't issue that amount of paper, take on that amount of credit risk, and sustain a very high credit rating. The margins in the business are just too thin. We put a stop to it. We've really written very little in the way of new funding business since then. We've frankly been surprised at the rates at which our competitors have been writing it," said Warren Thomson, who had been at Manulife from 1987 to 1994, left, then rejoined in 2001 to work in investments.

As the new regime slowly improved the portfolio, Manulife also got out of $1 billion worth of hedge funds in which Hancock had invested. "Hancock had one of the largest private placement books in the United States. They had a variety of credit issues. A lot of their privates had very good covenants and good collateral coverage, but you needed to have the capital and the patience to stick with a lot of the holdings and work with the borrowers," said Thomson, executive vice president, U.S. investments. "We wound up doing very well. It was a classic example of not trying to pull the trigger too quickly. Surprisingly, we were either able to get a lot of things repaid in full, or repaid early. Today that book is in great shape. It was one of the many elements of the Hancock transaction that proved to be a very pleasant surprise for Manulife."

Other investments in oil and gas, timber, and agriculture worth $10 billion were immediately embraced. As a result of buying Hancock, Manulife produces forty-one thousand barrels of oil and gas a day in Western Canada, operates processing plants, and delivers natural gas to pipelines. There's also a portfolio of timberland in New Zealand, Australia, and the United States that amounts to about one-quarter of all the world's managed timber. Agricultural crops in the portfolio include almonds, walnuts, pistachios, and cranberries. Manulife owns land in the Napa and Sonoma areas of California and is the largest U.S. producer of fine wine grapes that isn't a vintner. Such investments have fared well. At the end of 2008, the five-year return for timberland was 6.4 percent, farmland 13.9 percent, and oil and gas 26 percent, far better than many other investment possibilities.

WHILE SUCH INVESTMENTS were welcome surprises, other merger-related news was not. On June 10, 2004, six weeks after the deal closed, David D'Alessandro—who had agreed to stay on and become president—announced he was leaving, effective November 30. When I later asked him why, he said, "When you sell a car, you don't want to ride around as a passenger." He has since shaved his moustache and has more time for his own investments, including Toscano, a Boston restaurant that's run by his son Andrew. In 2008 he published his third book, *Executive Warfare*, in which he recommends that any executive passed over for a promotion should immediately move elsewhere.

David D'Alessandro's decision to decamp was quickly followed by the departure of most Hancock executives. Nine of the ten members of the policy committee—Hancock's top group—left. Twenty of the twenty-six senior vice presidents fled; so did nine of the top ten female executives. "The speed of the exodus has surprised Hancock veterans. The main reason for the stampede is basic: Hancock was the seller, Manulife was the buyer. Manulife already had a sizable executive core in Boston, and virtually all of the best jobs went to them. Some Hancock executives were nearing retirement, and many had close ties to [David] D'Alessandro," said *Boston Globe* columnist Steve Bailey.

Money was the major propellant. David's severance pay was the highest at US$16.5 million plus $22 million in Manulife shares. The top ten executives shared $60 million in Manulife stock; in addition, each received severance of up to three years' salary plus bonuses. "Frankly, given the financial deals they had, if they'd stayed you'd wonder whether you wanted them. These offers were so compelling, you had to assume, and we did assume all along, they were all going," said John DesPrez.

Dominic D'Alessandro's pay packet soon caught up with the Hancock crowd despite his protestations about "outsized rewards." In 2003, his annual compensation doubled to $7.5 million from the previous year and then took off in 2004, when the board hiked his compensation for that year to $16 million. In addition, the board declared that each year of future service would count as two years for credits toward D'Alessandro's pension upon retirement, when his annual pension will be $3 million, more than most people make in a lifetime.

———•———

WHILE HANCOCK EXECUTIVE departures were expected, no one anticipated how many employees, even those two and three levels down in the organization, would also leave. The reason was not due to any lure of the lucre but because they'd been made to feel unwelcome. "Some of the [Manulife] corporate guys were heavy-handed. We lost a fair amount of talent that in the final analysis might have been helpful. [They] basically said we don't need these guys and in fact eliminated a lot of them prematurely in the integration process," said DesPrez. "We're still having issues today on some of our legal entities and getting everything cleaned up. To at least some degree, it's because we lost a lot of the history." In all, about 350 staff left, reducing total employment in Boston to 3900. The number is now back to the same level as in pre-merger days, at 4200. Community donations have grown from US$7.5 million to US$11 million annually.

Two departments in particular suffered: systems and finance. "In these kinds of situations everybody thinks the other guy is going to get his job, so there's not always the most accurate and reflective of evaluations of who would actually be helpful," said DesPrez. Happily, from Manulife's viewpoint, the numerous consultants retained by Hancock were no more. "They had a whole entourage of consultants around, most of them from Monitor Group," said Bob Cook, who headed U.S. insurance for Manulife prior to the merger, as well as in the merged company. "In the Manulife culture there's no consultants."

As part of the deal, Dominic D'Alessandro promised to add as many as five Hancock directors to the Manulife board, but only two wanted to join: David D'Alessandro and Richard DeWolfe, managing partner of DeWolfe & Co., a real estate management and investment consulting firm in Milton, which is part of Greater Boston. After resigning his executive position, David did not stand for re-election as a director at the May 2005 annual meeting.

In the one situation where a senior Hancock officer remained, the arrangement didn't last. David was replaced by two senior vice presidents—James Benson from Hancock and John DesPrez from Manulife—with both reporting to Dominic. "It was an unwieldy structure. Both guys had been used to having one guy in charge and making decisions. There are a lot of decisions that are not easily compartmentalized by product line. If you're going to make branding or human resource decisions, everybody wants a say in that. If you've got two guys disagreeing, too much stuff has got to go to Dominic for resolution. I don't think any of us expected that was a long-term structure," said Bob Cook, who worked for Benson. Benson retired in August 2005.

———◆———

MANULIFE ALSO ALTERED Hancock's real estate portfolio. Many insurance firms lease space. Manulife is a rarity in the business; most of the real estate they occupy, they own. As a result, Manulife owns the head office in Toronto, Canadian headquarters in Waterloo, Boston headquarters at 601 Congress Street, as well as half of First Canadian Place and 100 percent of North American Life Centre, both in Toronto. Manulife also owns trophy buildings such as 1100 New York Avenue in Washington, D.C.—which surrounds a former Greyhound bus depot with its art deco facade—plus buildings containing Manulife offices in Los Angeles, Atlanta, Bangkok, and Kuala Lumpur.

Hancock had sold off three head office buildings in 2003, a decision that Manulife set out to reverse. As with any such sizeable transaction, Dominic D'Alessandro was intimately involved. On real estate, Warren Thomson can approve anything up to $35 million; Donald Guloien's consent was needed on deals up to $100 million. A credit committee consisting of Thomson, Rubenovitch, Guloien, and chief risk officer Bev Margolian had a limit of $250 million, and D'Alessandro could go to $500 million. The board of directors saw anything bigger.

In December 2006, Warren Thomson recommended to D'Alessandro that Manulife pay US$540 million for the Stephen L. Brown Building at 197 Clarendon Street and the Berkeley Building at 200 Berkeley Street. D'Alessandro said the market was overheated; he didn't want to pay anywhere near that much. Thomson suggested a lowball offer of US$400 million and D'Alessandro agreed. Beacon Capital Partners of Boston, the company that had acquired the buildings from Hancock, didn't even respond with a counter-offer.

That same month, Beacon sold a portfolio of properties that included those two buildings to Broadway Real Estate Partners of New York. Broadway in turn offered Manulife the Brown and Berkeley buildings. The price negotiated was US$454 million, a saving of US$90 million on the number Thomson had originally proposed. "Our putting in that initial low bid probably facilitated the ultimate purchaser coming back to us with an offer that was much lower than we would think the market might have otherwise ascribed. A year later they were appraised for a value much more similar to our initial bid price, so we had a very nice gain," said Thomson.

The Hancock Tower was not part of the deal. In 2005 John DesPrez moved from his temporary office on the fifty-ninth floor of the Hancock Tower to Manulife's first U.S. headquarters, a fourteen-storey building with a six-storey atrium at 601 Congress Street in the Seaport District. The building, which had been under construction since before the merger, has been ranked as one of the "greenest" in Boston, with a double-skin window system and a rooftop garden with grasses and flowering plants that helps insulate the building and manage storm water run-off. About 1700 employees work at 601 Congress; 2300 are in the Brown and Berkeley buildings.

The name Hancock Tower will continue until 2015. "We've been approached with the idea of selling the naming rights. I can't believe anybody's going to pay much for it, given the fact that everybody calls it the Hancock Tower despite the fact that there are no Hancock people in the tower," said DesPrez. "I think everybody's going to call it the Hancock Tower forever. If we can have that without having to pay for it, that would be dynamite. Hancock has an image and presence in Boston that is disproportionately large to the company."

—•—

I'M SITTING IN the Pavilion Club section, between home plate and third base at historic Fenway Park, munching on a frank and drinking a beer. The weather couldn't be better on this fine summer's eve in August 2008. Jon Lester's on the mound for the Red Sox and all's right with the world. The home team jumped out to an early 8–0 lead and went on to post an 8–4 win over the Texas Rangers.

The billboards shout Coke, Ford, and Budweiser—easily among the most recognized brands in America. But rising above them all, perched high atop the centre field scoreboard where every fan in the crowd of 37,876 looks at least a dozen times every inning, is what has to be the most recognized signature in the United States: John Hancock.

As if that twenty-four-foot tall, sixty-eight-foot wide insignia that costs $1 million per year weren't reminder enough of the insurance giant, just to the right, a mile away on the downtown skyline and glistening in the setting sun, rises the sixty-storey Hancock Tower, the tallest building in New England. There's also the Berkeley building, home to Hancock employees, with its illuminated beacon that forecasts the weather with blue and red lights.

> Steady blue, clear view.
> Flashing blue, clouds due.
> Steady red, rain ahead.
> Flashing red, snow instead.

In October 2004, for the first time ever, both blue and red lights flashed to signal the first World Series victory by the Red Sox since

1918. Not since Paul Revere's ride to warn about the British troop movement—one if by land, two if by sea—had lights been utilized locally to send a signal to so many about so much.

Here in Fenway, home to legendary players, such as Ted Williams, Carlton Fisk, and Mo Vaughan, John Hancock sponsors an annual Fantasy Day, when two hundred individuals try to blast a ball over the left-field wall, known as the Green Monster. In June 2008 the event raised more than $500,000 for the Dana-Farber Cancer Institute.

The Hancock, as the insurance company is called, is all-pervasive. In addition to Major League Baseball, the company sponsors numerous local charities and sends its employees into schools to teach. "We didn't have much of a profile before we bought Hancock. We were small," said DesPrez, who ran the U.S. division of Manulife for five years before the merger. "Because Hancock had this disproportionately large public role, I've had to assume that role over the last two or three years. I try to keep a low profile personally, particularly in contrast to David D'Alessandro. He spent most of his time tooting his own horn, which had its benefits. He raised the profile of the company dramatically. He also was a very controversial figure. I've spent a lot of time in the last few years unwinding the various conflicts."

One of them was a dispute with the United Way. David D'Alessandro got into a contretemps with the United Way and did not allow the organization to raise funds at Hancock. DesPrez has rebuilt that relationship; employees contribute again. DesPrez, a Republican in a state dominated by Democrats, has taken Manulife into new areas of interest by steering a corporate donation of $1.5 million to the Institute of Contemporary Art. He is on the board of the Institute, which is two blocks from his office at 601 Congress.

The Manulife–Hancock merger was one of those unusual unions in which one plus one actually ended up equalling three. In 2004 the combined companies ranked fifth in the United States; by 2006, they were number one. In the two years 2007 and 2008, Hancock added fifteen new products. Three-quarters of all sales now come from those new products.

In the United States, 99 percent of consumers recognize the John Hancock brand, up from 95 percent at the time of the transaction. "It's sometimes difficult to measure how much brand means. But for those of us that are from the legacy Manulife side, it was an impediment to sell with the [Manulife] brand," said Jim Boyle, executive vice president, U.S. insurance. "We had pretty much everything we needed to compete with the exception of brand, and we used to get the Manu-who? Or the Manu-what? Brokers tend to show two or three products to customers. We know we lost in some ties. We don't lose those ties anymore." Dominic D'Alessandro wouldn't have it any other way.

SIXTEEN

Green, Green Grass
of Home

HEAD OFFICE LEADERSHIP matters, of course, but where business growth actually occurs is out on the street, one client at a time. From weekly policies at the factory gate to Wi-Fi laptops, insurance sales methods have changed dramatically over the years. Today's general agent is well educated and represents numerous companies in order to find the best deal for the client, whether for insurance products, mutual funds, pensions, group health, or estate planning. Agents use high-tech software systems, hire staff to handle the back-office administration, and run entrepreneurial businesses that can pay them incomes of more than $1 million a year.

In August 1897 Manulife gathered its agents at head office for the first convention of top producers. The official photograph showed men of serious mien who wore high starched collars and sported drooping moustaches. The three-day event featured papers on such arcane topics as "Impaired Risks" and "The Relation of the Medical Referee to Agents and Medical Examiners," as well as more practical subjects like "How to Keep a Good List of Prospects" and "Illustration of Canvassing the Average Man."

There was time for frivolity, too. Attendees enjoyed a tour of the city in tallyho coaches, an outing to Niagara Falls, and an evening garden party at the residence of General Manager J.F. Junkin at 40 Glen Road in the swanky neighbourhood of Rosedale. According to a report published in *The Economist*, "The grounds were beautifully illuminated with Chinese lanterns while Mr. Bailey's String Band discoursed sweet music. The Quebec representatives sang several songs to enliven the party. Refreshments were served on the grounds and a most delightful evening was spent."

In 1912, the company honoured the highest achievers at a separate gathering. The first outing of the Hundred Thousand Club was held on the French River in northern Ontario and was limited to those agents who had produced $100,000 of paid-for business on ten or more clients during the year. Thirty-two agents exchanged ideas and participated in fishing contests. The following year, winners met in Algonquin Park for more of the same.

In Canada, individual success is still celebrated, but Manulife products are now sold through 7400 financial advisers, 17,600 stockbrokers, and 22,900 general agency brokers. Manulife does not sell direct. In the case of John Hancock, the company had 5000 captive agents in 1991. By 2000, Hancock products were sold by 66,000 stockbrokers and financial planners, as well as through internet sites and online aggregators, such as Quicken and Quotesmith. "It's a tough business. People selling insurance are very special. I couldn't do it. The rejection factor is enormous. I thought they were all ridiculous, these conferences, but really what they are is an ego replenisher because they get so worn down doing what they do day in, day out," said D'Alessandro, pointing to the modern-day equivalent of wilderness fishing trips, the Million Dollar Round Table, an international organization of high achievers that meets annually. "They need the gratification that comes periodically with the reward. They need other people like themselves who are earning their living successfully, so you can encourage one another. Unless you've done it, and I never have, you can't really appreciate it."

Founded in 1927, the Million Dollar Round Table (MDRT), based in Park Ridge, Illinois, is made up of thirty-five thousand high-performing life insurance agents composing the top 1 percent of all agents in the world. To be a member, and attend the meetings, an agent must make at least US$80,000 in commission income annually. The June 2008 meeting, held in Toronto, was the eighth in Canada in MDRT's history, and the fourth at the Metro Toronto Convention Centre in the last two decades. All delegates at this five-day event were so eager to attend that they paid their own way. They arrived raring to be recharged, to be reminded how relevant they are, to learn a few sales tips, and to make contact with someone who might offer helpful counsel on the phone the next time sales dry up, as they most assuredly will no matter how effective the pitch.

Among the other eighty-five speakers that week who described their triumphs or their ability to learn from failure included Tom Flick, a Rose Bowl champ and ex-NFL quarterback; Patrick Henry Hughes, who was born without eyes and cannot walk but has excelled as a student and a musician; Dave Williams, an astronaut who logged almost seven hundred hours in space, including three spacewalks; Mary Lou Retton, an Olympic gold medallist in gymnastics; and Neal Petersen, who sailed solo around the world in a homebuilt boat. An agent from Milwaukee captured the mood of most attendees when he told me: "If they can overcome their problems, I can overcome mine."

———•———

UNDER D'ALESSANDRO, high achievers know no bounds. Jim Rogers, president of MDRT, is a thirty-five-year member from Vancouver, British Columbia. He doesn't just qualify at the entry level; for each of the last twenty-seven years he's been Top of the Table, the *crème de la crème*, which means his annual commission income is at least US$485,000. Rogers is only the second Canadian to head MDRT. The first, Ron Barbaro, was president in 1985 when he had his own firm, Win-Bar Insurance Brokers Ltd.

Rogers has an economics degree from the University of British Columbia and a Master of Business Administration in organizational theory from Simon Fraser University. The firm he founded in 1973, Rogers Group Financial, has fifty-one investment advisers, portfolio managers, and insurance agents. As an independent agency, Rogers Group can sell products from any firm but uses Manulife and two dozen others for about 80 percent of all transactions. He admires D'Alessandro for retaining Moshe Milevsky, associate professor of finance at York University's Schulich School of Business, to help create retirement products. "I have a very high regard for Moshe; he does excellent work. The fact that Moshe designs products is confirming, in my mind, that they are on top of it as opposed to taking the position, 'We're big, we've got lots of people internally, we can design our own stuff, thank you very much.' That is, to me, narrow thinking. If I sound like a fan of D'Alessandro, you're right, I am."

MDRT gives agents the opportunity to compare products, learn methods, and generally expand their world. Twenty years ago, when Jennifer Borislow attended her first MDRT meeting, she was one of John Hancock's leading producers. "When I got to MDRT I was just a little fish. It was very humbling," said Borislow, who runs Borislow Insurance in Methuen, Massachusetts, thirty miles north of Boston. "Going to the annual meeting is a shot of adrenalin that keeps you pumped up and moving forward. They call it adult camp, but it really is a wonderful opportunity to reconnect with friends and to also share in not only ideas but business practices."

Borislow Insurance employs twenty people, earns $5 million in commissions on $450 million in annual premium income, and does 85 percent of its business in employee benefits with firms other than Hancock. Seventy percent of the rest of the business, which is mostly individual life insurance, is placed through a general agent that in turn deals with Hancock. "The strengths of Hancock are clearly the name brand recognition, their product portfolio. We could jump ship for better compensation but I just have a very comfortable relationship. Because I am a long-standing producer, we have the ability to get things done," said Borislow, who started as a career agent selling for Hancock in 1982 and in 2012 will become president of MDRT.

Getting started is the biggest hurdle of all. Insurance companies measure the retention rate of new agents; the proportion that last five years can be as low as 10 percent. Betty Alejandro, who has been a Manulife agent in the Philippines for more than twenty years, tells new agents that they need to conduct a minimum of four face-to-face interviews with prospects every day, five days a week, non-stop, until they create a book of business with five hundred clients. "Mind you, some new agents stumble onto jumbo cases and earn huge sums of money in their first year in the business, but those are often happy accidents and hard acts to follow and do not guarantee lasting success," said Alejandro.

Success in Alejandro's case means having nearly 1500 clients and a staff of three: an administrative assistant, a runner, and an information technology assistant who manages her client database. Like all agents in the Philippines, Alejandro is a "tied agent," meaning that she can sell insurance products only from Manulife. "Manulife has a strong image of professionalism and integrity. Because of the quality of Manulife's training programs and its insistence on recruiting only full-time agents, the company has earned a reputation for having the most professional agency force in the country," said Alejandro.

Alejandro wouldn't say how much she makes annually, but her income is split fifty–fifty between Manulife commissions and earnings from clients in the form of financial planning fees. "Let's just say that I've been able to purchase a 560-square-metre home and two condominium units while being totally debt free." She lives in a three-bedroom high-rise condo, about twenty minutes from the Manulife head office in the Makati financial district of Manila. "The thing I enjoy most about being an independent financial adviser is the total control it gives me over my time and my income. It allows me the freedom to choose my clients, and I'm paid in direct proportion to my performance—not on the basis of what somebody else thinks I'm worth."

———◆———

IN THE CORPORATE CULTURE that is Manulife Financial, freedom comes in many forms. Of all the jobs at Manulife, the most unusual must be that of chief horticulturalist Derek Lelievre, who gave me a tour of the head office grounds on a sunny September afternoon. The 7.5 acres are home to specimen trees, a bright palette of flower beds, benches from which to admire the surroundings, sculpture, and an octagonal greenhouse for growing hostas, ferns, and annuals.

Lelievre, forty, a former golf course groundskeeper, obtained his Bachelor of Science in horticulture from the University of Guelph, and has worked at Manulife for five years. He has a staff of three, two of whom graduated from a similar program run by the Niagara Parks School of Horticulture. "I've got the best office in the company," says Lelievre. "I spend seven and a half hours of my eight-hour day outside. It's a joy to come to work, even on the minus 20 days when we're shovelling snow." There used to be a cottage for the groundskeeper, but that's long gone, and Lelievre commutes like everyone else.

The first thing Lelievre does every morning is to walk the grounds to see what needs to be done. He checks the flower borders that in 2008 held rudbeckia, anemone, coleus, canna lily, and impatiens. He looks closely at his American elms, one of which is ninety feet tall, which escaped the scourge of Dutch elm disease that devastated the species across North America in the 1960s and 1970s. There are also three lindens, a dawn redwood, a Kentucky coffee tree, a gingko, and a shining stand of silver birch.

But of all the garden features, the most eye-catching is the grass. For years I've been curious about how they get their grass to look like a golf putting green. Turns out it looks like putting green grass because it is putting green grass, known as Penncross creeping bentgrass.

In 1925, when Manulife first moved to its current site, the groundskeeper drove thirty minutes to Scarborough Golf and Country Club where he loaded his car with Penncross creeping bentgrass sod and laid the rolls in front of the building. He went back at least once more for another load.

You can grow bentgrass from seed, but it also spreads on its own. So over the decades the lawn has expanded across the front of the building, around the corner, and down the east side. There are now twenty-six thousand square feet of bentgrass. Bentgrass requires regular mowing, so groundskeepers cut the grass twice a week, Monday and Friday, to a height of just a little over one-quarter of an inch. The direction of the walk-behind mower alternates; one time it's north–south, the next time east–west. The result is an eye-catching checkerboard appearance. They apply fertilizer at half strength every three weeks all summer to maintain a constant rate of growth. The other twenty-six thousand square feet of lawn, on the rear portion of the property, is the more familiar Kentucky bluegrass.

Animals are regular visitors. Raccoons come foraging from nearby ravines. Squirrels and chipmunks scurry about, and once Lelievre spotted a white-tailed deer, a four-point buck, that stayed long enough to have his picture taken. And, of course, there are the dogs. He speaks to their owners about keeping them on a leash and asks them to scoop, but his pleas often fall on deaf ears.

The favourite spot for dogs is the grass in an open area near Bloor Street around a statue that was commissioned by D'Alessandro. Titled *Community* and created by artist Kirk Newman, the work on a rectangular base consists of twenty-one life-size figures in bronze— each weighing one hundred and eighty pounds—representing members of a community, such as a businesswoman striding with a briefcase and cellphone, a father hoisting a child, and a boy Rollerblading. Daily the grounds crew carefully washes the work with soapy water and carts away a bucket of dog feces from the grass nearby. "It's only going to get worse," said Lelievre, pointing across Bloor Street. "They're going to build two 44-storey condos over there, so that means more dogs being taken for a walk."

Vandalism is rare. The grounds are protected by a nine-foot wrought iron fence and video monitoring. Every year, a dozen wedding parties—after applying in advance—take commemorative photos on the grounds. Each spring, six thousand tulips bloom. Some years it's a mixture of colours, but in 2008 Lelievre presented a solid colour—all pink. Manulife employees take a keen interest in what colour is planted every fall. "They bug me to know the colour and then when I do tell them they're upset because I've broken the secret." Tulips in the spring of 2009 will probably be blooming by the time this book's published, so I can safely reveal that Lelievre plans a solid colour again: dark red.

Inside the head office complex, the groundskeepers tend two thousand potted plants; jade pothos is the most popular vine. The next most prevalent plant is dracaena—the Lisa Cane and Janet Craig varieties—because they do well under fluorescent lights. Hallway displays in December feature poinsettias. Every office on the executive floor gets a poinsettia, the only time of year the top brass receive special floral treatment. After Christmas, the poinsettias are donated to hospitals. The annual exterior/interior budget, not including salaries, is about $150,000 for plant materials, equipment, fertilizers, and fees for a tree pruning service.

No one is more interested in what the horticulturalists are doing than the boss himself. One time Lelievre and a colleague were changing some planters, putting in chrysanthemums for fall. Suddenly, a voice behind them said, "How are you? What are you guys up to today?" They turned and there was D'Alessandro. "He sneaks up on you," said Lelievre. "Myself and Matthew were covered in mud, with dirt and plant material all around. Matthew said to me after, 'Can't you get someone to tell us when he's coming?'"

Such surprises don't bother Lelievre. After all, he knows D'Alessandro is a supporter. "I've been told that Mr. D'Alessandro comes with his wife on a Sunday and has lunch on a bench." Like many people who spend a large part of their lives in gardens, Lelievre radiates serenity, an inner calm that comes from creating beauty on such a large canvas. Sure, you fight fungus and pests and bulb-eating squirrels, but so what? They're all part of God's good earth.

THE DAY AFTER MY TOUR, the grounds were transformed for the annual United Way barbecue. Hundred of employees gathered outside at noon to celebrate the end of the staff fundraising campaign for the community charity. Dance music boomed from speakers. Two huge inflatable games sat on the Kentucky bluegrass, as I now know to call it. The first, The Wild One Obstacle Course, was like a roller coaster without the cars. Individuals clambered up steep inclines with handholds and then slid down the other side. There were also channels with posts to slow the progress of participants and narrow openings through which they squeezed. It's harder than it sounds; even keeping your footing was difficult. The wise ones doffed their shoes for a better grip. Employees formed four-member teams for relay races against other squads. Some groups arrived wearing matching outfits, in one case black T-shirts and billed camouflage caps.

The other game was Gladiator Joust. Two participants, who were both wearing the equivalent of protective goalie masks, stood on pedestals. Using a padded pole, each tried to knock the other off the pedestal onto the padded area below. Men lambasted women, usually winning easily. It's hard to know what was more amazing: the men so desperately needing to be victors or the women agreeing to play even after watching their female friends be so mercilessly pummelled.

In the midst of the frivolity, some speeches were delivered from a mahogany podium set on a temporary platform. The emcee announced that two thousand of the three thousand head office employees had participated in the campaign and given a total of $1,645,438.44, a new record. In addition to raising money for the United Way, in 2007 Manulife donated more than $25 million to six hundred non-profit organizations around the world and eighteen thousand employees put in sixty thousand volunteer hours.

D'Alessandro was expected but at the last minute was replaced by Katherine MacMillan, executive vice president, John Hancock retirement plan services. Hardly had she finished speaking when D'Alessandro showed up. "I wasn't supposed to be here, but I heard the good news so I snuck out of another meeting. When we set the target I wasn't sure we could deliver, but we exceeded it. I think every year I've been here we've exceeded our target. I'm very proud of you." Unlike most CEOs, D'Alessandro knew enough to keep his remarks brief at such events. Employees are happy he's made an appearance, but they don't want to listen too long.

Two food stations offered hamburgers, hot dogs, pasta salad, soft drinks, and water. Volunteers made cotton candy, popcorn, and snow cones for long lineups of employees. Midway games included beanbag and ring toss. There was also karaoke, run by none other than Sweet Daddy Siki, a professional wrestler from the 1960s, famous for finishing off his opponents with his trademark airplane spin. Some of the singers were off-key, while others were terrific. The one that drew the biggest reaction from the crowd was a young woman in see-through white pants and top, her belly bared, who treated this as her best shot at becoming a contestant on *Canadian Idol.* Friends videotaped her vocal performance and dance routine, which consisted mostly of suggestive hip gyrations.

The party lasted about ninety minutes before everyone headed back to work. Manulife's corporate culture has real appeal. There's clearly a camaraderie; office friends are important. As with every workforce in Canada, the staff grows more diverse every year. One of the lucky draw winners was Jeff Wong. When the name was announced, a man standing near me said to his companion: "We've probably got more than one Jeff Wong here." There was no rancour or racism in his voice; it was just a statement of fact. How the place has changed since the days of Sir John—or even Syd Jackson for that matter.

While the many games were tempting, I had something else in mind, something I'd thought about since my tour with Derek Lelievre when he told me that the *Toronto Star* had called Manulife "The best place in Toronto to go barefoot." I walked over to the manicured Penncross creeping bentgrass and sat down. Now that we'd been properly introduced, I took off my shoes and socks, and then placed my bare feet reverently on the cool, meticulously maintained surface. Now, that's entertainment.

SEVENTEEN

The Next Generation

THE TOPIC OF SUCCESSION had been moving higher on the board's agenda ever since Dominic D'Alessandro signed a five-year employment contract that ended on December 31, 2008. As is often the case at large companies, the board asked D'Alessandro to recommend which senior officer he thought could best become acting CEO if he were to get hit by a bus, someone who could hold the fort while D'Alessandro recuperated. D'Alessandro wrote the name of his emergency fill-in on a slip of paper, put it in an envelope, and gave the envelope to chairman Arthur Sawchuk.

D'Alessandro wouldn't tell me the name of his designee, but he did reveal that it was one of the two men eventually considered to replace him: John DesPrez III and Donald Guloien. My hunch was Guloien. After all, Guloien had long been seen within the company as D'Alessandro's protege. But even if that were the case, it didn't mean Guloien was D'Alessandro's favourite to succeed him. "I've made it clear that this name was put there for emergency replacement. It's not necessarily the same guy you should choose to be CEO," he said.

D'Alessandro's five-year contract included the possibility of an automatic extension. In 2006, D'Alessandro told the board that he might not be renewing; he was considering retirement. As directors began thinking about succession, the board hired recruiting firm Egon Zehnder to provide a list of possible external candidates. Most names were from the United States and Europe, citizenships that did not sit well with Chairman Sawchuk. "Art really felt that this was a Canadian company and if you brought in somebody to be CEO who wasn't Canadian, the first thing he'd want to do is start moving the head office elsewhere, and that's not a road they wanted to go down," said Robert Swidler of Egon Zehnder. "If this had been done five years ago, the board would've gone outside to find a successor worthy of the scope this company had attained. With the passage of time they felt that it would send the wrong signal to the marketplace to have to go outside again for a CEO. A financial institution of this size and scope should be able to produce succession from within," said Swidler.

Most organizations really are pyramidal in shape and come to a sharp point at the top. It's amazing how often a board goes looking within the company for a successor and is lucky to find even one executive worthy of the name, despite numerous efforts to broaden the field. Succession is biblical. Many are called, few are chosen.

In the case of Dominic D'Alessandro, having more than one candidate was extremely improbable. Not since Bill Mulholland churned through a multitude of senior executives in the 1970s and 1980s as he resuscitated the moribund Bank of Montreal had any financial services CEO practised such a machine-gun management style as D'Alessandro. Just look at how many members of his management committee didn't last. That group of top officers, averaging twenty-eight members from 1999 through 2008, included seventeen individuals who made it through only one or two years before dropping off the hallowed list for various reasons and being replaced by fresh troops. Only seven officers survived all nine years.

In the fall of 2007, D'Alessandro advised chairman Arthur Sawchuk that he would not be renewing his contract. Sawchuk convinced him to stay the extra five months until the annual general meeting in May 2009 and then got busy with succession. Directors did not look seriously at anyone on their list of outside candidates. They had a bounty of two executives who had been groomed by D'Alessandro: John DesPrez and Donald Guloien, both fifty-one.

On D'Alessandro's recommendation, the two men were given expanded duties in June 2007 to round out their experience and provide the board with more scope to assess their capabilities. In addition to his role as head of the U.S. division, DesPrez was put in charge of Canada; Guloien was given Asia on top of his job as chief investment officer. The announcement was made during the annual retreat for senior executives held at Langdon Hall, a Relais & Château hotel near Cambridge, Ontario. The previous year, the retreat had taken place in Laguna Beach, California. The sessions last two and a half days and include an informal presentation by D'Alessandro about where the business is going. Leaders of the different business units give speeches and respond to questions. The gathering provides an opportunity for senior executives to play a little golf, talk directly to each other in an informal atmosphere, collaborate on ideas, and hear about products and ideas that might be exported to other regions. "The Japanese annuity business really emanated out of the business in the United States. It uses the same administrative system. We had some of our distribution people go over. That is happening much, much more. That's one of the more successful things that Dominic's done," said Hugh McHaffie, executive vice president, U.S. wealth management.

Less successful has been the promotion of women to senior roles. Twenty-five years ago, Syd Jackson had three female senior officers reporting to him. Even as recently as March 2006, D'Alessandro had no women on his nine-member executive committee, the most senior group in the company. In the next level down there were three women out of twenty officers: Diane Bean, Bev Margolian, and Marianne Harrison, executive vice president and controller. This group, combined with the executive committee, made up the management committee. By March 2007, all three had been elevated to the executive committee. By the end of 2008, Harrison had received a new role: executive vice president and general manager, long-term care, and was moved down to the management committee. During the same period, D'Alessandro expanded the management committee to thirty-two. The group included three more women—Katherine MacMillan, Lynda Sullivan, executive vice president and controller, and Angela Shaffer, vice president and corporate secretary—thereby raising the proportion of women on the management committee to 19 percent (six out of thirty-two) in an employee population where women make up 60 percent of the total.

Looking at the next rungs down in the organization, the proportion of women rises only slightly. Among all 336 officers with the title vice president and up, there are 74 women, or 22 percent. Among the 790 assistant vice presidents are 275 women, or 35 percent. If there is a glass ceiling at Manulife, that's where it shows. Fewer women than men are promoted from assistant vice president to vice president. "I have investigated this a million times and I don't believe there is any systemic bias other than the fact that it is an extremely demanding environment and not everybody wants it," said Diane Bean. "Not all men want it either, but if you're trying to have a family and do some other things it's an even harder nut to swallow."

THE MANULIFE EXECUTIVE COMMITTEE gathered as usual on Friday, May 9, the day after the 2008 annual meeting at which D'Alessandro let fly his thunderbolt announcement. D'Alessandro outlined his plans for the months ahead and then said, "Now, I don't want to walk around to any of your offices and see calendars with Xs marking down the days until I'm gone." Donald Guloien pointed out the window at some excavation work that had just begun on the lawn below and said, "So I guess the floral clock we're building is not a particularly good idea." Everyone laughed, including D'Alessandro, who then asked, "What is that damn hole for anyway?" Turned out it was for waterproofing repairs to the underground tunnel between Manulife's South and East Towers.

Prior to picking a new CEO, the board had chosen a new chair to replace Arthur Sawchuk, who was turning seventy-two, the mandatory retirement age for Manulife directors. In the spring of 2007 Sawchuk appointed a committee of three directors—Lino Celeste, Pierre Ducros, and Allister Graham—all of whom were due to retire within a year or two and so had no personal ambition for the job. After meeting with their fellow directors and ranking several possibilities from among the board on a first-, second-, and third-choice basis, the committee arrived at a decision; in December 2007 they chose Gail Cook-Bennett, sixty-seven, who joined the board in 1978 and is the longest-serving director. For the previous ten years, Bennett had been chair of the Canada Pension Plan Investment Board. The job of chair at Manulife pays $375,000 a year. The other directors receive an annual retainer, plus fees for attending meetings of the full board and its committees, for an average total compensation of $150,000 a year.

The timing of the CEO selection process was set so that the name of the CEO-designate could be announced prior to Sawchuk's own retirement on September 30, 2008. While it was an administratively neat arrangement, there was a risk: D'Alessandro could become a lame duck by staying around until May 2009. "I'm already noticing there's more traffic into those two offices than there used to be because people are paying their respects," he told me in July 2008, only two months after his public announcement and fully ten months before the official transfer of power. "I mean—that's life. I'm not under any illusions. I don't think these guys would be abusive of the fact that I'm a lame duck. I think they have respect for me. At the end of the day, these are mature individuals. They have no interest in pushing me out the door or down the elevator quicker than I need to go. Maybe I flatter myself that they might think I'd be useful."

Manulife was ripe for a change. "The strange thing about Dominic is that he's not a natural about being CEO of a large corporation. As effective as he's been, it's probably time for them—and he would be the first one to admit it—to move to a more modern-day style of manager," said Robert Swidler. "Although he got great use out of his people, he's always had trouble working with such a wide span of control and working through others. I don't want to say he's been a one-man show, because that would be unfair to him and it would be incorrect, but he's got a more old-fashioned style of management where you hear the views of your people, you decide, and you go out and do it. He's not as inclusive as modern-day management techniques call for. He's wanted to be relieved of this for a while."

IN THE WEEKS LEADING UP to the board's decision about the next CEO, D'Alessandro spoke to all of the senior executives to see if there were any worrisome undercurrents about either candidate. "Everybody had a *slight* preference, but it was a slight preference. No one said, 'That guy could never do the job,'" said D'Alessandro. Ironically, it was the 1995 takeover of North American Life—in which Donald Guloien was intimately involved—that delivered to Manulife the candidate against whom Guloien now squared off for the top spot: John DesPrez III.

DesPrez's Huguenot ancestors had left France for Quebec and then, 125 years ago, moved to Cleveland, Ohio, where he was born. DesPrez, who is six feet tall and weighs two hundred pounds, played hockey in high school, graduated from Harvard in economics, took law at Georgetown University, and then practised securities law. Since 2005 DesPrez has worked in Manulife's U.S. headquarters at 601 Congress Street, in Boston's snazzy new Seaport District. Hanging on the wall outside his office are a series of framed historic items that include a photo of the attendees at the first Two Hundred Thousand Club convention in Cocoa Beach, Florida, and a specimen policy from North American Life dated July 12, 1912.

Floor-to-ceiling windows provide him with spectacular views of downtown Boston, the three towers of Fidelity Investments across the street, the fish pier, and beyond the harbour, Logan Airport.

Everything is perfect except for the door to his office, which is electronically controlled. He never closes the door, always keeping it slightly ajar, so that it can never malfunction and trap him inside. DesPrez doesn't trust the fail-safe panic button, doesn't even want to test it.

NASL, the arm of North American Life where DesPrez worked in the early 1990s, was like a small business, so he gained broad experience. "NASL in those days didn't have any of the corporate infrastructure. If we needed a new phone system, the top four guys would listen to the guy from the phone company and decide what we were going to get," said DesPrez. "We did everything. I worry a little about some of our younger executives who don't ever have anything like that. It divorces you from the nuts and bolts of business realities."

WHILE DESPREZ SPENT his entire life insurance career far from head office, Donald Guloien was always connected to the corporate umbilical. A graduate of the University of Toronto, Guloien worked at Household Finance for four years before joining Manulife in 1981 to do strategic research. When D'Alessandro arrived in 1994, Guloien was running the 1500-employee U.S. individual life division from Toronto.

D'Alessandro put Guloien in charge of a new department called business development. Initially, Guloien sold off businesses, helped with the North American Life merger in 1995 and demutualization in 1999, and then oversaw Manulife's investment in Japan with the purchase of Daihyaku Mutual Life. In 2001, he was named chief investment officer. "He was being groomed for the president's job. He was being positioned to be able to grow into that role," said Richard Coles, who had previously run investments and was still in that department when Guloien was put in charge. Although Guloien operated closely to D'Alessandro for years, he denied having any special status. "Dominic doesn't have fair-haired boys or girls. You're as good as what you're producing at the time, so I don't think anybody's got a sinecure. Dominic was trying to impart his wisdom and experience. I've learned a lot from him," said Guloien.

Guloien, whose name is of Norwegian origin, is married with two children and has a cottage at Thunder Beach on Georgian Bay, north of Toronto. He owns two Boston Whalers—a twenty-two-footer for water-skiing and a thirty-two-footer for longer jaunts. When I interviewed Guloien in July 2008, he'd had his first interview with the board in June about succession and was preparing for the second round in August. For someone who should have been under serious stress, he seemed remarkably at ease. Here's what he said when I asked what kind of company he'd run if chosen. "I love Manulife. It's a great company filled with great people. I think we've got a very healthy mix of values at Manulife. I'd like to see it be a strong, reliable, creative organization. I think we have the capability to do more things and some different things but not stretch too far. I'm a realist about being ambitious about the number of businesses and the number of geographies that we can operate in, but we have a great team. We've delivered a great track record and avoided—not every pitfall—but many, many, many pitfalls that have hurt other companies. We're in a fantastic position to grow both organically and through acquisition. I'd be excited about leading the enterprise through that."

As answers go, it was good enough, but it was neither passionate nor polished. I thought by then he'd have a ready-made response with a little more meat, like a politician on the hustings. Moreover, after talking to me about several diverse topics with some animation, Guloien delivered his vision in a soft voice, almost a monotone, as if he were measuring the words so carefully that he had eliminated all heft. Perhaps he didn't want to reveal his hand or jinx his chances.

When I put the same question about the company's future to John DesPrez in August 2008, shortly after the two men had completed their second and final round with the board of directors, his answer was far more fully formed. He laid out an action plan that included investing more money in Asia, getting Manulife into India, and doing another takeover. "We've gone a bit into a coast mode. We need to do another significant transaction. It's one thing to integrate the actual businesses, then there's a period of cultural integration, so the whole thing probably takes about four years. The four years [since the Hancock acquisition] is up and you cannot achieve the kind of growth rates that we've achieved over the last ten to fifteen years without making acquisitions," said DesPrez.

D'Alessandro did not have a vote in the selection of his successor, did not reveal his choice to other directors, did not attend the meetings between the board and the candidates, and professed he could support either man. "Depending on the day of the week or the last interaction I've had with them it's 49–51, or 51–49. It's not like one guy's a bum and the other's a hero. I think I've groomed two very worthwhile candidates," he said.

IN HIS ROLE AS CEO of the Canadian Council of Chief Executives, Manulife director Tom d'Aquino has watched twelve hundred CEOs come and go at their firms. "The process that was put into place by the board, the chair, and Dominic, was among the very best that I have seen in twenty-five years. The careful analysis of strengths, talents, and skills of the people who would eventually bubble to the top—having spotted them quite some time ago—nurturing those people forward, then creating an environment where the actual succession process was extremely carefully defined in terms of timing, benchmarks, not done in haste," said d'Aquino. "The fact that there are two very able finalists and both have chosen to remain with the company, I think in itself was truly remarkable. That does not happen very often. The final coup is the fact that we all said to ourselves: Either one could run the company and run it well."

At the June 2008 meeting of the full board, Guloien and DesPrez each met separately for three hours with directors. Each of the hopefuls made a presentation about his vision for Manulife and then answered questions. Relations between the two were so gentlemanly that when Guloien was finished, he warned a waiting DesPrez there was no water available, to be sure to bring along his own bottle. He also let his rival know that if he wanted to use PowerPoint, there were no technical facilities. The lack of equipment did not matter to DesPrez; he was not planning to use slides anyway.

In his presentation to directors, DesPrez not only laid out his vision but also promised that, if selected to be CEO, he would move to Toronto and become a Canadian citizen. Both candidates told the board that they would be prepared to work with the other candidate if he were willing to stay on. By the end of the meeting, no director had declared either for or against either man.

At the next board meeting, in August, each candidate spent another ninety minutes with the directors covering points not previously addressed. Once those final interviews were completed, and the candidates had left the room, board chairman Arthur Sawchuk took soundings. He did not ask the directors who they favoured but how they *felt* at that point in the process. Individual directors talked about the strengths and weaknesses of the two candidates. Sawchuk could sense a consensus emerging in favour of Guloien, but he said nothing. He sent everyone away, telling them to continue thinking about the two candidates as they prepared for a third and final meeting in September that would be held without the candidates present.

Concurrently, the U.S. economy had begun to tank. IndyMac Federal Bank, a large mortgage lender, collapsed. As the contagion spread, the U.S. government was forced to prop up the Federal National Mortgage Association (Fannie Mae) and the Federal Home Loan Mortgage Corporation (Freddie Mac). At the Manulife board meeting in early September, each director spoke twice during two rounds of comments. After everyone's views had been thoroughly aired, Sawchuk declared that, in his view, the consensus choice was Donald Guloien. There was no hands-up vote, no secret ballot. "Sometimes in getting to a consensus, you're better off not putting it to a vote because then you have the 'nays' as opposed to the 'yays.' Unless somebody wants to really stand up and scream, that's probably a more collegial way of doing it," said Diane Bean, executive vice president, corporate affairs and human resources. "You have to go forward with 100 percent support. If you actually had to take a vote, you've crossed that line. You couldn't have a camp that was still unhappy."

After consensus was declared, some directors reiterated the qualifications of DesPrez, noting his talents for sales and distribution. But, everyone agreed, the company was about more than just the liability side, designing and selling products, where DesPrez held the edge between the two men. There was also the asset side, capital and investments. That's where Guloien excelled, and given the parlous state of business and markets, Manulife needed a CEO with expertise and experience in that area of sudden prominence.

———◆———

ON SEPTEMBER 8, 2008, the board announced its decision: Donald Guloien would be CEO. In order to harness the talents of both candidates, DesPrez was named chief operating officer. While D'Alessandro believed that both Guloien and DesPrez were equal as candidates, he could understand the board's choice. "Insurance companies don't get into trouble because their liabilities are misstated or they promised too much to their clients, they get in trouble because they take money and invest in improper ways. Marry that up with the volatility and turmoil in the markets, they put a premium at this time on the investment skills," he said. DesPrez may also have suffered in the minds of directors because of his personality. "John's not necessarily his own best salesman. He thinks he is, but he could be a little warmer and fuzzier. Maybe he didn't cultivate some directors as much as he should've," said D'Alessandro.

D'Alessandro believes that Guloien and DesPrez, who will remain in Boston, will be able to work well together. "John's got a lot of psychic reward. He's chairman, president, and CEO of John Hancock. In his community and in his world, he's a CEO. He's treated like that—he's got the visibility and respect in the community. Would he leave if somebody offered him three times the salary to run a bigger company? Probably, who wouldn't? Does it have the prospect of working? Yes, it does: fifty–fifty. I told the board they'll know within a year." In many succession battles, picking a chief executive officer and then naming his rival chief operating officer (COO) doesn't last; the loser often leaves to run another company. "If they'd done it the other way round, I don't think they could have kept Guloien. That might be part of the reason that they did it in this way," said Robert Swidler. "Don's personal goal was to be the CEO of a major financial institution and [COO] would not have satisfied that goal. It might have worked in the short term, but he would have found a way to fulfill that goal," said Diane Bean, who has known Guloien since he joined the firm.

That desire to be in charge of something was instilled in Guloien as a boy. As the youngest in his family, he had three older brothers, with a four-year age gap between Guloien and the next oldest. "They were typical older brothers. I spent a good part of my life being tied up and beaten up. My sister was ten years older and that was even worse, more psychological than physical, you know, 'Pesky little brother.' She'd have to babysit me when she wanted to go out. Somewhere along the line, I said I'd really like not to be at the tail end of it but the other end."

As it turned out, Guloien's appointment as chief investment officer in 2001 was crucial. "He had no investment experience when he was given that role. It was quite a roll of the dice, but through that he got to understand all sides of Manulife as opposed to John DesPrez. He's a wonderful business guy, but he's been on the liability side principally," said Richard Coles.

Moreover, the role expanded Guloien's contacts in the Toronto business community. After seven years in business development and then seven years in investments, he got to know all of the investment bankers and pension fund managers. He is a member of the Granite Club, Royal Canadian Yacht Club, and Rosedale Tennis. The only item missing from his resumé was golf. Guloien does not golf and regards the game as a waste of time, abnormal behaviour in the Manulife culture.

There have been occasions when American business leaders scoffed because they regarded Guloien's compensation—$5.4 million in 2007—as modest. Guloien saw his situation differently. "They say, 'What are you working for that for?' I bring them to my office and point to where I live," said Guloien. He's in the same nearby neighbourhood as D'Alessandro, although Guloien's commute takes a few minutes longer. Such proximity means that at the end of the workday Guloien can slip away to watch his son play hockey and still return to the office in time for a dinner meeting. It's not unusual for him to join the group only to have someone call out, "So, who won?" If he'd been chosen CEO, DesPrez could have built a similar life in Toronto, but it would have taken a while.

The global financial crisis continued to intensify after the board's September announcement of Guloien as CEO. Within a week, the choice of Guloien with his experience in investments seemed prescient. In one tumultuous weekend, Bank of America bought Merrill Lynch and Lehman Brothers filed for bankruptcy. DesPrez might even have felt a sense of relief that he did not get the nod as he watched the insurance world change so drastically that long-time competitor AIG had to be rescued by a $150-billion transfusion from the U.S. government. As country singer Garth Brooks puts it, "Some of God's greatest gifts are unanswered prayers."

DesPrez was divorced in 2006. He married Angela Quinlan, a former meeting planner at Hancock, on the Saturday following the announcement of Guloien as CEO. DesPrez had told the board that win, lose, or draw, he wanted to take a three-month sabbatical with his new bride. The honeymoon lasted a month. When stock markets turned nasty in October, DesPrez cut short the celebrations and returned to work.

EIGHTEEN

Sideswiped

AS THE SEVERAL DOZEN money managers, brokerage firm analysts, and members of the ratings agencies gathered at Manulife headquarters in Toronto for the annual Investor Day meeting on September 29, 2008, the problems caused by deteriorating markets still seemed manageable. Many at Manulife were congratulating themselves on avoiding the plight of other financial firms that were plunging into the abyss. Dominic D'Alessandro was headed for a graceful exit; his successor, Donald Guloien, was a popular choice.

The daylong event featured six Manulife executives, all giving forty-five-minute speeches about their lines of business. Earlier in the month, Manulife had delivered a similar five-hour detailed presentation focused solely on Asia and Japan. D'Alessandro tried to set a positive tone in his opening remarks. "We think Manulife is in an excellent position compared to everybody else in the financial services industry to weather the storm no matter what happens. Our leverage is rather modest compared to other companies in the financial services sector, and our deposit base is very, very stable. However, we're not immune from the events," he said.

Indeed, that very morning, Citicorp had made an offer to take over an insurer in trouble, Wachovia Corp. Manulife was on the hook for US$600 million invested with Wachovia, but given the fact that there was a saviour, Manulife presumed its money was secure. (It was, but not because of Citi; Wells Fargo eventually bought Wachovia.) Manulife's total losses as a result of investments in failed companies amounted to $253 million after the collapse of Washington Mutual Inc., Lehman Brothers, and AIG. "I think it's well within the ability of Manulife to withstand the cumulative impact of those four failures," D'Alessandro told the meeting. The Lehman money is long gone, but Manulife may eventually get back its investment in Washington Mutual and AIG. The company's only previous loss was in WorldCom, which filed for bankruptcy in 2002.

The financial chaos surprised CEO-designate Donald Guloien. "A lot of people said, Did you see this coming? Did you see what was going on? We were very concerned about what had been going on in credit markets around the world but particularly in the United States. But I will have to admit that we did not see the depth to which this would go and the degree to which institutions have loaded up and leveraged up on the underlying exposures that, in and of themselves, were deemed to be risky. That has been a revelation for anyone who's been a participant in capital markets, and a great lesson for all of us as we go forward with our careers," said Guloien.

Toward the end of Investor Day, Michael Goldberg, an analyst with Desjardins Securities who has known D'Alessandro since his time twenty years ago at the Royal Bank, rose to congratulate D'Alessandro on what he'd achieved at Manulife. It was an unusual public accolade from someone paid to grill senior officers and present a hard-nosed look at the numbers. The room erupted into applause.

On Investor Day, the closing price of Manulife shares was $36.25. Over the next two days it rose to $39, about the same level that it was at the beginning of the year. In contrast, Sun Life shares were down by one-third during the same nine-month period.

Apparently, Manulife's risk-averse corporate culture had inoculated the firm against harm.

———•———

BEGINNING OCTOBER 2, however, Manulife share price started to slide, falling to $26.63 on October 10. D'Alessandro released a brief statement saying, "Manulife remains conservatively reserved, has a high-quality balance sheet and strong and leading business franchises around the world. We are well positioned to weather these difficult times and continue to build for the future." On October 14 he conducted a conference call with analysts. "When you see your stock drop by 25 percent in two days, it sort of focuses your mind that maybe you ought to pay attention to reassuring and making your investors understand your position," he said. "We think that Manulife was sideswiped by the meltdown in the markets in a way that grossly exaggerates any impact that they're going to have on us. I want to put that to rest." Share price briefly bounced back over $33.00 but then began falling again, even though Standard & Poor's had just reaffirmed Manulife's AAA top financial rating. The only other firm with life insurance subsidiaries that has the coveted AAA rating is Warren Buffett's Berkshire Hathaway.

What was happening to other firms shouldn't have been happening to Manulife. Donald Guloien, as chief investment officer, and Bev Margolian, as chief risk officer, had for years followed D'Alessandro's directives. Manulife did not drink from the poisoned chalice of asset-backed commercial paper (ABCP), special investment vehicles (SIVs), credit default swaps (CDS), or collateralized debt obligations (CDOs). "Many of the innovative instruments at the centre of the current crisis are fiendishly complex, not properly understood by anyone, and certainly not well controlled by any of the risk management systems in effect at many of the world's largest financial institutions," said D'Alessandro.

All credit and investment decisions were the prerogative of Guloien, based on rules in a three-hundred-page binder; the decisions are then reviewed by a credit committee that includes chief financial officer Peter Rubenovitch and also Bev Margolian, whose department has grown to ninety employees from three people when it was established in 2001. "The way the credit cycle works is you have no defaults for a number of years, then peak defaults for a number of years, then no defaults. The defaults we've incurred are well within our expectations," said Margolian. "Of course, it frustrates me. I would have liked to have a perfect record on never having had a default, but that's not a reasonable expectation nor one that we count on."

Analysts who had only recently praised Manulife's performance began to beat up on the company. Mario Mendonca, of Genuity Capital Markets, downgraded Manulife to a hold from a buy, a strong signal that investors should bail out. Mendonca said that Manulife might have to sell businesses or raise capital because of wrong-headed procedures in the past. "The decision not to hedge the variable annuity business during the growth phase was, in hindsight, a shortcoming in the company's risk management process and perhaps culture," he said.

Manulife had indeed decided in 2004 not to bother backstopping variable annuities—products for which they accept someone's lump-sum of money and promise to begin paying it back at an agreed-upon point in the future through pension-style payments guaranteed for twenty years or more. Manulife invests that money in stocks and bonds in the expectation that the holdings will provide funds for the eventual payments, as well as some profit along the way.

D'Alessandro couldn't see the point of paying some other insurance firm high-priced premiums for coverage against a worldwide calamity when Manulife was an insurance company and could assume the risk itself. "The mistake we made is we didn't fully appreciate the impact on our capital the way these formulas work. We didn't understand that once you get into a shortfall, it's an exponential consumption of capital. They were tested for a 30 percent decline [in the stock market] and nothing above that. At 50 percent, it's not linear—it becomes almost geometric. That was a mistake," said D'Alessandro.

In Canada, those long-term variable annuity plans included IncomePlus. Launched in 2006—and four years earlier in the United States—IncomePlus attracted $7 billion during the first two years, far more than most mutual funds accumulate in a decade. For every $100,000 a client invests, at age sixty-five she gets a $5000 per year pension with the possibility of receiving more if the investments do well. If markets fall, the $5000 is guaranteed, just like a company pension plan. Clients pay dearly for that guarantee; annual management fees are 3.5 percent.

Beginning in 2007, D'Alessandro changed his mind and ordered hedging on some of the U.S. variable annuity products. By the end of 2008, however, only US$5 billion of the entire US$72 billion U.S. variable annuity portfolio was protected. Those companies that hedged earlier in the cycle have suffered more, according to D'Alessandro. "All of the insurance companies that hedged have got bigger problems than I do. Look at Hartford, Principal, Met, and Prudential. Their stocks are even lower than mine." In the future, clients will pay more for these annuities, and the products will have fewer features, such as resets and bonuses, as all companies batten down the hatches on a business that caused so much woe.

Manulife needed to look no further than its own Investor Sentiment Index to be aware of the new world order. The quarterly index, based on a consumer survey and released October 24, was down 16 points to +8, the lowest level since the survey began in 1999. The company responded to the deteriorating environment by putting the brakes on spending. Hiring was frozen, except for call centres and claims, where there's always a high turnover. All discretionary spending was curtailed; anything that could be deferred was deferred. The annual spring retreat for senior executives, which had been rescheduled for November in Miami, was cancelled. So was the October 2009 board meeting in Asia, an out-of-Canada event that occurs every three years.

———◆———

AT FIRST BLUSH, the damage to Manulife was inexplicable; the company's balance sheet was worry-free compared with most. The total loss of $253 million—out of a portfolio of invested assets of $164 billion—was a minuscule 0.0015 percent. But if a rising tide raises all boats, a killer tsunami spares no one. At a time when the U.K. banks were all partially nationalized, the financial flood wreaked havoc on every company, no matter how high and dry it appeared to be perched.

Manulife didn't have a cash problem caused by the $253 million in losses—Manulife had an accounting problem. "Our problem is not credit exposure to any of the instruments that are causing everybody else problems. Our problem is that we've sold people pension plans. The value of equities collapsed 50 percent in the space of two months. There's a gap between the assets you gave us to manage for you and their value today. That's where the problem lies. The reserving that has to be done with respect to that shortfall is astronomical. If it was a sponsored pension plan like IBM or DuPont with a funding deficit, we would have to set aside $660 million dollars. We have to set aside $11 billion," said D'Alessandro. Where was that money to come from?

The relentlessly grim tidings wore down D'Alessandro. In mid-October, he had lunch with former Manulife executive Richard Coles. As D'Alessandro's first recruit in 1994, Coles ran the investment division, so he understood the global crisis better than most. Said D'Alessandro to Coles, "Why didn't I leave a year ago?" Coles took the comment to mean D'Alessandro wished he'd left in May 2008 at the time of his departure announcement, rather than remain for another year. "He wouldn't leave the place in the lurch and I'm sure the board puts him under a lot of pressure to stay. It's a hard job at any time. It must be incredibly difficult now, especially when you've got events storming around you and there aren't any real answers. I know I'd say, 'Who needs this?'" said Coles, who retired in 2001. "He was frustrated he wasn't able to convince people or get the full message out. What people think is he has to raise his capital to keep his ratios up."

On October 27, analyst Mendonca wrote a research note to clients on that exact topic, saying that Manulife's financial position was so weakened that the company would miss out on acquisition opportunities as beleaguered firms unloaded lines of business at bargain prices. By then, Manulife share price had fallen to $21.17, off 46 percent for the month, after holding firm all year. The drop meant that Manulife's market capitalization had plummeted in October from $58 billion to $32 billion. Sun Life was in worse shape. Share price was down 54 percent in 2008; the market cap fell from $31 billion to $15 billion.

There was a certain irony in the fact that Guloien had just been named CEO-designate in September on the strength of his capacity to keep Manulife safe, only to see the company fall prey a month later to the same disease suffered by companies that had allowed greed to dominate their agendas.

TO ACHIEVE STABILITY and stop the carnage, D'Alessandro lobbied Julie Dickson, superintendent of financial institutions, the regulator of banks and insurance companies, about the requirement for Manulife to beef up regulatory capital. The regulator agreed to a modest break on October 28 that had the effect of improving capital by $2.3 billion. The rules, established ten years earlier by the regulators in concert with the industry, were geared to kick in if there were a 50 percent drop in markets. Under the strict regime, insurance companies had to assume markets would stay at that depressed level forever, rather than wait for them to rise again as they usually do. In addition, insurers also had to factor in a further 25 percent fall—and assume that additional loss would also persist forever. As if all that weren't sufficient punishment, they then had to double the result of those calculations.

The relief given by the Office of the Superintendent of Insurance (OSFI) amounted to a minor change to one of the calculations: The additional 25 percent had previously been 40 percent. "Think about what we're talking about here. Let's say the market goes down 50 percent, and then another 25 percent, so the market goes down 65 percent in aggregate and stays there for ten years. If that happened, it would be like nuclear winter. And you're not allowed to recognize revenue you might have in connected businesses or the franchise value of your operation. It's just as if you were a stand-alone business—all you did was sell these pension plans, and didn't have anything else," said D'Alessandro.

D'Alessandro had expected more relief from the regulators. During the 1980s, when the Canadian banks were left holding billions in bad loans to less-developed countries (LDCs), such as Mexico, Brazil, and Argentina, D'Alessandro was the point person for the banking industry during talks with the federal government. As a result of those negotiations, the Canadian government permitted the banks to write off the bad loans at a rate of 10 percent a year rather than forcing them to swallow the losses all at once. The banks then set out to increase their spreads—the difference between what they pay for deposits and what they charge for loans—to cover the loss. "The spreads on the consumer business went from 200 points to 450 points. Two and a half percent on $40 billion is a billion dollars a year. We used that billion dollars to build up the reserves to deal with the LDC problems," said D'Alessandro. "Irony of ironies, in 1987 they actually gave us a tax deduction for all the goddamned reserves even though those loans were on our books in offshore tax havens. That was the extent to which the government went."

Similar help was granted during the Great Depression, when the Canadian stock market fell by 84 percent. Sun Life was heavily invested in stocks and was technically bankrupt. In 1931, the federal government saved Sun by giving special values to its investments that had lost so much value. This time around there was no bankruptcy, nor was there any similar forbearance despite pleas by D'Alessandro to Finance Minister Jim Flaherty and Deputy Minister of Finance Rob Wright. OSFI gave a break to pension funds by cutting in half what they were required to come up with to offset losses in investments. OSFI did not, however, give the same leeway to the pension fund portion of any insurance company's business. "This could have been solved with the stroke of a pen. The number of technical solutions to this are legion. But we dealt with a particularly entrenched regulator who was unwilling to make compromises that would have made life a little easier for us. We live in a different era. People are suspicious. They didn't want to interfere with the structures that we set in place," said D'Alessandro.

Manulife had been through tough times before. In 1929, the company had its best year ever; total insurance in force reached more than half a billion dollars. Top-selling agents established records that would not be toppled until 1944; such was the depth of the Great Depression. New business at Manufacturers dropped from $93 million in 1929 to $53 million in 1933. "As the depression lengthened and deepened, spreading its withering tentacles into virtually every niche of industry and commerce, the effects began to appear in many aspects of the company's affairs," said *The First Sixty Years*, a company history published in 1947. "Terminations by lapse and surrender mounted steadily as did the volume of policy loans. The investment officers were faced with declining interest earnings, defaults of interest, especially on farm mortgages and, in consequence, the necessity of taking over numerous properties on which money had been loaned."

But policyholders also learned the strength of life insurance. "They saw that Life Insurance companies were little bothered by the decline in the market price of the securities they owned, for they had no need to dispose of them," said the corporate history. "They saw friends and neighbours tided over financial chasms and the families of unemployed men kept from the relief rolls by the emergency values of their Life Insurance. They saw that, even in March 1933, when the banks of the United States closed their doors and a virtual panic swept the country, Life Insurance companies went on paying claims and granting loans."

Because the modern-day Manulife needed still more capital as a result of the stringent accounting rules, D'Alessandro called the

CEOs of Canada's six-largest banks and asked for a loan—the first time in his career he'd taken such a drastic step. All six readily agreed to participate in the loan, but at the last minute TD Bank's Ed Clark demanded tougher terms. D'Alessandro had to phone Clark at home to get the deal back on track. On November 6, Manulife was able to announce a five-year $3-billion bank loan, the proceeds of which provided additional capital. The impact of the modest regulatory relaxation by OSFI and the loan was to boost the Minimum Continuing Capital and Surplus Requirements (MCCSR). MCCSR is a ratio created by regulators that compares an insurance company's actual capital to the minimum amount regulators require. They demand a ratio of at least 150, meaning that Manulife's capital has to be at least 50 percent more than the figure set by the regulators.

Manulife's capital—assets minus liabilities—was $29 billion in the third quarter, about where it had been a year earlier. So far, so good. But as equity markets fell, OSFI increased the amount it designated as required capital. Without the bank loan, Manulife's MCCSR would have been 193, down from 221 at the end of 2007. While 193 was within the company's 180–200 target range and well above what OSFI wanted, D'Alessandro was not satisfied. The bank loan had the effect of raising MCCSR to a much healthier 225, back to the levels enjoyed before the crisis began.

Analysts, such as André-Philippe Hardy of RBC Capital Markets, John Reucassel of BMO Capital Markets, and Mario Mendonca of Genuity, weren't impressed, saying that Manulife needed to raise even more capital. It was as if they were measuring Manulife for a shroud. Any further drop in the market would cause regulators to raise their capital requirements again, said Mendonca, a step that could trigger downgrades by ratings agencies and cause more worry among investors, as well as concern among clients.

Analysts, who as recently as Investor Day had been misty-eyed fans of Manulife, began circling for the kill. Citibank analyst Colin Devine chastised D'Alessandro in a conference call on the day the bank loan was announced. "Why was some sort of proactive action not being taken in October while all of this was going on? What would you have done if [the regulator] effectively hadn't moved the goalpost for you? Because it seems you might have had to raise $5 billion of equity," said Devine. "You're entitled to your view, Colin, that it was a breakdown," replied D'Alessandro. "We didn't expect the volatility in the markets that actually transpired. We didn't expect the markets to be as unsettled as they turned out. We didn't expect all of these financial institutions to fail. In one week we had massive reorganization of the financial sector. Maybe you guys saw it at Citibank, but we didn't." (Citigroup lost US$20 billion in 2008 and received a US$45 billion bailout.)

On December 2, in an attempt to get all the bad news out, Manulife pre-declared a loss of $1.5 billion in the fourth quarter, the first such loss since the company went public in 1999. In fact, when the official results were released in February 2009, the loss was much worse, $1.9 billion, despite record insurance sales, such was the impact of the market crash. That same month, Manulife lost its cherished AAA rating when Standard & Poor's downgraded the company to AA. With markets at a six-year low, share price fell below $10, a far cry from the halcyon days in 2004 when it reached $50. On that occasion, Warren Thomson invited D'Alessandro to his Boston home, where he'd been keeping a special single malt, The Macallan, from the year of D'Alessandro's birth, 1947, to celebrate that stock market milestone.

The poor results in 2008 meant no bonus for D'Alessandro or any senior executive. Return on equity, D'Alessandro's favourite measure of success, fell from 18.9 percent a year earlier to an anemic 8.2 percent, barely above the 7 percent level when he'd joined in 1994. D'Alessandro relented to demands for more capital. The regulatory relief and the bank loan weren't enough. Manulife issued $2.3 billion worth of new shares. Half of the new money went to pay down the $3 billion in debt recently arranged with the banks. With credit markets again willing to do such deals, other institutions—TD Bank, Royal, Bank of Montreal, and Great-West Life—also began issuing equity to add to their capital. Manulife's share issue lifted its MCCSR to a robust 235 percent, one of the highest levels in company history. As far as D'Alessandro was concerned, Manulife was back in business. D'Alessandro had raised more than $6 billion in capital through a loan, share issue, and regulatory relief. The other $5 million required to reach the $11 billion demanded by the regulator was already held in the corporate reserves. Capital had been bolstered, analysts could relax, and he could go trolling for acquisitions again.

———•———

D'ALESSANDRO CITED GREED and the lack of regulation as the major causes of the market meltdown. "It drives me nuts to see these people, supposedly educated and wise to the ways of the world, espousing these stupid theories that if you just stay out of the way and let the market work it'll solve everything. This calamity that has befallen is the result of no regulation of whole sectors of the economy," he said.

The trouble with such calamities is that sophisticated investors and hedge fund managers earn billions and don't suffer along with their investors. "The perpetrators are getting away to their homes in the Hamptons. The people who got hurt are you and me. You own shares in the Royal Bank, you own shares in the CIBC. Every pension plan was affected. It never should have gotten that bad. A society like ours should have the mechanisms—not to strangle anybody or stifle innovation—but we police our highways, we police our airports. We should have the mechanisms to ensure that we're not exposed inadvertently to systemic risk."

It's a topic on which D'Alessandro had been holding forth for months. "How the hell did they get this stuff certified? How did they get somebody to put a rating on it? How did they get it marketed? How did they get it understood? It's quite clear that it wasn't understood. The banks themselves ended up losing most of the money. Slow down the pace and make sure we understand before it's introduced to the market. It's no different than a drug. Manulife was different. We've made money in an admirable way. We haven't stolen it from anybody, we haven't shortchanged anybody, we haven't sold stock to people that turned out to be worthless. I wouldn't want to make money that way."

And make money he has, although like most investors, his personal net worth is far from what it was a year ago. In early October 2008, before Manulife share price began tumbling, I interviewed D'Alessandro on the same day that *The Globe and Mail* published a ranking of CEOs and their shareholdings. According to the list, D'Alessandro owned $188 million in Manulife shares and options. "Isn't that terrible? It is true and I'm probably worth more. I have other assets. That's everything I've earned here. I've reinvested my short-term incentives, my long-term incentives. I believed in the company. Maybe I believed in it too much with what's happening in the market. I can't believe this, a total meltdown. It's the culmination of so many years of excess that I've been railing about."

As Manulife share price fell 46 percent that month, the impact on D'Alessandro's personal net worth was catastrophic. His 5.4 million stock options, which had been valued at $93 million, were suddenly worth almost nothing. Some of his options had an exercise price of $15, so they still had some value, but most were issued at higher exercise prices than the actual market price so were "under water" as the saying goes. His Manulife portfolio, which also included 2.4 million shares, had in one month gone from being worth $188 million to $50 million, a calamitous drop of 73 percent. D'Alessandro was not alone in his losses. In October 2008, Warren Buffett led all the losers, down almost US$10 billion. The crisis might only be temporary, as D'Alessandro believed, but a lot of hard work had been wiped out.

NINETEEN

Leaving a Legacy

AS HIS LAST FEW MONTHS in office wound down, Dominic D'Alessandro began turning over responsibilities to the new team. In November 2008, John DesPrez produced the 2009 operating plan, the first time in fifteen years that D'Alessandro hadn't led the process, although he and Donald Guloien massaged the numbers before sending the annual budget to the board for approval. As usual, the plan set out specific targets for return on equity, profits, and earnings per share. At the end of 2009, the actual results will be measured against those predictions in order to decide the size of bonuses. For example, assistant vice presidents in North America make approximately $125,000 a year and can earn a bonus of anywhere from 0 to 62 percent of that amount. Each executive also sets non-financial goals that are factored into the bonus.

Given the international turmoil, Guloien worked even more closely with D'Alessandro than he otherwise would have during a normal transition of power. "This has been a wonderful baptism by fire for him. Given the state of the financial markets, he's the right man for the job. I involve him in everything I do," said D'Alessandro.

In the past, Guloien attended board meetings along with the rest of the senior executives, but as CEO-designate, he also began sitting in on the one-hour in camera session that D'Alessandro held with the board. To free up more time for his new duties, Guloien passed along his responsibilities for investments to his number two, Warren Thomson. John DesPrez assumed some of Guloien's day-to-day operational duties by adding Asia to the U.S. and Canadian divisions already in his roster. Jim Boyle, who previously ran U.S. wealth management, replaced DesPrez as head of the U.S. division.

Throughout, D'Alessandro remained firmly at the helm, reminding his underlings at meetings, "Let's not forget who's in charge around here." In subtle ways, however, Guloien had begun to assume the reins and responsibilities of power. Executives would quietly check with Guloien first before promoting someone or making other major changes in their business units.

Once Guloien officially takes charge in May 2009 and moves into D'Alessandro's former office, Manulife's corporate culture will begin to alter. "It's important that it does change because it has become synonymous with Dominic," said Diane Bean. "A company has to be more than a single person, more than an iconic CEO. That's Don's challenge, to make sure that happens, that it is a more broadly based leadership and a more broadly perceived strong management team."

Their differing personalities will propel that change. Guloien is more outgoing than D'Alessandro, who is reclusive by comparison. Both are the same height—five feet seven inches—but Guloien, who weighs 204 pounds, is 30 pounds heavier than D'Alessandro. "I'm not overweight, I'm underheight," Guloien likes to say. He has a lighter touch, loves to make jokes, quick retorts, and puns, and will suddenly show up at someone's office, a management-by-walking-around technique that D'Alessandro did not employ. "He's a very smart guy and he can be very, very funny. He's always been a little round, like the Pillsbury Doughboy. Don is perhaps more approachable than Dominic. Dominic can be scary; I don't think Don's so scary," said Bean. "He knows all of the people in the company and I think he will harness them across the balance sheet divide in a very effective way."

There is one other home truth. Although he may be just as demanding as D'Alessandro, Guloien won't blow up at people in quite the same way. "He'll probably be a little bit more collaborative, not as confrontational as I am. He's a friendlier guy," said D'Alessandro. "His ability and his approach to dealing with people will be different than Dominic's," said Bev Margolian, chief risk officer. "I think that probably will be welcome by some. Some people won't get tongue-lashings. The basic culture of the company, the high performance and integrity and professionalism won't change. Don's very outgoing, very jovial, but at the same time he can sift through information and make a tough call."

Under Guloien, Manulife will continue to focus on wealth management and continued expansion in China. Just as D'Alessandro stayed away from India because foreign firms, such as Manulife, can own only 26 percent of any operation, so will Guloien. As CEO, Guloien will also be on the lookout for acquisitions in Asia and in the United States, where Hancock is number one in individual insurance but has only 7 percent of the market among 1100 insurance companies. The implosion of so many financial service firms in 2008 will provide numerous opportunities.

Because DesPrez will take over daily operations, Guloien will have fewer people reporting to him, perhaps six rather than D'Alessandro's nine. For Guloien, the biggest adjustment may well be how to distance himself professionally from colleagues with whom he has worked closely. Twenty years ago, Guloien was in the U.S. division on the fifth floor of the South Tower, toiling with the likes of Bev Margolian and Bob Cook, who are now senior officers. Before any of them had families, they'd stay after work, play basketball using hoops tacked onto the back of office doors, or go across the street for a few drinks at the local pub, The Spotted Dick. "There's negatives and positives about being here a long time, but I've had to deal with people who were my boss's boss, who ended up reporting to me. I've been there before—I know how to deal with that. It's nothing magic, it's a combination of sensitivity and inclusiveness but at the end of the day being pretty clear about who's boss, if it comes down to a difference of opinion," said Guloien.

D'Alessandro has urged Guloien to acquire a corporate jet, an expenditure that D'Alessandro studiously avoided but no longer sees as an extravagance. Guloien agrees that a company plane would be a useful business tool but worries about the optics. "There's general support. This company has grown quite large. A number of board members spoke to me and said, 'You really ought to do this and make life easier on yourself. Don't feel you have to be Superman.' It certainly wouldn't be the first thing that I would do," said Guloien. "You can't tell people to get by with less, work a little harder, go for productivity, and then be spending unnecessary amounts."

In some areas, the changeover from D'Alessandro to Guloien will be seamless. Guloien intends to continue the weekly management meetings, although he might alter the day they are held so that executives based in Asia don't have to stay up late on a Friday night, due to the twelve-hour time difference. "There are people who say that you've got to quickly establish that it's a different situation from the last guy. I don't subscribe to that. I'll change something if I find it's not working or I'm convinced that it'll work more effectively a different way," said Guloien.

One aspect that he won't vary is the investment strategy. "Don's thought process on diversifying our asset base and understanding the risk-return on assets is his legacy. We've taken his asset allocation philosophy. We're not just buying bonds and equities, we're in timber and oil and gas," said Hugh McHaffie, executive vice president, U.S. wealth management. "We've taken that expertise and brought that asset allocation philosophy to our mutual funds."

While his colleagues admire Guloien's easygoing nature and the fact that he is a "people person," the incoming CEO believes he is as tough as D'Alessandro. "Dominic is a wonderful manager for those who truly understand him. He can be challenging. Some people are not up to that and find that, especially when he's being demanding, off-putting. But I'm pretty demanding too. We just do it different ways," said Guloien.

For all his people skills, like D'Alessandro, Guloien can be a solitary man. Guloien's father and his many aunts and uncles are all musical. A cousin, who took the stage name P.J. Perry, plays bebop saxophone and has won two Juno awards. Guloien also plays the sax, but he says he has no sense of rhythm or timing, so he cannot play in a band. Twenty years ago, when he was taking weekly lessons, his teacher told him to leave his sax at home. In an attempt to improve his timing, Guloien spent the next four lessons clapping his hands to a machine with flashing strobe lights. "You're hopeless. I've got a three year old who could do better," said the instructor. "Are you really trying?"

Guloien's self-confidence was destroyed; he stopped playing the sax for a number of years. "Then I thought, 'I never intended to play in a band anyway. I don't have the time. The hell with him.'" He bought a sopranino, a small sax that can fit in a briefcase and has a high, shrill sound that doesn't travel very far. He takes the instrument with him when he's travelling on business. In the evening, he'll relax by playing in his hotel room, all by himself, confident that he's not disturbing the other guests.

A HIGH-PROFILE SPONSORSHIP that will not continue under Guloien is Manulife's support of the Olympics, a program that Hancock's David D'Alessandro began in 1994. The sponsorship, which cost US$55 million over each four-year cycle, ended with the Beijing summer games in 2008. The firm will not be involved in the Vancouver Olympics in 2010, a decision that was taken prior to Guloien's appointment.

In a final hurrah, D'Alessandro and outgoing chairman Arthur Sawchuk attended the first week of the Beijing Olympics—the week that Canada won no medals. D'Alessandro was taken aback by the changes that had occurred since he first visited China in 1994. Skyscrapers had replaced low-slung buildings; there was a new subway, two new airports, and Olympic facilities that took his breath away. Changes in the Manulife workforce in the dozen years since the licence had been granted in 1996 were equally amazing. "The first batch of agents looked like they just came off the farm. They were eager and shining eyed. You were giving them an opportunity to do something. Six months later they were better dressed and more self-confident. Today, they look just like you and me. They're talking about the kids they've got, the schools—it's really wonderful. I remember coming to this country and starting out, and remembering how important it was when my mother got a new this or a different that."

D'Alessandro has decided he will become a director on three boards but will wait until he steps down to choose from the numerous offers. Friends have told him to be careful. Knowing that he is an impatient former CEO, they worry that he will find board work frustrating because all he can do is offer advice after being used to making the decisions. He will do some pro bono work, continue to build his art collection, and read even more books than he does now. He may establish a family foundation to handle his philanthropic activities, or he may just make specific bequests to causes and avoid the costly administrative arrangements that a foundation entails. "I've made lots of money, more than I ever expected and more than I'll ever need. I'll often reflect on my life and how circumstances have changed. I'll spend more in a day now than my family would earn in a year when I was a kid. I'm starting to learn how to use my wealth."

D'Alessandro, who has been a Canadian citizen since 1954, recently reacquired his Italian citizenship so that he could live for an extended period in the country of his birth if he so chose. "I don't know that I could retire there. My home is here. I feel a deep attachment to Canada. I love everything about the country—except the climate." In addition to milder Mediterranean conditions, Italy offers balm for his soul. On a recent visit to Fiesole, just outside Florence, he and Pearl stayed at Villa San Michele. One day, while Pearl was at the pool, he wandered off to find a place to smoke his favourite cigar, a Montecristo No. 4. He came upon an opera singer rehearsing with a pianist for a concert. D'Alessandro sat in a corner, an enraptured audience of one, as she sang famous arias from *Carmen* and *Madama Butterfly*. "I had one of these out-of-body experiences. It was one of the most beautiful twenty or thirty minutes of my life. It was just so magical."

D'Alessandro will not stay on the Manulife board; the company's corporate governance rules don't permit a former CEO to remain a director. For the next five years, however, he'll work out of an office provided by the company in a different building in the head office complex. He and Pearl plan to sell their house and move into a condo in Toronto's Yorkville area. Five years ago he joined the Royal Montreal Golf Club, the oldest golf club in North America, so he could play there after he retired. They may also buy a pied-à-terre in Montreal, but most of the reasons for Dominic and Pearl to visit their childhood home are gone. D'Alessandro and Pearl's children and grandchildren all live in Toronto; D'Alessandro's mother and his brother Felix, and many of his and Pearl's Montreal friends, are dead.

———◆———

ANALYST MICHAEL GOLDBERG, who has watched D'Alessandro for more than twenty-five years, puts D'Alessandro's leadership on a par with Canada's best bankers, past and present—CEOs such as Scotiabank's Peter Godsoe and TD's Ed Clark. "I'd rank him ahead of the management at the Royal, and that's probably one of the reasons that he set out on his own. Part of it was being able to prove to himself and to other people what he eventually did and feeling that he probably wasn't going to get the same chance at the Royal. I think he did a great job," said Goldberg.

Still, the share price drop in his final months did tarnish what he had accomplished. "I can't control the market. The market went down 50 percent. What could I do about that? If you tell me that insurance companies shouldn't be exposed to equities, well, who should? I don't feel personally culpable that I was asleep at the switch. Nonetheless, I'm disappointed that this should happen," said D'Alessandro. "I don't know how long it will take for this money being poured in by governments to stabilize and start to create activity again where we have growth. We're in a contraction mode now."

The work he did to right the ship by lobbying regulators, obtaining a bank loan, issuing new shares, and trying to reassure employees and markets alike, took its toll. His pride and self-respect suffered. "I felt pretty shitty. They're not the two or three months that I'm going to remember with the greatest fondness in my life," said D'Alessandro. When he was not at the office, he holed up at home, went for hour-long walks with Pearl, and drew strength from his mother's capacity to manage as a single parent. "I was very close to my mother. I was the only one who could relate to what was happening. My sister was too young; my brothers were otherwise preoccupied. I tried to imagine this poor woman, with four kids, she didn't speak English or French, in a strange country, no money—and she coped. She didn't abandon herself to welfare. You have no idea what an example that is for me. When I have problems, I think, what problems do I have? How the hell can you possibly compare the challenges that I had? You have to put it in perspective. It wasn't life or death. At the end of the day, I just had to go and get some money."

AMONG HIS MANY SUCCESSES, Dominic D'Alessandro did not achieve the goal everyone believes he desired—a dream he denies ever having. He did not run or buy one of Canada's Big Five banks. What he accomplished instead was a far greater individual success story than clawing his way up through a bank bureaucracy. How much better it was to build his own brand-new summit than climb someone else's well-worn path. "He's driven, but he's not financially driven. He likes to make good money, but he does not want to be the richest guy in town," said Mickey Cohen. "There's part of Dominic that says 'I could have and should have been president [of the Royal].' Deep down, he set out to make a company that was bigger than the Canadian banks, and he did. Dominic's view of business is a lot like his view of the golf course. He doesn't play for money, he doesn't play for score—he loves the game. Business is the other game."

In that game, D'Alessandro was a winner who achieved far more than his corporate peers. He took over a strong but small company, surpassed all of his life insurance rivals, went head to head with the Big Five banks, and carved out a more commanding place on the global stage than any other financial services firm in Canada. On his watch, the number of Manulife customers grew from 2.8 million in 1994 to 20.9 million today, 8.1 million of whom are in the United States. Three-quarters of all Manulife's premiums and deposits come from outside Canada—up from 60 percent when he joined. D'Alessandro will demur and say any success he's had was due to the team, but the plain fact is that every CEO leads a team. Some leaders are simply better than others.

After all, he moved Manulife so far up the achievement ladder that the company became the biggest insurer in North America and the third largest in the world. D'Alessandro also took Manulife to an entirely new level by making the company larger, in terms of market capitalization, than two of Canada's Big Five banks—CIBC and Bank of Montreal—and about the same size as The Bank of Nova Scotia. After the Hancock merger, Manulife was for a time bigger than D'Alessandro's former employer, Royal Bank. Toward the end of D'Alessandro's regime, Manulife shares had a better track record than those of Royal Bank: a five-year total return of 118 percent versus 101 percent for the Royal, as of September 30, 2008.

D'Alessandro's tough-love management methods brought about other achievements. "When I joined this company [in 1986], it was like all the other mutual companies—big and sleepy. We didn't have the mentality of excellence. While we wanted to do well, we weren't rigorous, we weren't metrics-driven, we weren't profit-driven," said Paul Rooney, general manager of the Canadian division. "We're a very disciplined company now. We make bets, but we do thorough analysis. We buy companies, but we buy them after exhaustive due diligence."

The international stature achieved by Manulife during D'Alessandro's era instilled pride in employees. "You have a sense of history working for Manulife in general. There was a sense of history going into Japan. We're the largest Canadian direct investor in Japan," said Craig Bromley, Manulife's general manager for Japan. "It's a great feeling to be a Canadian company in a knowledge business who is a world leader. Every time I go to Boston or Hong Kong or Tokyo, I think we're here running these things because we're the best. Canadians don't get to say that all that often."

D'Alessandro's vision for the company has remained consistent since 1994. Few mission statements survive so long; fewer still make it out of the framed version on the wall that no one bothers to read or heed. It's worth looking again at the words he wrote shortly after joining the company: "Manulife will be the most professional life insurance company in the world, providing the very best financial protection and investment management services tailored to customers in every market where we do business."

In 2001 those values were turned into an acronym, PRIDE, devised by D'Alessandro and Guloien, which D'Alessandro then imprinted onto the body corporate like a tattoo artist. "Coming from the banking industry, I always thought that insurance was a little flim-flammish. People really didn't know what they were buying and it was so hugely complex. We wanted to sell products that we were pleased to sell or proud to sell to our grandmothers," said D'Alessandro. "The financial strength just followed; professionalism was something I believed in. Even when I ran Laurentian, that was its raison d'être, too. Don and I weaved these into a story and came up with the PRIDE."

PRIDE stands for Professionalism, Real value to our customers, Integrity, Demonstrated Financial Strength, and Employer of Choice. "The PRIDE values really do come from him," said Roy Firth. "That's what he is all about. His imprint is on the organization and it's not going to leave for a long time. That's his legacy, on the type of people we hired, the type of products we offer. Most people around here believe that were it not for Dominic, this organization would be a shadow of what it is now."

A well-run business depends upon a CEO's sense of self. "My motivation in life was I've always been curious. I've used my mind to secure my independence and live life the way I want to lead it, which is not beholden to anybody," said D'Alessandro. "Old-fashioned values mean a lot to me: loyalty, constancy, friendship, keeping your word, integrity. I'm very proud that I've come so far. I have a very good appreciation of where I started off and the circumstances of my family. It's one of the reasons I'm so besotted by the country; I've been well treated by it. I've had opportunities it is not reasonable to expect. I'm leaving behind a far better company than I found. I feel quite fulfilled professionally."

———————

THERE ARE THOSE who worry how well Donald Guloien will do replacing D'Alessandro. "Dominic is a one-in-a-generation type of person. I've never seen anybody in my life as decisive as Dominic. He's extraordinarily decisive after being extraordinarily analytical. Whether Don can match that performance, we hope he can, we think he might, but time will tell," said Manulife director Tom Kierans.

At the time of demutualization in 1999, the role of Richard Coles in the investment division included oversight of real estate, not only office towers in Los Angeles, but also the lawn and plantings for which Manulife head office is renowned. "I remember being out there walking, a week before we took the final decision to [go public], thinking, 'I wonder if this is the end to that lawn and these facilities and the ability to have something as comfortable and unusual, because corporations typically aren't allowed that level of frill,'" said Coles in 2008. "It survived because Manulife has been so successful.

I wonder if it will survive the next one or two CEOs. Laurentian Bank really hasn't taken off since Dominic's not there. It's doing a little bit better this year, but it certainly went into a bit of a slide. Dominic is a very hard guy to replace."

Of all D'Alessandro's accomplishments, his greatest is handing over a company that's in good shape compared with so many other former high flyers. After all, it's not the man that matters—it's the office. Any CEO is just a steward. When one leader leaves and another assumes the mantle, it's the strength and solvency of the franchise that counts, particularly in the case of an insurance company that has promised millions of clients that it will pay designated retirement amounts for the next twenty years or a death benefit in fifty years. "The things he's put in place are obviously going to keep on going. The vision and the continuous improvement and the search for excellence, that's not going to dissipate, that's hard-wired into the system. It's a performance culture," said newly appointed chair Gail Cook-Bennett.

Most CEOs don't create anything like that solid a legacy. That's why so many leaders donate money to etch their names on hospital wings or university buildings; they want to make sure that they are remembered for something. In fact, the ultimate tribute occurs when the firm they ran has no further need for them. The question that remains is this: Has Dominic D'Alessandro, like those in earliest civilizations, created a tool that can be used over and over again? There's no way of knowing the answer for certain until after he's gone. "One way or another, this turmoil will accrue to the benefit of the strong, and we are the strong. Some of the largest players in our industry have fallen by the wayside. There will be a flight to quality and we will be the quality that they will be looking to do business with. I always wanted to run and build a great company and I think I've done that. I've done it in an honourable way, without rolling the dice or taking risks that happened to work out," D'Alessandro told analysts at Manulife's annual Investor Day in 2008.

Someone asked, given the stock market turmoil, whether D'Alessandro might stay on a little longer than planned. "I do intend to retire in May of '07. I don't see anything...." Then he suddenly realized he'd got the year wrong and corrected himself, saying, "'09, sorry. Gosh, that may have been a Freudian slip."

Dominic D'Alessandro was ready to go; Manulife was ready to let him leave.

EPILOGUE

THE SESSION STARTED SLOWLY but picked up speed. "I'm not at my best at this time of morning," said Dominic D'Alessandro of the 8:15 A.M. start. "Please excuse me if I look a little dazed," he added, sipping from a glass of Diet Coke, seeking a kick-start. The speech during the two-day Canadian Division Leadership Conference at the Renaissance Toronto Airport Hotel in October 2008 was one of D'Alessandro's several swan songs given to Manulife employees in Toronto and Boston during his final months, detailing his triumphs and tragedies.

He began in an ironic mood, recalling how he'd joined Manulife on his birthday, January 18, 1994, only to have one of the ratings agencies downgrade the company that very day. "I'm proud that Manulife is third largest in the world. But I'm more proud that we did it the right way. We did it without compromising our values, without risking our future, and without screwing anybody. We're tough business people, but we've always kept our word."

While long-term performance was sound, employees might have felt a bit singed that month when Manulife shares fell by 46 percent. Some people in the room had options that were suddenly worth nothing. Others, with shares bought through payroll deductions, watched their hard-earned compensation go down the drain. "We came dangerously close to having a total meltdown in our financial system—not the Canadian financial system—but the world financial system. In every major industrialized country, governments have had to step in to refinance all of the large financial institutions. On the weekend, [Dutch insurer] ING had to get 10 billion euros, that's about $15 billion, of fresh capital from their government. You see what's happening in the United States with the Troubled Asset Relief Program. They're going to use about $200 billion of that to inject into the large banks. In the United Kingdom, all the large banks have been semi-nationalized. On the weekend, the Swiss authorities injected $60 billion into UBS. No one would ever have imagined that this would have come to pass."

There were two causes. "We've had it good for a long, long time, and we fell in love with the idea that there might be a free lunch. Societally, everyone was for instant gratification. The old verities of spending less than you earn, saving for a rainy day, seem to have gone away. The other development is that we've had an explosion in financial instruments and financial engineering in a manner that's completely uncontrolled."

In the face of further catastrophe, he held out hope for recovery. "The huge amount of capital injections seems to be working. We're going to get over this problem. I believe that markets will correct and we'll look back on this episode and say, 'What an adventure!' But I'll tell you, it doesn't feel like an adventure some days."

By the halfway point in his hour-long presentation, D'Alessandro had come alive. He'd gotten a few laughs. He was animated, rarely referred to his notes, and spoke off-the-cuff without hesitation. This was a man in full—confident that he'd done all he could, achieved all he would, and had nothing to hide.

The final twenty-five minutes were given over to questions. The first: What did he consider his greatest accomplishment? His answer: the Hancock acquisition. "Canadians aren't supposed to do this. It's supposed to be the other way around." What about regrets? He feigned difficulty answering, ducked, put an arm protectively in front of his head, and said, "Oh geez, I'm like George Bush now."

After the laughter had died down, his response was surprising. If he had one thing to do over, he would have taken Manulife public in 1999 at a lower price. At the time, the investment bankers pushed for just such a course, but he said no, he wanted to deliver as much money as possible to policyholders. "I regret that because no one's ever given us credit for it and it allows some of our competitors to say that since they became public companies they've had growth equivalent to ours. They came into the world as runts," a dismissive description that produced chortles from the audience. "They went public at less than book value; both of them, 90 percent of book value. We went public at 150 percent of book value. If you start off life at 150 percent of book value, your future growth is going to be measured by that condition you were in when you came into life. If you came in at 90 percent of book, it's a heck of a lot easier to get to 150 percent than it is to go from 150 per cent to 225 percent of book." He was nothing if not a competitor to the end.

D'Alessandro then poked fun at the very trait for which he was notorious—his tough-guy management style—as if he were kneeling in a confessional instead of standing at a podium. "I've demanded a lot of the people I've worked with. I think everybody that's worked with me has worked very, very hard, very, very well. Some have not worked very, very long." After the laughter subsided, he added, "I don't regret that. Everybody was treated fairly and properly."

What advice would he give someone starting out in a career? "There isn't a day I don't learn something new. My kids say, 'God, Dad, it's not possible.' My wife says, 'No, no, don't believe him, he's such a liar.'" Another laugh line. "But I really do. The best advice I could give you all is to keep learning. It's such a great, interesting world. If you have a choice between going through life with a narrow view or a broad view, why wouldn't you choose a broad and generous view of the world and try to understand. It's a beautiful world in many ways."

And what advice would he give to his successor, Donald Guloien? "Don has got to be Don. Don's got a super energy level. He's a very intelligent guy. I've worked with Don for a long time. I think he's got to become a little tougher. When you're in these jobs, you can't please everybody all the time. It's all about making priorities and making decisions. When you have a group of strong-willed people around you, you're not going to get stories about the Boy Scouts at the Jamboree, and they all decide. It really doesn't work that way. Somebody has to say, 'OK, I heard you all, this is what we're going to do.'"

In case they missed the message the first time, D'Alessandro took pains to remind them. "Don has all the tools. He's just got to learn to be tougher, which he will do, because if he doesn't, he's going to die. I don't mean die physically—it's going to exhaust him. These are great jobs; don't get me wrong. Being CEO is wonderful. It beats everything else, but it's not a cakewalk. There are a lot of moments that are tense and a lot of decisions you have to make."

The final question took him to the source of his greatest strength: hearth and home. Around the dinner table, someone asked, what guiding principles did he share with his family? "It's very tough for me to answer this question. I intimidate my children so terribly." Everyone laughed. "So I talk to my grandchildren." More laughter.

D'Alessandro then opened up to them in the same way he had during an interview with me, as if he were airing his personal issues while there was still an audience. "My kids grew up watching me work. They travelled the world with me. I was sort of a CEO when I was thirty years old. I worked in Arabia then. I was the general manager of this company so everybody around the organization deferred to me, so they're used to seeing me scowling and giving orders."

Reading about their father's success over the years further intimidated them. "I have son who is a CFA, I have another son who is a golf pro—in reaction to my situation." By now, the audience was in sync with his thinking. After all, they have family issues, too. Many of his lines brought laughter, not the polite kind for a boss who told a feeble joke, but the laugh-out-loud kind that came from the shock of self-recognition. "I have a daughter who wants to write and she's dating a guy who also wants to write." Laughter. "We have a very happy domestic life." More laughter.

Then he became serious. "What I try to teach my children is to be ambitious, to do their best, to be generous in their spirit toward people. I tell everybody this: You can go through life being cheesed off at everybody and regretting and resenting everybody that you see. Or you can say, hey, you're only here for a little while, have a good time."

AMONG ALL THE WORKS by Canadian artists that Dominic D'Alessandro bought for the halls and walls of Manulife, he chose a select few paintings to hang in his own office. Most are colourful, vibrant works by artists such as A.J. Casson, David Milne, and Arthur Schilling. His favourite, displayed in a small boardroom that forms part of the suite, is a canvas by Jean Paul Lemieux called *La Nouvelle France*. As is typical of Lemieux, the colours are mostly muted, the feeling serene. Usually Lemieux has just one figure in the foreground, a beseeching individual who demands eye contact and understanding from the viewer. In this painting there are three people: a seated woman holding a baby wrapped in swaddling clothes and a girl standing beside them wearing a long red dress. In the background is a valley with tree stumps.

The woman is wearing a hat that could belong to the flying nun. "Most people think this is a religious painting," D'Alessandro said to me as we stood admiring the canvas. He then waited to hear what I thought. "She looks like a hard-working mother," I said. "And the background is obviously land that's been cleared for farming." D'Alessandro turned, hit my upper arm with the back of his hand and said with a broad smile, "It's the immigrant experience."

Being a CEO is not a contact sport. Of the hundreds of CEOs I've interviewed over the years, not one of them has ever sent such a specific message via physical means. D'Alessandro wanted to make sure I understood the relevance of the immigrant experience in his life—that's why he whacked me. "It's only the last ten years that I realized how thoroughly my personality, character, and attitudes have been shaped by the experiences I had as a child," he said.

Immigrants try harder than native-born Canadians as they seek respect and recognition. "There's no question that Dominic was heavily motivated by his humble roots. He's always been driven to prove that he's as good or better than anybody else," said Robert Swidler, who has shared so much of D'Alessandro's thinking throughout his career that he could be a personal therapist, not just an executive recruiter. Events at the Royal Bank further fuelled that inner force. "What happened at the bank with Cleghorn drove him to prove that he was as least as smart as those people and they made a mistake by not picking him."

That experience would have derailed or embittered lesser lights. "Dominic's too smart just to do things for ego reasons. There are lots of people who are trying to get back at others, but he never let his emotions get the better of him. He always stayed under control. What happens to most people is their egos overtake them and they make foolish decisions just to get back on top and they're paying the price for it," said Swidler. "The thing that differentiates all these titans is not how many successes they have, but how they avoid failures and how they cut their losses as soon as they do something wrong. As an entrepreneur, [Power Corp.'s] Paul Desmarais stands alone, and as a business executive, Dominic stands alone."

Canada has always been a nation of immigrants, a wide-open place that needs more leaders like D'Alessandro, men and women with ideas in their heads and hope in their hearts. Meanwhile, Dominic D'Alessandro is a beacon to others. Adversity and heredity need not hold anyone back; drive and determination can conquer all.

SOURCES

MOST OF THE QUOTES in this book are from my dozens of interviews. Those that come from other sources, such as books, newspaper articles, or speeches, are listed below with citations.

p. 15 *"It took only ... beneath herself."* Speech to the Ivey Business Leader dinner, October 29, 2008, p. 3.

p. 16 *"What their recruiting ... background education."* Speech to Canada's Outstanding CEO of the Year 2002, Toronto, November 21, 2002, p. 3.

p. 22 *"There were very few ... for your actions."* Ibid., p. 4

p. 24 *"D'Alessandro, that's Italian ... to ask him."* Ibid., p. 5.

p. 34 *"Say nothing ... fee in advance."* Gwyn, Richard, *John A.: The Man Who Made Us*. Toronto, Random House, 2007, p. 46.

p. 35 *"He acquitted himself ... first to last."* *The Empire*, January 21, 1888.

p. 36 *"If there was ... remembered her."* *The First Sixty Years: A History of the Manufacturers Life Insurance Company*, Toronto, privately published, 1947, p. 37.

p. 38 *"I was literally ... managers and agents."* Vista, Winter 1987, p. 7.

p. 39 *"Our staff are ... years to come."* Financial Post, August 28, 1925.

p. 41 *"It would be ... stood her ground."* Information for this incident was drawn from the Winter 1987 issue of *Vista*, a company publication, as well as the one-hundredth anniversary book about the Philippines, *From Sea to Sea*. This quote is from page 24.

p. 43 *"In effect, the ... public address system."* The Telegram, September 26, 1953, p. 21.

p. 44 *"Oh, he didn't ... the 650 to him."* Vista, Winter 1987, p. 18.

p. 45 *"The present level ... any business man or woman."* The President's address, eighty-third annual meeting, January 15, 1970.

p. 46 *"There were a large ... between them."* Vista, Winter 1987, p. 2.

p. 47 *"Life firms have ... painful changes."* Financial Post, August 12, 1972.

p. 48 *"It must have been ... danced all night."* ROB Magazine, March 1986, p. 56.

p. 48 *"There was a percolating ... place to be."* Vista, Winter 1987, p. 22.

p. 51 *"In retrospect ... more aggressive."* ROB Magazine, March 1986, p. 59.

p. 55 *"I didn't authorize ... could find it."* Kitchener-Waterloo Record, October 20, 1988.

p. 56. *"The dinner held in November ..."* For the retelling of Tom Di Giacomo's departure, I have relied on recent interviews, as well as a feature article I wrote for the *Financial Post* that was published on November 27, 1993, three months after the incident.

p. 90 *"I have two pieces ... consulting actuaries."* McQueen, Rod, *Who Killed Confederation Life?* Toronto, McClelland & Stewart, 1996, pp. 195–96.

p. 107 *"Your question for ... a moderate smoker."* Manufacturers Life Insurance Co. of Canada: The First 65 Years in South China, Hong Kong and Macau, 1898–1963, pp. 1–2.

p. 110 *"It is not important ... mutual trust."* D'Alessandro's speech to the Financial Services Institute, Toronto, January 22, 1997, p. 6.

p. 115 *"The Indonesian minister ... break the fortress."* "Manulife in Indonesia," a case study prepared by Ulla Fionna, research associate, and Douglas Webber, professor of political science, INSEAD, 2002, Part B, p. 4.

p. 115 *"We have to handle ... with the IMF."* Ibid., p. 5.

p. 116 *"I'm very proud ... they've started."* National Post Business Magazine, November 1, 2002.

p. 117 *"I first went out ... on Monday afternoon."* Vista, Winter 1987, pp. 3–4.

p. 173 *"He is well aware ... below the line."* Ashforth, R.V., *and all the past is future*, Toronto, published privately, 1987, p. 17.

p. 178 *"Executive compensation ... our best shot."* The Boston Globe, September 30, 2003.

p. 178 *"I'm doing better ... right about this."* The Boston Globe, April 24, 2008.

p. 191 *"Hancock established ... are his legacies."* The Globe and Mail, May 8, 2008.

p. 192 *"My people ... curtailed that business."* Manulife Investor Day, September 29, 2008.

p. 194 *"The speed of ... D'Alessandro."* The Boston Globe, July 6, 2005.

p. 200 *"We had pretty ... those ties anymore."* Investor Day.

p. 229 *"Many of the ... financial institutions."* Speech to the Ivey Business Leader Dinner, October 29, 2008, p. 17.

p. 235 *"As the depression ... and granting loans."* The First Sixty Years, pp. 136–37.

BIBLIOGRAPHY

Ashforth, R.V., *"and all the past is future": Commemorating the Hundredth Anniversary of the Manufacturers Life Insurance Company*. Toronto: Published privately, 1987.

Bliss, Michael, *Northern Enterprise: Five Centuries of Canadian Business*. Toronto: McClelland & Stewart, 1990.

Bruce, Harry, *Never Content: How Mavericks and Outsiders Made a Surprise Winner of Maritime Life*. Toronto: Key Porter, 2002.

Creighton, Donald, *John A. Macdonald: The Old Chieftain*. Toronto: Macmillan, 1973.

D'Alessandro, David, with Michele Owens, *Brand Warfare: 10 Rules for Building the Killer Brand*. New York: McGraw-Hill, 2001.

———, *Career Warfare: 10 Rules for Building a Successful Personal Brand and Fighting to Keep It*. New York: McGraw-Hill, 2004.

Everatt, Donna, and Trevor Hunter, *Manulife Financial: Adjusting International Strategies in Response to the Asian Crisis*, case study for Richard Ivey School of Business, The University of Western Ontario, London, 1999.

Fionna, Ulla, and Douglas Webber, *Manulife in Indonesia,* case study, INSEAD, Fontainebleau, France, 2002.

Gwyn, Richard, John A.: *The Man Who Made Us.* Toronto: Random House Canada, 2007.

Lento, Camillo, Philippe Grégoire, and Bryan Poulin, of Lakehead University, *Manulife Financial and the John Hancock Acquisition,* Journal of the International Academy for Case Studies, Volume 13, Number 2, 2007.

Manulife Financial, case study for Darden Graduate School of Business Administration, University of Virginia, Charlottesville, 1997.

McQueen, Rod, *Risky Business: Inside Canada's $86 Billion Insurance Industry.* Toronto: Macmillan of Canada, 1985.

————, *Who Killed Confederation Life? The Inside Story.* Toronto: McClelland & Stewart, 1996.

Orendain, Joan, *From Sea to Sea: The Manulife Philippines Century.* Manila: Manufacturers Life, 2007.

Schull, Joseph, *The Century of the Sun: The First Hundred Years of Sun Life Assurance Company of Canada.* Toronto: Macmillan, 1971.

Swainson, Donald. *Macdonald of Kingston.* Don Mills: Thomas Nelson & Sons, 1979.

The First Seventy-five Years: John Hancock Life Insurance Company, published privately, 1937.

Winter, L.A., et al., *The First Sixty Years: A History of the Manufacturers Life Insurance Company.* Toronto: Published privately, 1947.

ACKNOWLEDGMENTS

THIS BOOK is not an authorized work, but it was created with the generous co-operation of Dominic D'Alessandro. He not only agreed to numerous interviews and made family photos available; he also opened doors among Manulife executives and directors by recommending my project.

At Manulife, Amelia Sia, D'Alessandro's executive assistant, accommodated my every request; Donna Murphy, manager, corporate archives, patiently provided research material and historic images; Jennifer Rowe, vice president, corporate affairs, guided me through the organizational labyrinth; and Roy V. Anderson, vice president, John Hancock Financial Services, helped immeasurably in Boston.

Scott Maniquet, chief librarian at the *National Post*, uncovered fascinating material about Manulife dating as far back as 1916 in the *Financial Post* archives.

At Penguin, Andrea Magyar, Karen Alliston, Sharon Kirsch, and Sandra Tooze provided excellent editing and an efficient process.

My thanks go also to my wife, Sandy, and to Tom Hopkins for their thoughtful comments on the manuscript.

As always, my agent, Linda McKnight of Westwood Creative Artists, cheerfully worked in my best interests.

Rod McQueen
February 2009

PHOTO CREDITS

INDEX